FAMILY EVALUATION

Mark A. Karpel, Ph.D.
Eric S. Strauss, Ph.D.

FAMILY

EVALUATION

GARDNER PRESS, INC.
New York and London

GARDNER PRESS, INC.
19 Union Square West
New York 10003

Library of Congress Cataloging in Publication Data

Karpel, Mark A.
   Family evaluation.

   Bibliography: p.
   Includes index.
   1. Mentally ill—Family relationships. 2. Mental
illness—Diagnosis. I. Strauss, Eric S. II. Title.
[DNLM: 1. Family. 2. Family therapy. WM 430.5.F2 K18f]
RC455.4.F3K37   1982   616.89'156   82-21118
ISBN 0-89876-038-0

Printed in the United States of America

Design by
Publishers Creative Services, New York

To our parents,
Anna and Larry Strauss
Sybil and Milton Karpel

Contents

Acknowledgments

We wish to thank a number of people who contributed in different ways to this project. Our interest in family evaluation began during our tenure in the Department of Psychiatry at Baystate Medical Center in Springfield, Massachusetts. We are indebted to the department and especially to its previous and current chairmen, Dr. William Linson and Dr. Benjamin Ianzito, for giving us the time to develop our ideas and the secretarial support to shape them into the present manuscript. Dr. Denise Gelinas co-directed the Family Therapy Program in the department with us and contributed to the evolution of our thinking about therapy and technique in family evaluation. Ms. Joyce Smith, Ms. Kathy Field and Ms. Kathryn Lenker typed the seemingly endless revisions of the book speedily and, to the extent humanly possible, cheerfully. We would like to thank those families with whom we have worked over the years who have taught us about family life and family therapy. In this context, a special debt is due to the "Turner" family. Finally, we are deeply grateful to Dr. Barbara Krasner who provided voluminous and valuable comments on the three theoretical chapters of the book.

Preface

This is a book about evaluating families. Our hope is to offer a theoretical framework for understanding families and specific guidelines and techniques for conducting the evaluation. This work is aimed at beginning and experienced family therapists, therapists who work in other modalities of treatment, clergy, physicians and nurse practitioners—in essence, any professional who identifies a need to assess and provide services for individuals and families. We hope to encourage professionals to see families for purposes of evaluation, and to increase the reader's sense of competence, confidence, and comfort in working with families.

On another level, the book is intended to provide a counterweight to what we consider several problematic trends in the field of family therapy. One such trend involves a deemphasis on family *evaluation*, as distinct from family therapy. We feel strongly that the evaluation process should be viewed as a clinical practice distinct from treatment. This is certainly the case for individually oriented therapies in which an abundant and detailed literature exists on most aspects of the evaluation process. In the training of individual therapists, there is usually a clear emphasis on mastering the demands of assessment before progressing to ongoing therapy. In the family therapy field, this has frequently not been the case.

Most family therapists receive little or no formal training in the area of family evaluation and the literature on the subject has been slow in developing. While there is a variety of accepted evaluative methods and formats to be used in assessing individuals, few clear and established guidelines exist for the difficult task of assessing a relationship system. Many therapists have chosen not to see families for evaluation owing to their anxiety about managing a group of people in a session. They have felt uncertain about what to look for in a family, what information to obtain, and how to obtain it.

One possible reason for the shortage of useful and practical literature on family evaluation may be the family therapy field's "action" orientation. Focusing on relationships, family therapists have spotlighted interpersonal behavior. There has been a general underemphasis on gathering information in an organized manner or reaching a diagnostic formulation. Indeed, the term "diagnosis" has been viewed as exclusively linked to an individual model of psychopathology. The emphasis on interactions, with the therapist actively observing and managing them, makes the family therapy field a lively and energetic one. Many therapeutic techniques have been developed, and the therapist's style of conducting the session has been closely scrutinized and highly valued. But evaluation has frequently been lost in the exciting interactive process, and has been done "on the run."

The family therapy field's relative lack of interest in the evaluation process is particularly unfortunate because the field itself has provided therapists with a concept of great importance for the art of clinical assessment—the significance of context. The essential point of the family theorists is that human beings do not exist in isolation from each other. Individuals are recognized as existing in a network of relationships, and are viewed as capable of changing the network by their own actions and of being affected themselves by changes in the larger system of relationships.

The implications of this conceptual system for the process of clinical or psychiatric assessment are striking. Each and every problem needs to be understood in its context. To understand a problem situation adequately, one must ideally hear the problem described by each family member from his or her unique, separate perspective, and one must observe the family members in relationship, interacting with each other in characteristic ways during the course of the evaluation meeting. The therapist then learns about both the particular presenting problem and the family system in which it exists and which it affects.

In summary, we believe that good family treatment has to begin with a careful and thorough evaluation of the family and that this first phase of treatment is important enough to merit consideration in its own right.

We do not, however, assume that family treatment must inevitably follow from a family evaluation. Our experience indicates that a thorough family evaluation can shed enormous light on and provide significant therapeutic leverage in a wide variety of cases which may never involve family therapy. These might include: crisis intervention by a psychiatric emergency service, individual inpatient treatment, psychiatric consultation in a variety of settings, and the routine evaluation of individuals or couples who request outpatient therapy. These family evaluations may or may not lead to a recommendation for family therapy. They will, however, yield a more detailed understanding of the presenting problem, and will contribute to more informed and more productive treatment recommendations.

A second trend which we consider problematic in the field of family therapy involves a reliance on concepts of competing self-interest, power, and dominance to explain what goes on in families. These "disjunctive" forces (Boszormenyi-Nagy and Spark, 1973) can give us at best only half the picture. In the actual daily and yearly life of families, in the development of pathological patterns and symptomatic behavior, and in the resolution of such problems, they coexist with "conjunctive" forces such as loyalty, devotion, trust, and fair treatment of the other. These forces have, until recently, been largely overlooked. We consider this the most significant oversight in the development of family therapies and the various theories which have guided them over the past twenty years.

A third trend which we hope to counter in this book involves the tendency to see intrapsychic and interpersonal dynamics as mutually exclusive, a tendency which, ironically, is shared by many individual and family therapists. The assumption, in its extreme form, suggests that people can be understood solely in terms of what goes on "inside" them (with no consideration of their relational context) or solely in terms of the properties of systems (without any need to examine how they feel and what they think). Our own position is that individual and relational dynamics are complementary and co-constituted. We can no more remove the person from the system than we can remove the system from the person. This has traditionally been an unpopular position as purists in both camps tend to see its advocates as members of the enemy camp in disguise. Nonetheless, our experience suggests that such a view most closely approximates the realities of human life and that it puts the therapist in the best possible position to understand and help families and individuals.

Finally, we hope to counter, or at least not to contribute to, the faddishness of family therapy. We have had experiences with training as well as practicing therapists which convey to us a sense that certain areas of clinical work, such as family therapy or work with death and dying, for example, are exciting because they are "in" at the moment. Often, one cannot escape the feeling in these situations that no particular skills, perspective, or experience are required for such work. Serious practitioners in either area know how mistaken this is. Unless therapists who are beginning family work are introduced to the ethics, perspective, and skills required for family treatment, they may feel they can or should simply imitate the often dramatic and flamboyant masters in the field, with predictably disastrous results. We hope to steer a sensible middle course between the positions that it is prohibitively difficult and frightening to see families in treatment and that it is something to be approached lightly or cavalierly.

This book is divided into three sections, generally corresponding to conceptual material, practical guidelines, and special problems associated with evaluating families. Part I introduces the basic concepts which we consider essential for therapists trying to understand families. These concepts do not represent any one "school" of family theory but, instead, an attempted integration of ideas from a variety of family approaches. Chapter 1 presents an analysis of family structure and Chapter 2 examines the predictable stages of family development—the family life cycle. Chapter 3 applies these concepts to one particular family in an effort to integrate this more abstract material.

Part II moves to practical issues involved in conducting family evaluations. Chapters 4 and 5 present guidelines for setting up the evaluation, before it even begins, and for structuring the opening phase of the meeting(s). Chapter 6 addresses the question of how the therapist goes about assessing the family, using observations and information on a variety of levels. Included here are a series of probe questions which are designed to assess some of the critical areas of family structure and development presented in Part I. Chapter 7 explores the issue of therapeutic alliances, examining different types of alliances which are commonly established between families and therapists during the evaluation. Chapter 8 presents guidelines for closing the evaluation, including the therapist's formulation of the problem and recommendations to the family.

Part III covers a variety of problems which can preclude, impede, or complicate family evaluations. Chapter 9 focuses on obstacles for the therapist, such as his or her own fears and possible misconceptions about evaluating families. Chapter 10 moves to common problems with family members, such as the dominating member and the resistant adolescent. Chapter 11 is devoted to the common and often complicated problem of managing family secrets. Each chapter examines factors which contribute to these "traps" and presents guidelines and techniques for managing them.

In summary, we hope to encourage thorough professional evaluations which do justice to the family that is seeking help. Such practical evaluations must be based on a general understanding of family life, and so we turn first to an examination of family structure and the family life cycle.

Part I
UNDERSTANDING FAMILIES

1
Family Structure

In this chapter, we are concerned with the structure of the family, that is, the overall pattern of relationships between and among individuals and subgroups within the family. But before proceeding to the elements of structure, we need to address briefly the question of what a family is. Most texts on working with families presume that we all know what a family is, and indeed for practical purposes we do, until we try to define it. The reader can, for example, consider the following questions and the implications of his/her answers for the definition of "family."

If a grown child moves away, is (s)he still "in" the family? What if (s)he renounces the family and has no further contact for twenty years? When parents divorce and father relocates without the children, is he still "in"? If mother then remarries, are both fathers in the family? Is it one family or two? Are adopted children part of the family? Are foster children? If one set of grandparents lives in the home and the other in another state, are both sets part of the family? Are grandparents ever part of the family? Are in-laws part of the family? Is the family outcast—that is, the person who plays the role of the outcast in the family—part of the family? Is (s)he less a part of the family than the person who acts as a loyal caretaker?

Table 1.   Alternative Concepts of the Family

MEANING OF "FAMILY"	NATURE OF BONDS	POTENTIAL FOR CHANGE IN MEMBERSHIP
The functional family	Defined by shared household living, shared activities, shared responsibility for daily life and child rearing	Great potential for change
The legal family	Defined by legal structure; altered by divorce and adoptive placement of children	Some potential for change
The family as seen by its members	Defined by the perceptions of its members; who is seen as "in" the family by family members	Some potential for change
The family of long-term commitments	Defined by long-term expectations of loyalty and commitment; trust, reliability, and fairness are basic expectations	Very little potential for change
The biological family	Defined by blood relationships; parent-child, sibling ties	No change possible

However differently we may answer these questions, what becomes clear is that we generally employ not one but several definitions of family. Webster's, for example, includes at least three definitions of the family in the sense we mean by it. These include: "a group of persons of common ancestry"; "a household (including the servants and kin of the householder)"; and "the basic unit of society having as its nucleus two or more adults living together and cooperating in the care and rearing of their own or adopted children." As these definitions and our questions imply, there are actually multiple meanings of the term "family" as we normally use it. Some of the most common meanings are summarized in Table 1 and described below.

Often, when we speak of families, we are referring to the group of persons living together in the household, the persons who see one another daily and coordinate the chores of shared living. This is the *functional family*. At other times, we are referring to the family as defined by law (adoptive parents, custodial parent, etc.), or the *legal family*. Sometimes, we use "family" to mean *the family as seen by its members*. Family members may include or exclude specific persons from the family in ways which diverge from both the legal definition of the family and the actual membership of the household.

In other cases, the term "family" is meant to imply long-term, in fact, essentially lifelong, relationships based on mutual commitments. These are relationships in which devotion and loyalty play major roles and trust and fairness are basic expectations. For lack of a better term, we can refer to this as *the family of long-term commitments*. Last, one of the simplest and most basic definitions of family derives from the fact of biological relatedness; thus, finally, the *biological family*.

In the case of a typical two-parent, nuclear family, these meanings overlap perfectly. The biological family is the functional family is the legal family, and so on. But in a host of other situations, there is less than total overlap. The reason we may have difficulty answering some of the questions posed earlier is that we become caught between these various meanings of family. For example, are adoptive children part of the family? Yes, they are part of the functional and legal family. No, they are not part of this biological family. And they may or may not be part of the family as seen by its members and the family of long-term commitments. As the divorce rate rises in this country, as families continue to split apart and to re-form with new members, there is even less overlap in these various meanings of family.

The major significance of these multiple meanings is twofold. First, the definition of the family determines its membership and is directly related to the clinical decision of who is asked to attend the family evaluation. Often, the degree of overlap is sufficient so that this decision is straightforward. Where there is less overlap, it becomes somewhat more complicated. Nevertheless, it is usually possible to involve family members in treatment in a way which respects the self-definition of the family and includes significantly involved members. The practical question of who should be included in the family evaluation is addressed in Chapter 4.

Second, the meaning of family that we employ has significant implications for the concepts we use to understand family relationships. Just as the bonds between members differ according to which meaning we employ, so do the patterns that are most characteristic of and most important to each.

One indication of these differences is illustrated in the third column of Table 1, which compares the potential for change in membership for each of the meanings of family we have discussed. There is great potential for membership change for the functional family since members can very easily join, leave, and return to the home. There is relatively less but still some change possible for the legal family and the family as seen by its members. The law moves more slowly than do those who may impulsively enter or leave a household and it is usually consulted less often about these changes as well. Likewise, engrained perceptions of who is "in" the family tend to change less easily and less quickly than does the actual membership of the home.

Even less susceptible to change is the family of long-term commitments. One simply cannot have more than a limited number of relationships at this level of importance in a lifetime. And lastly, there is no possibility of changes in membership for the biological family. We can no more divorce our biological parents or children than we can choose new ones.

These last two types of bonds, derived from the facts of biological connectedness and long-term commitments, are sufficiently different from functional, legal, and psychological bonds that, in our minds, they require a different level of analysis. In view of their essential permanence, we can call these relationships "life relationships." And this permanence is a major factor in what makes family relationships different from social or occupational relationships. The analysis of family structure can proceed on a number of different levels but it must, in some way, address the uniqueness of these "life relationships" and their central role in families. We will return to this concept in the final section of this chapter which addresses the ethical dimension of family structure.

In spite of these multiple meanings of the term "family," it is still possible and helpful to frame a definition of family which respects its complexity. For purposes of discussion in this book, we define the family as a group of persons related by biological ties and/or long-term expectations of loyalty, trust, and commitment, comprising at least two generations and generally inhabiting one household during the period of childrearing.

Having briefly addressed the membership and definition of the family, we can move to an examination of its relational structure. One way to suggest the complexity of this structure is to consider the moment when family members enter the interview room for the first time and arrange themselves in the various seats in the room.

This relatively simple and brief event is filled with a complicated series of individual moves, checks, and reactions, by and between each member of the family. Mother and father may head for the same seat, look at each other briefly, and somehow agree nonverbally that mother will take it. Father heads for another seat, but sees older sister walking towards it and chooses a seat on the other side of the room instead. Younger brother waits because he wants to sit next to older brother, wherever that is. Somehow, out of all these moves, doublechecks, silent signals, and reactions, family members finally arrange themselves in one particular pattern.

In a sense, similar processes determine the "invisible" structure of the family. In this case, however, the stakes are not simply the family's seating in a room for an hour or two. They involve such fundamental factors as: patterns of emotional closeness and distance, boundaries and subsystems, personal identity and intergenerational legacies, interlocking roles, obligations, and entitlements. Obviously, the jump in complexity is formidable. To complicate things even further, bear in mind that family structure is not static and invariable, but is susceptible to change and is in fact constantly changing in response to developments outside the family and changes within it.

This analogy of the family being seated highlights an important aspect of family structure. Just as no one person dictates the seating arrangement of the family, no one person dictates the family's overall structure. Each member contributes in some way and is influenced in turn by the contributions of other members. Structure evolves from a sequence of relational processes, not simply from the orders or initiative of any one person.

Families may be complex but they are not unknowable. Those who work with families can generally come to understand not only the relational structure of a particular family, but the role of specific problems within that structure. This requires, however, a conceptual framework for family structure within which specific situations can be examined.

We feel that a thorough understanding of the family requires consideration of several different levels, or dimensions, of family structure. Specifically, the four dimensions we consider most important in understanding family life, first organized and proposed by Boszormenyi-Nagy (1979) (and slightly retitled here) include:

1. the factual dimension;
2. the individual dimension;
3. the systemic dimension; and
4. the ethical dimension.

The first dimension addresses the particular facts of a family's life. For example, the number of children, physical illnesses, death of or abandonment by a parent, or financial reverses. This dimension describes the givens of reality with which the members of the family must contend. In this sense, it provides the immutable ground for the other dimensions.

Each of these last three dimensions has been explored by particular schools of thought in the history (and prehistory) of family therapy. Each is associated with one or more of these schools and their particular treatment approaches. And each to some extent redefines concepts associated with the other dimensions.

Our intent in spelling out these dimensions is not to develop a strict categorical organization so much as it is to validate the importance of each one. Particular schools of therapy often focus exclusively on one particular dimension. Longstanding debates between schools are often, at least in part, over which of these dimensions are valid. Our own clinical and personal experience convinces us that each of these dimensions counts. While therapists may choose to intervene on one particular level (individual experience, systems forces, or relational ethics), they will understand the family best when they understand and acknowledge all of them.

We hope to illustrate the validity and congruence of these four dimensions in the discussion which follows and by means of a case discussion in Chapter 3. The "Turner" family will be introduced as they appeared for family evaluation and will be examined in the light of the theoretical material presented in this and the following chapter. We begin our analysis at this point with the factual dimension of family life.

THE FACTUAL DIMENSION

In the analysis of relational structure, facts come first. This is expressed in its most mundane form when an intake worker asks, first of all, who are the members of the family—names, ages, sexes, and so forth. These, among other facts, provide the ground from which particular family patterns proceed. These facts impose conditions which are essentially unchangeable, although there is room for enormous variety in how individuals and families respond to these conditions.

Circumstances of Birth

The most commonplace of these facts involve the context surrounding one's origins. A person is born either male or female. Born at a particular point in both parents' lives and in a particular position in the birth order of the children in that family, (s)he becomes part of a particular racial, religious, and ethnic group in a particular national, political, and economic context.

Beyond these fairly general factors, the influence of the circumstances of one's birth can be suggested more specifically by considering any of the following real-life situations:

A teenaged girl discovers she is pregnant. She and her boyfriend decide that, although they had no previous plans, they must marry. They are unprepared for marriage and family and both feel miserable and trapped. Often silently and sometimes openly, they blame the child for their misery.

Twins are born in a large family. The girl grows up to be a successful career-woman. The boy, who is delivered second, suffers congenital injury and is functionally retarded. This fact contributes to a situation in which all the children in the family feel guilty in relation to their brother, although certainly it is none of their faults. The twin sister feels most guilty of all.

In a large immigrant family, one son fills the role of the family savior. He is his mother's favorite and is being groomed for a life of success which will bring pride and better life circumstances to the family. He dies in his first year of college. After a long period of depression, his by now somewhat aged mother finds to her surprise that she is pregnant. The daughter she bears is given a name related to the dead son's and feels pressed to and does in fact succeed in ways which are normally quite difficult for a woman of her day.

These facts of birth are unchangeable, although their implications for one's life are by no means fixed. One is born, for example, either as a female or as a male. This is a given. It leaves room, however, for a tremendous degree of variety in terms of what kind of woman or man one will be. The individual and the family as a whole are faced with the resources as well as the limitations of these legacies of birth throughout their lives.

The facts associated with an individual's birth are obviously not the only ones which affect him or her. Individuals and families are subject to an ongoing stream of events which have a profound influence on their lives. Any one of these events can drastically alter the life circumstances and life-style, the roles and patterns, the opportunities and resources of the family.

Illness

The fact of illness, especially serious illness, is an obvious example of such a life event. Whether such an illness is suffered by a child or a parent, its impact can be enormous. Serious illnesses in children, such as renal failure, diabetes, and seizure disorders, may limit the child's social relationships, disrupt his or her education, complicate the normal parent-child separation process as the child ages, and limit the resources (both relational and financial) available to all family members.

The younger of two children in a family is mentally retarded, apparently as a result of lead poisoning at age 4. With both parents working, his 8-year-old sister becomes largely responsible for his care. She spends a good deal of time looking after him. When he is teased by other children, she comes to his defense. Both children are largely ostracized by other children in their small town. As an adult, the sister has great difficulty forming friendships and has a repetitive pattern of becoming involved with men who are dependent and irresponsible in their relationships with her.

When one of the parents suffer a serious illness, the consequences for the family may be even more drastic. If a breadwinner becomes ill, the family can be devastated financially. Whichever parent becomes ill, the relational and financial resources of the family are likely to suffer. Role patterns and responsibilities within the family may shift and the individual hopes of its members may have to be diminished, postponed, or even abandoned.

A 38-year-old married mother of four children, ages 8 to 17, suffers an intensification of a longstanding diabetic condition. She experiences visual deterioration and renal failure, requiring dialysis three times a week. She is essentially bedridden for long periods of time. The cost of treatment requires an overall tightening of finances in the family and leads her 17-year-old daughter to give up plans to attend a more expensive, prestigious four-year college in favor of a local two-year junior college. The woman's husband feels overwhelmed by the responsibilities of working, caring for his wife and parenting the younger children. He turns increasingly to the 17-year-old daughter for help, at first only for parenting functions, but increasingly for emotional support and day-to-day decisions regarding the family. The daughter's disappointment at having to give up her original plans for the future turns to resentment as her mother becomes increasingly jealous of what she feels to be her daughter's usurping her role in the family. Conflict between mother and daughter increases with father feeling trapped in the middle.

Aging

The aging of parents is another fact which confronts all families. The parents themselves are faced with multiple losses—relational (as old friends, siblings, and possibly spouses die), physical, professional, and financial. Their adult children may experience the psychological stress of seeing the once-strong parent grow weaker. They may be called upon for much greater availability and help for the parent and may have difficulty dealing with changes in mood or functioning in the parent—confusion, complaining, suspiciousness, or regression, for example.

In a family with three adult married children, the widowed mother, in her late 70s, becomes physically ill and requires daily care. Her daughter, with husband and 10-year-old son, move into her home. One son lives in another state and the other nearby the mother's household, with his own wife and child. Within a few months, their previously reasonably amicable relationships become actively hostile and accusatory. Mother complains bitterly to her son of her treatment at the hands of her daughter and son-in-law. Son rushes in to protect and defend his mother, resenting both mother and daughter for the stress this imposes on him. Daughter feels overwhelmed by the demands of caring for her mother, unappreciated for her efforts, and furious at her mother's inteference in her efforts to raise her own son. Son-in-law feels unable to assert himself as a husband and father, and mother feels neglected and tyrannized in the home.

Death

All families face the fact of death repeatedly in the generational cycle. Even when a parent is quite aged and his or her death has been long espected, it can have a profound impact on surviving family members and, in some cases, can be devastating. The impact may ripple through the family as in the following situation:

The mother of an only child loses her own aged mother. She had been extremely dependent on her mother and continues to feel lonely and neglected by her husband. She now becomes both less available to give to her child, in view of her depression and grief, and more in need of care and comfort from the child.

In other cases, the death of a parent in old age is less disruptive than other deaths since the family has at least to some degree been preparing for it and because there has often been a gradual reduction in contact with the aging grandparent.

The deaths which usually exert more disruptive and decisive influence on the family are those of younger family members—middle-aged parents and young or grown children—deaths by injury or sudden illness. The death of a parent knocks out one of the two main pillars of the family. Its irrevocable impact on the family is so severe that to speak of its influence seems inadequate. In a very basic sense, it is not the same family. A vital part which can never be replaced has been taken away.

In a large family with children from 10 to 28 years old, the 56-year-old father dies in his sleep of a heart attack. While he had received treatment in the past for a heart condition, he had recently been declared quite healthy by his doctor. Family members describe themselves as having been quite unprepared for his death. The following changes are reported within a matter of weeks. The family decides to sell father's business, which they do not feel they can manage without him. The eldest son (28 years old) immediately begins to take on a more parental role in the family, especially with the younger children. Mother and 15-year-old daughter, who have always had a poor relationship which was to some extent buffered by father's mediation, become embroiled in escalating conflicts. The 19-year-old sister is so upset by these arguments that she moves out of the home into her own apartment. The eldest son, who has thought about leaving home but never done so, is now more than ever determined to stay.

When a child dies, whether in childhood, adolescence, or young adulthood, a different but similarly severe loss is suffered by the family. This event, like the death of a parent, drastically alters the life that the family has been leading and imposes upon it a very different life, with different experiences, different resources, and different consequences.

In a family with five daughters, ages 3 months to 15 years old, the 3-month-old child dies of meningitis. The next youngest sister, then 3 years old, reports later in life that her mother never seemed to recover from this. She describes feeling that she herself was "kept a baby" for years after this event and that although she tried desperately to get her mother's approval, she never felt she did. She also describes a lifelong feeling of guilt in her relationship with her mother which she has never been able to understand. As grown women, each of these sisters is reported to have a photograph of the dead child (whom some of them can barely remember) in their homes.

The impact of a death in the family derives from the fact (and the experience of the fact) of loss. But death is not the only way in which families can lose a member. Parents can and do abandon their families. And when parents divorce, the result can sometimes be the virtual loss of one parent to the children, and the children to that parent.

The Physical and Social Environment

The family is embedded in a particular physical and social environment. This environment presents the family with a very different, but nonetheless real, order of facts from those we have discussed above. These facts, often implicit in more general statements about political, economic, sociological, and ecological forces, can seriously affect the structure and life of the family. Those who have been made refugees by war, natural disaster, or change in political regime understand this well, as do those who have experienced racial or religious discrimination and those who have lived through the Depression or the Dust Bowl.

Work

The fact that the family is in some way connected to the world of work, either through one or more breadwinners or by the fact of unemployment, makes it vulnerable to changes in that world.

The J. family consists of mother, 46 years old, stepfather, 53 years old, mother's 16-year-old daughter from a previous marriage, and the couples' 10-year-old daughter. The parents have been married for ten years. Mother works as a teacher and father as a sales representative for a large company. They live in a well-to-do neighborhood. Two years earlier, Mr. J. was laid off and remained unemployed for one year before securing his current job. Since that time, family members describe a number of problems in the family, including frequent arguments between father and both daughters, especially his 16-year-old stepdaughter, as well as marital conflicts. Father's complaint is that his daughters no longer show any respect for him. It quickly becomes clear in marital therapy sessions that they are at least in part following their mother's lead. The couple agree that Mr. J. was so demoralized during the period of his unemployment that he gradually gave up and his wife gradually took on most of the executive and emotional aspects of parenting. Each silently blamed the other for this. Mr. J's status as a stepfather of the older daughter may have made the family more susceptible to this kind of shifting and subsequent conflict over roles, but it is noteworthy that no such conflicts are reported prior to his unemployment.

Mr. and Mrs. B. are both in their early 40s. Their four children range in age from 13 to 20 years old. Mr. B. has worked for twenty years on an assembly line in a munitions factory. He is described as always having been prone to worry but this apparently never interfered with his work or private life until five years ago. At that time, the company he worked for instituted a new work program. Groups of five workers were now expected to work together on one piece with their pay directly related to the number of pieces they turned out and therefore the speed of their work. If one worker was slower than the others there was now not only financial but interpersonal pressure. Mr. B. experienced what in retrosepct appears to have been an agitated depression. He had difficulty sleeping, felt anxious, lost weight, and became less and less interested in sexual relations with his wife. He was later diagnosed as having developed a serious case of ulcerative colitis and became dependent on Valium. His wife assumed more and more responsibility in the home in an effort to take extra burdens off him. The work program was recognized by management as a disaster and discontinued after some time. But at this point, Mr. and Mrs. B. fought frequently over their roles and responsibilities and Mr. B. avoided sex. He interpreted his loss of libido as proof of not being a man and feared impotence. Secondary impotence, in response to these fears, did occur on several occasions which only intensified his fears.

Finally, in order to complete the cycle, it is worth noting that the birth of the child is not only the first fact in the child's life but a major one for a relational context into which the child is born. We will have more to say about the impact of children on couples and families when we discuss normal crises of family development in the next chapter. For now it will suffice to point out that a variety of facts, some more unusual than others, which revolve around pregnancy and birth can have lasting consequences for the family. An unplanned pregnancy (in an adult or especially a teenager), the unexpected birth of twins or other multiple births, a miscarriage or an abortion, illegitimacy where this is culturally proscribed, a child conceived in a secret extramarital affair, the birth of a child with serious disabilities—each of these constitutes a fact that cannot be undone or denied. What the family makes of it will depend on their resources and their actions.

If there is any last point which should be stressed concerning these facts, it is precisely this: facts in themselves do not determine the future of the family or its members. They impose conditions to which the family can and must react. Their significance for the day-to-day life and for the long-term development of the family depends on how family members react to them. Whether a particular fact erodes or renews the vitality of a family, whether it undermines or rebuilds trust will depend largely on what the family does with it. The future of a family depends not only on the hand that it is dealt but on how it plays that hand.

THE INDIVIDUAL DIMENSION

The family is composed of individuals, a fact often minimized or ignored in some of the family systems literature. The essential contribution of what has been called "family system theory" has been the recognition that individuals are not unrelated atoms that are motivated only by internal urges and instincts, but that they are parts of larger systems which exert considerable influence on their thoughts, feelings, and actions. Nevertheless, even in the language of system theory, individuals are also whole systems with internal dynamics which mediate their reactions to systems forces. No system theory has ever adequately explained the dynamics of a relational system without some reference to individual dynamics.

Usually, such references are implicit. However, they are never really absent. For example, communication theorists whose vocabulary is largely based on concepts such as "open" and "closed systems," "positive feedback," "homeostasis," and the like, have found it necessary to consider the individual's "punctuation" (Watzlawick, Beavin, and Jackson, 1967) of a communicational sequence—that is, their internal sense of who started the sequence and who is merely reacting. Instances of this implicit recourse to individual dynamics are as numerous as are supposedly "pure" systems theories. And this is really quite natural. Even if individuals are parts of larger systems, they are still separate human beings. If we grant that they are not completely interchangeable with parts of other systems (such as gazelle, bees, bodily organs, or atoms), we acknowledge something different or unique about them. Some of these differences can be described and, we feel, have significant bearing on family structure.

Our purpose in this section is not to offer a neatly packaged compendium of "everything you ever wanted to know" about individual psychology. Instead, we want to highlight several important aspects of individual psychology in order to illustrate the significance of the individual's contribution to the relational network.

Feelings

Probably one of the most obvious statements which can be made about individuals is that they have feelings. Feelings have been explored in some therapies, almost worshipped in a few, and rigorously banished from others. The fact remains that, although little understood, they are a constant in human life. Feelings of affection, love and anger weave through the day-to-day life of families. They are implicitly relational and are inseparably connected to systemic and relational patterns, but they are experienced and expressed by individuals. Feelings of pride, shame, guilt, jealousy, and resentment in one individual, above and beyond their origins in one relational system, can exercise a powerful influence on the structure and development of another relational system. Later, we will examine these feelings in the context of transgenerational legacies. Nevertheless, the individual remains the transmitter of such legacies.

The biographies of the famous provide numerous examples of individuals whose lives and achievements are dedicated to an effort to "live up to" the example set by a courageous or successful forebearer. One of the most well known examples might be the Kennedys, whose recent family history includes: the rise of Joseph P. Kennedy, the grandson of a poor Irish immigrant, to a wealthy national and international figure, the heroism and death of the oldest son, Joseph, Jr., in World War II, and the subsequent ambitions and accomplishments of John, Robert, and Edward Kennedy.

Conversely, individuals (and generations) of a family can be haunted by a particularly intense experience of shame or guilt in one generation. The rise of the Krupp family in Germany to unparalleled international wealth and power begins in the early 1800s with a teenage son who, after his father has driven the family into poverty and himself to an early death, resolves to redeem the family's fortune and status.

Hope

Individuals have hopes and, for this reason, they are susceptible to disappointment and discouragement. Anyone who has seen the impact of a parent's personal disappointment on a family or the hopes aroused by and invested in a child can attest to the power of these forces in family life.

Loss

One of the most powerful feelings, in terms of its impact on family life, is that of loss—whether threatened, anticipated, denied, or actually experienced. This could apply to material losses (occupational or financial), physical losses (injury, illness, aging), social losses (status, professional identity, community role), or, often most powerfully, relational losses. The impact of the loss of a family member on the family (and its course over more than one generation) has been especially noted by Paul (1967). Examples of such losses have been discussed earlier in this chapter.

Trust

One of the most frequently discussed and least understood aspects of individual psychology is that of trust. Trust is generally recognized as a cornerstone of individual psychological development and as an essential basis for lasting, healthy relationships. We will discuss the feeling of trust, along with its necessary relational complement, the condition of trustworthiness, in detail when we address the ethical dimension of relationships. For now, we simply want to note the importance of trust, as a feeling within the individual, for the maintenance of close relationships.

Needs

Attempts have been made to spell out what are considered to be universal needs of the individual. Generated from biological, ethological, psychodynamic, social, political, and spiritual frameworks, a veritable smorgasbord of hypothesized needs have been articulated. Again, our concerns are less ambitious. We simply want to remember that individuals, in general, feel a need to belong to some social grouping or to some one person—to be part of some human relationship. We have a need to master some area, that is, to be able to act or perform effectively in some endeavor, and to be successful and competent in some task, whether in our own eyes, in those of others, or both. In some cases, the particular expressions of these needs may be contradictory, even mutually exclusive. Whether or not this is the case, these personal needs influence relational networks.

Stress

Individuals experience and must cope with stress. They may be more or less successful in doing so. Stresses can be imposed by political, economic, or social forces which surround the family and the individual, or by special burdens imposed on them, such as the loss of a parent or the birth of a seriously ill child, requiring extensive and expensive medical treatment. Or, simply by the passing of time which inevitably confronts individuals and families with new challenges and losses. Or by such immaterial factors as prolonged uncertainty, whether about health, financial security, neighborhood safety, or relational dependability. The degree of stress a person experiences and the success with which (s)he copes with it will be felt in the network of relationships of which (s)he is a part. The example given in a previous section of this chapter concerning the reaction of a man and his family to a stressful change at work provides one illustration of this.

In this context, it should be noted that while a relational system can be "dysfunctional" or stressed, still it is often individuals who manifest symptoms. And especially when individual psychiatric symptoms are severe and potentially dangerous, such as psychosis or profound depression, the therapist has a responsibility to be at least reasonably knowledgeable about and extremely attentive to them. These particular aspects of the individual—biological signs of depression, indications of disorganization and thought disorder, lethality of suicidal impulses—should be of great concern even to systems-oriented therapists.

Identity

Much has been written about the concept of identity and its importance for the functioning and development of individuals. And if we assume that anything which is important for the individual is important for the relational system and vice versa, the vicissitudes of an individual's sense of identity are intimately tied to the dynamics of his or her family relationships. The concept of identity is virtually synonymous with the name of Erik Erikson, who more than anyone else has signaled its importance and charted its development over the span of a person's lifetime.

Even in Erikson's view of identity, which derives from an essentially psychoanalytic framework, the relational system is implicit. He describes identity variously as "a conviction that the ego is learning effective steps towards a tangible collective future, that it is developing into a defined ego within social reality" (1959, p. 23) and as "an identity of something in the individual's core with an essential aspect of a group's inner coherence" (p. 102). In discussing the systemic dimension, we will examine in detail some of the connections between identity formation in the individual and the dynamics of relationships in the family.

Defenses

One last aspect of individual psychology which we consider significant for family relationships involves the operation of psychological defense mechanisms. It was Freud's recognition of these dynamics which laid the basis for virtually all psychodynamic therapies. At the risk of oversimplification, this involved a recognition that people employ a variety of psychological processes in order to "prevent [a particular] mental process . . . from penetrating into consciousness" (1952, p. 304). Presumably, this occurs because the "mental process" in question is unacceptable to the person on a conscious level and because accepting it would mean major and seemingly frightening changes in how they see themselves. They may "repress" the particular thought, impulse, or memory so that they are literally unaware of it. Or they may "project" it onto another person, thinking that it is the other who feels this way or wishes for this thing.

This tendency of individuals to avoid awareness of certain material is an essential assumption of all individual psychodynamic theories and an implicit focus of the treatment approaches founded upon them. Note that in these individualistic formulations, persons are seen as operating on their own experience in order to accomplish this. "Mental processes," such as impulses, feelings, and memories, are the objects of transformation.

This construct has had important implications for the conceptualization of relational structure. The British psychoanalyst, R.D. Laing (1969), has pointed out that individuals operate not only on their own mental processes but that they can also operate on the mental processes, or experience, of others. For example, in order to avoid an unacceptable thought or feeling, they may have to prevent another person from being aware of it. The "attributions" they use to accomplish this will be discussed in the following section.

And while Freud limited himself to considering the denial of feelings, thoughts, and memories, Boszormenyi-Nagy and Spark (1973)* have pointed out that often it is not only these internal processes which are denied or avoided but that real relationships with real people may be denied or avoided as well. The evolution of treatment from helping individuals to face their internal experience to helping them to face and take

* The authors of this book make clear in their foreword that Boszormenyi-Nagy is primarily responsible for the book's theoretical chapters and Spark for the chapters on clinical application. Citations for Nagy, 1973 in this book refer to this source.

action to repair their relationships with other persons charts the movement from individual through systems to contextual therapy.

THE SYSTEMIC DIMENSION

Concepts and theories which focus on the individual provide a wealth of information about individual dynamics and behavior. In this sense, they resemble a pair of binoculars which a spectator at a sporting event focuses on one player on the field. The spectator can observe the player's movements and expressions in fine detail. Yet the drawback of focusing the binoculars in this way is clear, and it eventually became apparent to many therapists. This focus on the individual screens out, for the most part, what goes on *between* that individual and others. It fails to take in the overall pattern of involvements among all participants. And in failing to do so, it is likely to deprive the spectator of the context which would render the behavior of the individual player, to use Laing and Esterson's (1964) term, "intelligible."

While individualistic theories acknowledge that individuals "react" to outside events, they see order, pattern, and predictability as being essentially "within" the individual, just as they see all critical motivating and determining forces as "within." The problem is that they overlook the motivating and determining forces as well as the order, pattern, and predictability of the larger social systems in which the individual is embedded. This realization led theorists to widen the lens on the binoculars, so to speak, in an effort to understand the connections between the individual and the system.

This recognition of the potential importance of the individual's relational context constituted a quantum leap in conceptualization which required a new language. Attempts to extend individual psychodynamic theory to dyadic or multiperson relationships seemed inadequate to this task, as did various applications of concepts from the fields of sociology, anthropology, and political science. A major conceptual breakthrough occurred then when a number of theorists and researchers began to apply the concepts and assumptions of General System Theory to the study of family relationships.

The concept of a "General System Theory" was developed by Ludwig von Bertalanffy (1968). When it was discovered by family therapists in the mid-1950s, General System Theory was already being applied to a variety of problems in the natural and physical sciences and Bertalanffy had suggested its utility in the social sciences as well. General System

Theory asserts that seemingly very different phenomena, such as cell structures, organ systems in the body, the body as a whole, social groupings, even the solar system, can all be viewed as systems and as such can be seen as having certain patterns or regularities in common. These properties of all (hence, general) systems, it is felt, can be observed and understood.

Because the properties of systems are seen as shared, what we learn from the study of one particular system or class of systems can shed light on puzzles which arise when examining seemingly very different systems. So, for example, the study of territoriality and "pecking order" in certain animal groups has contributed to particular theories of human behavior.

Bertalanffy and others describe a system as "a complex of interacting elements" (1968, p. 55); the key word here is "interacting." What differentiates the ecosystem of a pond (with fish, insects, plankton, etc.) from a pile of rocks is that changes in one element of the pond produce changes in other elements. The parts are interrelated. This is the fundamental criterion of a system.

Subsystems

One characteristic of all systems which has significant bearing on the family is that of subsystems (Minuchin, 1974). The family is composed of a number of smaller units, or subgroupings. These are called subsystems by family system theorists because they are also "complexes of interacting elements" which in turn constitute elements of the larger system. Theoretically, each individual is considered one such subsystem. Other subsystems may be formed by generation, by sex, by function, or by a variety of other factors. In most families, the therapist will observe parental and sibling subsystems. Many family therapists like to distinguish between the parental and the marital subsystems, even though they most often involve the same two members. This is because the necessity of balancing marital and parental roles is considered so important. In larger families, there may also be a distinction between younger and older sibling subsystems.

In addition to these generic family subsystems, each family may contain its own particular set of different subsystems. Often called alliances or coalitions, these subsystems are defined by particularly close bonds between certain members, who are likely to feel closer, to do more together, and to be especially loyal to and protective of one another. They may be more likely to share opinions, to see things the same way in the family, and to support one another when disagreements with other members arise.

Boundaries

It is impossible to discuss subsystems without discussing the concept of boundaries. Boundaries exist on a variety of levels, from the very concrete to the very abstract. What they all have in common is that they define who participates and in what ways in different subsystems (Minuchin, 1974).

At the most concrete level, boundaries can be, literally, walls. The wall and the closed door which separate the parents' bedroom from the children's room are both symbolic and real boundaries between the marital and sibling subsystems. They say, in effect, that there are some activities of the marital subsystem in which the children are not included, and vice versa.

As another example, consider the change in boundaries which occurs between parent and child as the child grows to be a teenager. This change is often worked out most conspicuously in a struggle over the teenager's room. For the first time, he or she may ask parents to knock before entering or may forbid entrance under any conditions. Parents may insist on going in and "tidying up" in the child's absence or they may allow a distinction between the room, which the child may decorate as he or she chooses, and the rest of the house or apartment, which must be maintained as they desire. The point is simply that the concrete reality of the teenager's room becomes the arena in which the subtle and complex negotiations over his or her emerging privacy are conducted.

Boundaries can also be rules which regulate *information, access,* and *activity,* in such a way as to include and exclude different members from certain aspects of different subsystems. For example, in a family in which mother is involved in an extramarital affair, the affair is open knowledge among mother and the two children who are close to her, while father and the child who is closer to him are ignorant of it. This secret—that is, this rule regulating *information*—creates a very real boundary between two subsystems. If one of mother's allies tells father's ally about the affair, the boundary changes considerably.

In another family, father spends a good deal of time working in his study. It is understood that none of the children, except one, is allowed to interrupt or even knock when the door to the study is closed. The one child who is excepted, the oldest daughter, can and does enter the study whenever she pleases. This differential *access* to father creates a boundary of which all members of the family are aware.

Last, in a large family, all the children perform some housekeeping chores but only the older children are given responsibility for babysitting for the infant children. In this case, differential *activities* create a boundary between younger and older sibling subsystems.

Boundaries also exist between the nuclear family as a whole and the social environment outside the family. Physically, the nature of these boundaries is determined by such factors as: whether or not the family locks its doors, whether or not curtains or shades cover the windows, whether the shades are left open or closed or whether this varies, and whether the house is left easily accessible or surrounded by locked fences, perhaps even protected by guard dogs.

Less concretely, does the family have a phone? Is the number listed or unlisted? Does a working parent routinely take business calls during dinner? Are children discouraged from visiting neighbors and friends or encouraged to spend as much time as possible elsewhere? Each of these and many other factors determines the kinds of boundaries which separate the nuclear family from its social context.

A very important boundary exists between the nuclear and the extended families. And this, like all other boundaries, is defined in a number of ways. Have family members made an effort to live near their extended families or as far away as possible? Are in-laws given a key to the nuclear family's house, and vice versa? Are grandparents available for babysitting? If so, do they come only when the parents request their help or are they free to come to the house and take the infant for extended periods whenever they wish? Does the family go for regular Sunday meals with one set of in-laws and never with the other?

Finally, what are the rules of privacy concerning the nuclear family vis-à-vis the extended family? A wife may feel, for example, that details of her marital and sexual relationship with her husband should be kept private between them. Her husband may create a very different sort of boundary around the marriage and family by routinely discussing this personal material with members of his own family of origin.

Every school of family therapy, despite various differences which may exist between them, shares some concept of the necessity of firm but flexible boundaries within the family for healthy individual and family functioning. Boundaries need to be clear and firm enough to allow all family members to carry out their functions without undue interference but flexibile enough to permit contact between members of different sub-systems (Minuchin, 1974).

When boundaries are unclear and diffuse, members become overly responsive to one another (Hoffman, 1975). Often members are extremely dependent on one another; they may feel they cannot exist without each other and fear any disagreements which might emphasize differences (Karpel, 1976). In other cases, there may be a good deal of anger and quarreling. However, this does not reflect uninvolvement or distance because members are still locked into these chronically hostile relationships (Boszormenyi-Nagy, 1965). In both cases, members are so closely connected that any move by one triggers strong and immediate reactions from another. These overly close relationships variously described as "enmeshed" (Minuchin, 1974), "fused" (Bowen, 1971) "merged" (Boszormenyi-Nagy, 1965) and "symbiotic" (Searles, 1965), may exist between two or more family members or they may encompass the family as a whole.

When boundaries are overly rigid, members are underresponsive to one another. In these "disengaged" (Minuchin, 1974) relationships, there may be little contact or there may appear to be little concern between members. Family members may astonish the therapist in their ability to tolerate the wildest deviance or symptomatology or the most extreme pain in a family member without apparent concern or intervention. Again this form of relationship may characterize a dyad, a triad, or the family as a whole.

In summary, firm but flexible boundaries preserve the differentiation of the family. Between individuals, they assure that members can feel and be recognized as part of the whole group but also preserve a measure of individual difference and autonomy. Between larger subgroupings, they assure that the different functions and activities of family life can be carried out by those members for whom they are most appropriate. Between nuclear and extended families, they allow for mutual aid and support as well as additional family resources (relational, functional, and financial) while permitting the nuclear family to establish its own independence and direction as a unit. Finally, between the family and the outside social environment, boundaries permit privacy and a sense of group togetherness while integrating the family into a larger social community.

Communication

As some of the foregoing examples illustrate, one of the major channels for regulating subsystems and boundaries is communication. When family therapists employ the word communication, they are referring to verbal or nonverbal behavior in the social context. Communication is more than just "talking." An individual's gestures, posture, movements, silences, facial expressions, tone of voice, and manner of dress are all communicative. All messages have two key components. The most obvious aspect of the message is its content: the information the sender wishes to transmit. But a more subtle level of communication is the message's intended influence on the behavior of the receiver. The sender of the message desires a response from the receiver, and there is a "request" built into all messages

(Watzlawick et al., 1967). The message is aimed at influencing the receiver to respond in a desired manner. Each message, therefore, affects and is affected by the relationship between sender and receiver.

If the content of a statement fully expresses its intent or "request," then there is little room for confusion. The question, "What time is it?" can be asked in an entirely straightforward manner, and can be aimed solely at obtaining a factual response. But when the purpose of a statement is not as explicitly or clearly disclosed, interpersonal misfiring may be the result.

Imagine the same question, "What time is it?" asked at 8:30 P.M. by an anxious husband to a partially dressed wife who was supposed to have been ready to leave for a movie at 8:00 P.M. His simple question is now rampant with unspoken messages. These could include: "Hurry up"; "Can't you ever be on time?"; "We're going to miss the movie"; or "Let's forget the whole thing." The wife in this situation may read in the correct implicit message, but then again she may make an error. She may or may not realize that he is angry, anxious, or even unhappy about her lateness, depending on the husband's nonverbal cues and her perceptiveness. The husband's intensity of feeling may be misperceived. When analyzed in this detailed way, one becomes amazed that interpersonal life proceeds as smoothly as it does. People are adept at developing communicational shorthands, reading cues and signs, and checking out confusing messages.

Certainly, no one would argue about the value of communicational virtues, such as clarity, consistency, openness, and directness. If the husband in our previous example had said what was on his mind, he would have increased the chances of his being understood and responded to appropriately. But there are myriad reasons why people are indirect in their communications, and it is in this murky realm of less than successful communication that the therapist toils.

A communicational problem of far greater magnitude occurs when there is a discrepancy between the content and process aspects of a message. A person's words may clash with his or her tone of voice or facial expression. "But we all care about you," said with saccharin sweetness and a malevolent glare is an incongruent message. Which message is the receiver to believe? When such mutually exclusive messages are sent through different communicational channels, the receiver is confronted with a paradoxical situation.

This type of paradox is typically referred to as a "double bind" (Bateson et al., 1956). A husband asks his wife for a kiss, then stiffens and almost imperceptibly turns away from her. When she in turn withdraws, her husband may ask, "Why are you so cold towards me?" The wife in this example is called upon to decipher a paradoxical pair of messages. Unless the paradox can be commented on openly and directly, the interactional sequence is likely to remain confusing and unsatisfying. Yet, it is difficult for a participant in this type of sequence to pull back from the interaction and comment directly on its quality. Consequently, the confusion and misfiring frequently snowball and increase in intensity.

While incomplete messages represent communicational inadequacy, incongruence or paradox indicate major communicational pathology. Another form which the latter may take is known as "disqualification" (Watzlawick et al., 1967). This refers to communicational sequences in which the speaker invalidates his or her own messages. This disqualification of one's own statements can take numerous forms: self-contradiction, change of subject, tangentiality, inconsistency, incomplete sentences, and obscure speech, among others. The net result of such disqualification is that the receiver is unsure about what the sender of a message is trying to say. Trying to communicate with a "disqualifier" is analogous to stepping into quicksand. You have no firm footing, feel trapped, and inevitably sink into a morass, and the more you struggle to extricate yourself, the faster you sink.

One other important form of communication pathology is called "disconfirmation" (Watzlawick et al., 1967). In this case the receiver neither accepts nor rejects the sender's message. Rather, he or she denies the legitimacy or reality of that message. A family member may say he feels angry and be confronted by another person in the family who tells him that he doesn't really feel that way: "You just think you're angry but you're really not. We've known you all your life, and you're not the sort of person who gets angry about that."

As can be imagined, the impact of repeatedly having one's experiences disconfirmed is devastating. These more extreme forms of communication pathology lead to a pervasive sense of ambiguity, vagueness, and confusion in the family, and the presence of these disturbed and disturbing communications in a family has been correlated with the existence of more serious systemic problems.

Communication theorists point out that interactional sequences can be "punctuated" (Watzlawick et al., 1967) in different ways, depending on one's perspective. The most commonly employed example is that of a nagging wife and a withdrawing husband. If this couple were to come in to treatment, the therapist would generally hear two different views of reality from the partners. The wife might state that her husband shows her no affection and continually distances himself from the family. She tries to draw him back into the family and ends up sounding like a nag. The husband tells another story, however. He would like to be with the family but whenever he makes himself available, he claims that his wife descends upon him with a list of complaints and demands. He tries to deal with these, but when the nagging continues, k.. says he withdraws to get some peace.

Both husband and wife have sliced the pie of their interaction in different ways. Each sees the other's behavior as having begun or caused a sequence, and both view their own behavior as an understandable response. To the therapist, the circular whole of their behavioral sequence is clear. It is usually impossible to determine where the circle began, and in this "chicken-or-egg" situation, both partners' behaviors are seen as crucial in maintaining the pattern. Mutual changes in behavior will be required for the pattern to be broken.

Roles

One highly significant aspect of family structure is its role structure—that is, the roles which are assigned to and assumed by individuals in the family and the relationships between or among those roles.* The term "role" is often used to describe those presentations of self that we all assume in social or work situations. These roles are usually fairly temporary or limited, and are consciously and deliberately assumed. In other words, there is actually very little overlap between who we feel we really are and whom we may act like with the corner grocer or a neighbor down the block.

When we speak of roles in the family, however, we are discussing a very different phenomenon. The roles we are given and assume in our families are more permanent, less flexible, and usually less conscious. In these cases, there is a great deal of overlap between who we are in our families and who we feel we really are. We can move in and out of the roles we play with our neighbor as easily as we may put on and take off a coat, but trying to change our roles in our families is more often like trying to struggle out of a straightjacket.

This is all to say that a person's role in his or her family is very closely tied to his or her sense of identity. Roles organize who we feel we are and how we act, who others feel we are and how they act towards us. Families may have nicknames or pet expressions which capture a member's role in the family. Someone may be described as "the golden boy," "the black sheep," or "the family worrier." Identifying nicknames is often quite helpful in treatment since they enable the family and the therapist to encapsulate all the complexity of role structure with a simple and fairly understandable shorthand.

---

* This discussion does not refer to family roles in the functional sense, i.e., the role of the mother or father, etc., but to roles in the sense of interlocking identities, such as the "little angel" or the "peace-maker."

There are probably as many different family roles as there are family members in the world, but there are also some very common roles which occur in seemingly different families. Some of these common roles, especially for children, are: (1) the infantilized child, (2) the parentified child, and (3) the scapegoat.

The infantilized child is one whose psychological growth is stunted in the family. He or she is, as one 8-year-old boy put it, "babyfied." Dependency and immaturity are encouraged and steps toward autonomy are discouraged. In one family, for example, the parents felt it necessary to wipe their 9-year-old son on the toilet because, supposedly, he could not do this for himself.

The parentified child, also called the "parental child," the "family worrier," or the "caretaker," is similarly kept tied to the family, but here the child is encouraged to grow up too fast. The child is entrusted with a "mission" in the family, often at an early age. He or she may be held responsible for taking care of younger siblings, for one parent, for the parents' marriage, or for the family as a whole. These children often function as a sort of family therapist or may be referred to as almost like a parent to the parent. They may look either like Cinderella or like the family savior, but in either case they are overworked. While giving a child some responsibility for others can often contribute to psychological growth and a rewarding sense of identity, pathologically parentified children are expected to be overresponsible, to devote themselves often to impossible tasks, and to sacrifice their own childhoods in the process.

The scapegoat in the family is much like the scapegoat in society. He or she provides a focus for blame and accusation which takes the heat off other problems in the family. It's not that Mom and Dad have a bad marriage, they have a bad kid. It's as though all of the problems and failures of the family were gathered up and "located in" one person. One interesting variant of the scapegoat role is sometimes the "Identified Patient" role itself. In these cases, the person is seen not exactly as "bad," but as "sick" (which often comes quite close). This does not mean that every Identified Patient is really just being scapegoated. A family member may have genuine and undeniable individual psychiatric symptoms which have a serious impact on the family. The importance of the family perspective is in alerting the therapist to the possibility of this process and to the role of these symptoms in the system.

The development of family roles is an extremely complex process which involves interactions between members, intrapsychic experiences within members, and multigenerational legacies. In order to keep things brief, we will highlight one or two major components of this process. The creation of a family role "begins" with one or more members who need someone to fill the role—a mother, for example, who needs a dependent, insecure infant; a father who needs a parent figure to care for him; a couple who need someone to blame for their own problems. When these needs exist, one of the most powerful and common ways to influence another member to assume such a role involves "attributions" (Laing, 1969). Instead of telling someone what to do, we can repeatedly tell them who they are. Jane is told, for example, that she is quiet, moody, and afraid of people. John is told repeatedly that he is "just like" his mother—wild, selfish, and bound to end up in trouble.

This does not mean, however, that roles are merely forced on certain members. As with our family entering the therapy room, each member contributes in some way to the overall structure of the family. The member who assumes a pathological role in the family is not merely a helpless victim. He or she may participate out of a sense of loyalty to other family members, understanding on some level that this sacrifice is necessary for the stability of specific members or of the family as a whole. In addition, even pathological roles usually have some specific rewards associated with them, whether it be freedom to act out, pampering and protection, or a sense of importance and responsibility. One final motivation for assuming even the most pathological of roles is that it brings with it at least some form of attention, identity, and belonging. Like a younger brother who is allowed to hang around with older brother's gang at the price of teasing, pranks, and put-downs, belonging beats exclusion and being the butt of all the jokes beats getting no attention at all.

One member's need for another family member to assume a certain role, discussed above, exposes one last critical point, which is that roles in relationships are often complementary. That is, in order for one person to assume a certain role, he or she may need the other to assume a complementary role. I can only be the "strong one" if you are the "weak one." I can only be the "cripple" if someone will be the "caretaker." I can only be the "good one" if someone will be the "bad one." When we consider this complementarity of roles together with the close relationship between identity and role, we see why family members often resist attempts to change another member's pathological role. If the Identified Patient can be freed up from his or her role as cripple, infant, or bad one, other family members may face a threat to their own reciprocal roles and, therefore, to their own sense of identity.

Common Patterns

In addition to certain roles which recur frequently in different families, families therapists and researchers have also identified several structural patterns which are often seen. Three of these common patterns will be described here. Each pattern involves a configuration of relationships in the family and forms, in a sense, the framework within which the content of any particular problem is enacted. Family therapists have found that family problems often involve a triad or triangle (Minuchin, 1974; Weakland, 1976; Haley, 1977; Bowen, 1978)—that is, a relationship among three people, usually parents and one child, with other family members more peripherally involved. Each of the patterns described below involves one form of what Minuchin (1974) refers to as a "rigid triad."

One typical pattern, alluded to in our discussion of scapegoating, is often referred to as "detouring" (Minuchin, 1974). This occurs when parents reinforce deviant or symptomatic behavior in a child because dealing with him or her allows them to detour or to avoid their own marital problems. Detouring may take the form of blaming and attacking the child or of pathologizing and worrying excessively about him or her, or both.

Another typical family pattern involves what some family therapists have called a "stable coalition" (Minuchin, 1974). In these cases the child and one parent form a close, rigidly bound alliance against the other parent. Finally, in a configuration variously referred to as "triangulation" (Minuchin, 1974) or a "split loyalty" (Boszormenyi-Nagy, 1973) pattern, the child is caught between two parents, each of whom enlists his or her loyalty against the other. The child cannot express loyalty, caring, and concern for one parent without betraying the other. He or she is, therefore, either paralyzed, because any move is seen as an attack on one parent, or torn apart by the warring spouses. The specific symptoms, problems, or complaints which are enacted within these relational configurations can vary widely. What the family evaluation provides is a look at the context which may encourage or maintain such problems and may even make them inevitable unless altered.

The concept of loyalty, introduced above, takes us out of the dimension of systemic patterns. While some system theorists may try to understand loyalty as an epiphenomenon of systems and subsystems, we view this as reductionistic and unhelpful, both to therapists and families. The significance of loyalty and betrayal, fairness and unfairness, obligation and entitlement in human relationships and especially in family relationships is so central and so different from patterns in nonhuman systems, that it constitutes a different dimension of relationships. We explore this dimension—the dimension of ethical balance—in the following and final section of this chapter.

THE ETHICAL DIMENSION

A 30-year-old married woman recounts the following story during the course of a marital therapy session:

She remembers during her childhood that her father was alcoholic and physically abusive to her mother. He would humiliate her mother by bringing other women home while she was there. When the girl was 15-years-old, her mother informed her that she intended to divorce her father and asked her to testify against him in court. The girl felt very guilty about this and was reluctant to do so, but her mother pleaded with her and finally convinced her. Divorce proceedings were initiated and she testified against her father, which she still remembers as an extremely upsetting episode. Before the proceedings were completed, her mother informed her that she had changed her mind and decided to take her husband back, meaning that they would all be living together again, after daughter's having testified against father. In addition, mother told her that the reason for her changing her mind was that a young girl needed to be with her father. The woman remembers that she left home within six months after this episode.

This incident touches on many of the elements of relationship which are most significant in family and individual life—trust and the violation of trust, loyalty, sacrifice, fairness, and exploitation. When we listen to individuals and families describe the most important incidents in their lives and the problems which often bring them to treatment, these and other related issues, such as concern, devotion, dependability, and commitment, are raised consistently. In many ways, they constitute the most basic questions which individuals address to one another, overtly and covertly, in close relationships. Can I count on you? Can I trust you? Will you be fair to me? Will I get what I deserve from you? Will you stand by me? Can I be counted on? Will I be fair to you? Can I give you what you deserve? And they are questions not only for the individuals in these relationships but for the therapists whose responsibility is to understand and to try to help them.

The problem is that these are not questions which can be answered either in terms of the properties of general systems or with concepts which only address the experience and behavior of one individual. Understanding relationships in which these most fundamental questions are either implicitly or explicitly addressed requires that we look beyond concepts which describe occupational, social, and accidental relationships. Introduced in the beginning of this chapter as "life relationships," these are relationships which, however positive or negative, are most central to the very life of a particular person. These include biological relationships (one's natural parents, children, and siblings) as well as other relationships which involve major life commitments (such as marriage and adoptive parent-child relationships). These relationships, which are so central to the definition of family relationships, require a different level of analysis.

Just as family theorists needed a new language to explore and understand the systemic properties of families, this aspect of family relationships requires a language which addresses what Nagy and his co-workers refer to as the ethical dimension in relationships. We feel that the concepts which he has developed over the past twenty years, now generally subsumed under the heading of "contextual therapy," provide such a language. The following discussion derives from this work (Boszormenyi-Nagy, 1972; Boszormenyi-Nagy, 1976; Boszormenyi-Nagy, 1979; Boszormenyi-Nagy and Spark, 1973; Boszormenyi-Nagy and Krasner, 1980; Boszormenyi-Nagy and Ulrich, 1981).

Entitlement and Obligation

An analysis of this ethical dimension of relationships begins with a recognition that mutual obligations and entitlements exist in all relationships. Much of the literature of individual and family therapy has either minimized this point, overlooked it, or contested it. The "Gestalt Therapy Prayer" of "I do my thing and you do yours" was only the most overt statement of a philosophy which existed in a variety of approaches. This philosophy derived from a recognition that many individual and relational problems seemed to stem from destructive and unrealistic obligations in relationships. In essence, the solution they proposed was to help people free themselves from these obligations. While the initial intention may only have been to free people from these destructive obligations, in practice it often meant encouraging people to free themselves from all obligations.

This was perhaps an understandable consequence of a lopsidedness in theory. Many of these approaches have a highly developed vocabulary and conceptual system for the process of individuating out of relationships with these destructive obligations, but virtually no vocabulary or theory for helping people move back into more or less satisfying, nondestructive relationships. Their vocabulary is extensive when it comes to describing the manipulative games and power moves used in such relationships. It is often weak and inadequate, however, when it comes to describing the underlying structure of balanced, fair, mutually satisfying and growth-enhancing relationships. These approaches have helped us to understand the importance of people taking individual responsibility for themselves, instead of trying to get others to take responsibility for them. But they have inadvertently blinded us to the plain fact that much of what we all value in our own lives and relationships depends on the willingness of people to assume appropriate responsibility for one another. Finally, they have provided an extensive vocabulary for individual and relational pathology but have offered very little concerning (and sometimes served to obscure) valuable resources in relationships. This gap in theory represents in our minds the most important challenge facing the family therapy field at this point. And it is a gap which Boszormenyi-Nagy and his co-workers, as well as other theorists such as Helm Stierlin (1974, 1977), have begun to fill.

The simple facts of life are that there are obligations in relationships and that not all of them are destructive. In fact, the recognition of obligations and the willingness and effort to fulfill them are among the most important elements of satisfying, healthy relationships. This is true on a mundane level, and on the most basic existential level of human life. The following are some examples of fairly commonplace, day-to-day instances of obligation in relationship.

A wife is grateful for her husband's having gone out of his way to get something she wanted, and so offers to make a phone call both of them have been avoiding.

A husband decides that it's "his turn" to change the baby since his wife has done it the last few times.

A mother feels badly that for two weeks she has been unable to take her daughter to the circus as she had promised, so she gives up her own plans for a long-awaited social engagement in order to do so.

A teenaged girl feels guilty for having made fun of her younger brother in front of her friends. She apologizes to him and offers to let him use her previously off-limits stereo.

Some more serious examples might include the following.

A young woman with severe diabetes in indebted, literally for her life, to her sister who gives up one of her kidneys for a transplant operation.

A man feels a lifelong sense of debt to the parents who adopted him as a child and provided him with the emotional and material resources to build a satisfying, productive career and family of his own.

A teenage boy steps in to protect his sister who is being beaten by their stepfather. The boy ends up taking the beating for his sister.

A mother, who knows that her 12-year-old daughter is being sexually abused by her stepfather, abandons the family, leaving her daughter unprotected. Years later, the mother initiates contact with her now-grown daughter. She asks to be understood and forgiven for having left and expresses a hope to make up for this somehow to her daughter.

Each of these episodes involves at least one person's *obligation* to the other. The sources of this obligation vary, generally involving either the *merit* of the other based on his or her helpful actions or sacrifices, or the *debt* of the person based on his or her actions which have in some way harmed the other. The other element of this balance, which is implicit in the above, is the *entitlement* of the other. Obligation and entitlement are inseparable. If we agree that I owe you something, then we agree that you are entitled to something, that you deserve something from me.

In any relationship between two people, the balance of obligation and entitlement fluctuates constantly in response to their actions towards one another. Actions which attempt to fulfill obligations, and which help the other, decrease one's obligation and increase one's own entitlement as well as the obligation of the other. Actions which ignore real obligations or harm the other increase one's own obligation and the other's 38titlement. The "give and take" which occurs between two people around these issues of entitlement and obligation is a constant and endless process which underlies all relationships. The reality and the significance of this process is confirmed in the everyday language people use to describe their relationships. They talk about what they "deserve" from and what they "owe" the other(s), about fairness and unfairness, about "making up for" something, "paying back for" something, and "getting even" for something.

An important consideration to bear in mind in this discussion is that issues of entitlement and obligation exist *both within and between* persons. If we have sacrificed for another person, we may *feel* entitled, deserving; if we have wronged another or if (s)he has sacrificed for us, we may *feel* indebted. But these feelings are only one aspect of this ethical balance—the "within" dimension. The critical conceptual leap involved in considering the ethical dimension of relationships is from the internal experience of one or more persons to the *real existence* of interhuman debts, fairness and trustworthiness, outside the experience of any one person.

For example, when a parent abandons his or her child instead of attempting to fulfill the responsibilities of parenthood as best (s)he can, the balance of fairness and the trustworthiness of the relationship is altered. Even where there may be compelling reasons for this action in the parent's own history, the fact of the abandonment changes the ethical balance of this relationship. And this is so even if both parent and child psychologically deny or minimize the significance of this fact in later life.

Acknowledgment and Claim

The concepts of entitlement and obligation begin to spell out the alphabet, as it were, of the ethical dimension of relationships. Two related concepts which add to this groundwork and have significant therapeutic utility are acknowledgment and claim.

Acknowledgment refers to the willingness of one party in a relationship to recognize and "give credit for" the entitlement of the other. It requires a willingness to consider the balance of give and take in the relationship.

The withholding of acknowledgment when it is due constitutes unfairness or ethical imbalance just as does active mistreatment of the other. This is true even when such withholding of acknowledgment is preceded by a similar refusal to give credit from the other. In this case, it merely compounds the imbalance which already exists. These refusals to acknowledge the genuine contribution of the other also serve to undermine trust and trustworthiness, which will be discussed later.

Examples of the withholding of acknowledgment include the following:

A convalescent father refers affectionately and proudly to the occasional visits of one grown daughter. The daily attentions of another daughter, who lives with and cares for him, are ignored or minimized by his saying that she has nothing better to do.

A man who is bitter over what he considers his father's neglect of him as a child refuses to consider what appear to be the father's efforts to repair this in recent years. The father's "feelers" are dismissed as somehow manipulative or simply calculating, an effort to appease his own conscience.

A married couple's endless fights force their 10-year-old son into a split-loyalty position, in which he is enlisted and tries to side with and comfort both parents. Instead of acknowledging the position in which they have put him and his efforts to help them both, they are able to unite briefly after the worst fights by agreeing that the boy is a "troublemaker" who sets them against each other.

The withholding of acknowledgment, the bitterness and resentment it evokes from the other, and the increased risk that the other will punitively withhold acknowledgment in turn, constitute core dynamics in stagnant, mistrusting, mutually accusatory, and cut-off relationships. Practicing therapists are familiar with what seems like a mutual deafness, an inability to hear the other, which comes to characterize these relationships.

Conversely, the willingness to consider and acknowledge the contributions and hence the entitlement of the other constitutes a critical component of "rejunction" (Boszormenyi-Nagy and Ulrich, 1981), of family members reconnecting with each other with the purpose of rebalancing fairness in relationships. This may take the form of being willing to sit in a room together to reassess their relationships, to surface their claims and hear one another's sides. The process may involve recognizing the sacrifice or merit of the other, admitting an act of unfairness of one's own (and therefore the legitimacy of the other's claim), or taking seriously the factors which may have limited the other's ability to be more fair (such as strong obligations in another relationship). Often, a therapist can help family members start to rebuild trust by encouraging them to try to acknowledge each other's care and contributions or by the therapist's offering acknowledgment for evidence of consideration on both sides of the relationship him or herself.

In discussing acknowledgment, we raise the concept of claim. The ethical dimension is concerned primarily with the fairness of give and take in relationships. In this context, claim refers to one person's asking for something from the other. Having asserted that people do deserve and owe in close relationships, we imply that they are *entitled to make claims* on one another and *obliged to consider other peoples' claims* on them. In fact, from the perspective of the ethical dimension, the ability and willingness to make and accept claims is a vital component of balanced give and take in relationships.

Examples of making claims include the following:

The divorced father of a 12-year-old girl makes no attempt to contact her for almost two years following his separation from the family. Nevertheless, when she is given his address, the girl writes to him, expressing her disappointment and asking him to call or write her.

A woman in her 40s, who had worked to put her husband through medical school, asks that he find a way to spend more time with the children so that she can return to school for career training.

A single mother, who has provided well for her three children in the past, is now unemployed. She asks the two working teenagers to contribute part of their earnings to the rent and upkeep of the family's apartment.

Claims are not inherently valid. People can and often do make inappropriate claims in relationships. Thus, the willingness of one party to capitulate to unilateral, excessive claims may be as harmful to the long-term interests of the relationship as an unwillingness to consider any claims. It is up to the partners in the relationship to assess which claims are valid and how they can be most fairly fulfilled. But the process which might lead to a consensus on the validity of claims and on how they can be met requires that both (or all) partners make efforts to stand up for what they consider their own legitimate claims and to consider the claims presented by the other(s).

Ethical Balance

Another important concept in the ethical dimension of relationships, already alluded to here, is ethical balance. In an ideal sense, ethical balance might refer to a situation in which entitlement and obligation stand in relative balance with each other in a given relationship. It would imply no serious imbalance in fairness, such as might occur when the merit or entitlement of one person is ignored, his or her sacrifices unreciprocated, or when one person keeps the other fixed in debt by giving without allowing them to repay or reciprocate.

In the real world, however, balance has a more complex, if practical, meaning. There is, of course, no such thing as perfect, static balance. The balance of fairness which is achieved through the efforts of both partners in a relationship can and will be altered by any one of many factors. One member may momentarily act more selfishly or inconsiderately. He or she may inadvertently mistreat the other while absorbed or preoccupied in a problem of his or her own. Both partners may have to redefine what they consider fair balance between them if factors are introduced that drastically alter the overall entitlement of one of them. This might occur if, for example, one person becomes ill with a serious disease or is seriously injured or crippled in an accident.

From this perspective, balance in relationships involves an *ongoing effort* to consider mutual obligation and entitlement, rather than a static condition of perfect parity. The process of attaining balance also requires attempts to repair damage, to acknowledge merit, and to fulfill debts. In other words, ethical balance implies a conjoint commitment on the parts of both (or all) members to try to correct imbalance in order to maintain fairness.

Unsettled Accounts and the Revolving Slate

Balances of obligation and entitlement between two or more persons are affected by events which occur externally to those relationships. For example, those who have suffered greatly or have been greatly deprived may consciously or unconsciously feel they are entitled to make others suffer or to deprive others—that is, others who may have had nothing to do with their suffering or deprivation.

It is well known, for example, that battered children often become battering parents. And while, on one level, this may reflect behavioral deficits in learned parenting, on another it appears to involve an effort to get someone else to "make up for" or "pay for" what was done to the child, now grown to parenthood. Boszormenyi-Nagy speaks of a "revolving slate" (1973), meaning that when a person is unable or unwilling to settle accounts of justice in the relationship to which they belong, he or she may try to achieve balance by making an innocent third party pay for that imbalance. Contextual therapists also speak of what appears to be a felt "immunity from guilty" (Boszormenyi-Nagy, 1973) which may develop in those who have been severely exploited and which may encourage this revolving slate.

The concept of the revolving slate resembles those of "displacement" in psychoanalytic theory and "scapegoating" in interpersonal and system theory. However, while displacement refers to the intrapsychic experience of one person, and scapegoating refers to an observable behavioral process between at least two persons, the revolving slate refers to a process which requires a minimum of three persons and which occurs both between and within persons in the ethical dimension which connects them.

The revolving slate often involves at least three generations. An unsettled account between parent and child can be transferred when the child grows up, to a child of his or her own. Unless rebalanced at some point, these unsettled accounts can continue to be transmitted across generations, with each recipient hating the way their parent treated them and hating themselves for now treating their own child in the same way.

A 35-year-old single mother of two sons, ages 12 and 9, was herself beaten as a child by her alcoholic father and abandoned by her mother in her early teens. Now separated from her husband (who provides no child support and has no contact with his sons), she works as a waitress, drinks heavily, and provides little in the way of structure or support for her sons, although she continues to feed and provide for them. Chronically angry and bitter, she frequently berates them for apparently minor complaints and misbehavior and has, on several occasions, shut the older boy out of the home and ignored his pleas to be let back in. In treatment, she remarks that this boy especially reminds her of her father and when encouraged to consider her treatment of the boys, she implicitly justifies her actions by stating that "no one took care of me."

The revolving slate highlights the importance of multigenerational patterns in a variety of presenting problems. One of the most basic elements of these multigenerational patterns is addressed at the ethical level by the concept of legacies.

Legacy

Legacies imply inherited obligations which derive from the facts and patterns of one's origins. For example, the legacy of parental accountability (the obligation to act responsibly toward one's children) derives from the fact of conception and childbirth, as does the legacy of filial loyalty (the inherent indebtedness of the child to the parent for his or her very existence).

Beyond these universal legacies, there are more specific legacies within particular families which derive from more idiosyncratic facts and patterns. In an earlier section, we referred to the Kennedy and Krupp families. In the Kennedy family, the accomplishments of Joseph Kennedy contributed to a legacy of striving and achievement in many of his children. The deaths of first Joseph, Jr. and then John and Robert Kennedy may have contributed to an "over-weighted" legacy for each of the surviving brothers.

In the Krupp family, it was not the accomplishments but the failure of one forebearer which led to the tremendous efforts of his son (only 14 years old at the time of his father's death) to restore the family's fortune, position, and good name. In the context of this son's phenomenal success, the Krupp legacy came more to resemble that of the Kennedys, an expectation that each generation would respect the rules of the patriarch, continue his efforts to build the firm, and live up to his example.

What differentiates the legacy from the facts from which it may derive is its ethical imperative. The accomplishments of the parent are facts; the expectation or obligation they impose on a child constitute the legacy. Legacies, which are transmitted from parent (and/or grandparent, sibling, or extended family member) to child, may vary regarding to whom the debt is owed. Particular legacies may be very much between parent and child or they may reflect the accumulated events and expectations of generations in a family. They may involve the major ethnic, religious, regional, or tribal group to which the family belongs. The legacies of hatred for an historical enemy, of revenge for past wrongs, and the prohibitions against marrying "outsiders" cut across cultural, national, and class lines.

Some of the most common legacies involve expectations that children will continue a family tradition. This may involve the world of work (taking over the family business, learning a parent's craft, working for the same company or in the same union). Or, the choice of a mate, who must be from a particular religious or regional or economic background. Or, the religious upbringing of children. Other legacies reflect the hard work and longed-for status of the parents, perhaps most familiar to us in the "my son, the doctor" scenario.

More specific legacies may arise from a variety of factors, such as a parent's abandonment of the family or from the frustration of their earlier cherished hopes and dreams. Many individuals who achieve outstanding success in some area, for example, are often found to have had a parent (frequently of the opposite sex) whose own early aspirations in that or a related area were in some way thwarted. Legacies often derive from the early death of a family member.

In one family, the mother of three children is killed with her son in a car accident. It is understood by the surviving family members that the older daughter is expected to conceive a child who will be named after the deceased mother. When this daughter proves unable to have children, her 14-year-old sister understands that this responsibility has passed to her.

Legacies of shame, when a parent or family ancestor has been disgraced in some way, can continue to affect the family for generations to come. Conversely, a legacy of pride and self-respect can sustain generations of a family, as was perhaps most dramatically expressed in recent years by the television serial, *Roots.*

Legacies shape the lives of individuals and the destinies of families. Like the "missions" which Stierlin (1974) discusses, like family roles and individuals' identities, with which they are obviously closely related, they both enable and limit. They encourage development of some aspects of being a person and discourage others. They pass on something of value and rule out other values. They can liberate and support as they can imprison and obstruct.

While the legacy presents a demand or a claim to be fulfilled, it need not dictate the terms, the timing, and the form of the repayment. The claim of the legacy must be balanced against a variety of other claims in the life of the individual, including his or her own entitlement to a satisfying and productive life. The legacy itself cannot be changed anymore than time can be reversed and the events and patterns which have contributed to it undone. Nevertheless, the individual does retain the freedom (in fact, the obligation) to consider the legitimacy of the legacy's claim in context and to exercise imagination in deciding when and how it can best be fulfilled. Legacies shape individuals and, by their actions, individuals in turn shape the legacies of the future.

While the content of a family's legacies are shaped by the facts and patterns of its history, their power derives from the loyalty of the child to his or her parents and forebearers. This notion provides an opportunity for us to consider the concept of loyalty in more depth.

Loyalty

The word "loyalty" derives from the French word for law. According to Webster's, it means "faithfulness to something to which one is bound by a pledge, a duty, or by a sense of what is right or appropriate." Boszormenyi-Nagy (1973) points out that loyalty has a double meaning, referring both to "external expectations and internalized obligations" (p. 37):

Loyalty as an *individual's* attitude . . . encompasses identification with the group, genuine object relatedness with other members, trust, reliability, responsibility, dutiful commitment, faithfulness, and staunch devotion. The expectation hierarchy of the *group,* on the other hand, connotes an unwritten code of social regulation and social sanctions. [P. 42, emphasis is in original]

In this sense, the concept of loyalty contributes to a theory of human life which addresses both the "within" and the "between" from one, coherent perspective.

In families, we see loyalty expressed in the "school phobias" of the young children who stay home to keep a needy and lonely parent company; in the functional somatic and psychiatric symptomatology as well as the peer-relation problems of children, adolescents, and young adults whose parents are so in need of them that they cannot bear to let them separate from the home; in the efforts of adults to care for their aging and dying parents and of children to protect and defend their younger or weaker siblings from other children.

Loyalty is in fact so universal a phenomenon in human relationships and especially family relationships, in what we define as health as well as pathology in these relationships, that its virtual absence until recently as a descriptive and explanatory concept constitutes in our minds one of the major deficits in current family theory. Family theory and therapy have generally been either implicitly or explicitly based on the concept of power. Analysis has focused on who's in charge. Who's struggling with whom to be in charge? Who's dominant? How do interactions reflect sequences of one-upmanship? And while there can be no question that power is an important and relevant dimension of family relationships, family theory has suffered by exaggerating its importance and minimizing or overlooking the importance of loyalty dynamics. What is needed at this point in the development of family theory is a perspective which is willing and able to consider both power and loyalty dynamics, both disjunctive and conjunctive forces, as they interact in the ongoing life of the family.

It is worth noting that loyalty often reflects the recognition of indebtedness. This may involve indebtedness for particular actions of the other, actions which increase the other's entitlement and the person's obligation. This is the case when someone says, in effect, "he stood by me when I needed him and it's my turn now to stand by him." In other cases the others may appear to have "done nothing" for the person, may even have hurt or misused him or her in some way, but the sense of loyalty persists, even if its source is unclear. In these cases, the person may say, "I know she's been rotten to me but she's still my mother." The person him or herself may find this continuing sense of loyalty bewildering. Most contextual therapists would see this as the natural expression of the child's loyalty to his or her parents, regardless of the merit of their actions. In a sense, they would say it reflects an existential indebtedness—that is, a recognition that one owes one's life to one's parents, no matter how they have acted. To the extent to which they have avoided subsequent responsibilities or exploited the child, the child derives greater entitlement regarding them. But this does not erase indebtedness related to birth and nurturance.

The relationship between loyalty and indebtedness leads us to consider the relationship between loyalty, in some ways an unfamiliar concept in individual and relational theory, and guilt, a very familiar concept. From an individual, intrapsychic perspective, guilt is often assumed to be both irrational and pathological. This is understandable given the cultural and historical context in which psychoanalytic theory developed and perhaps inevitable in a framework that is grounded in internal individual experience.

This perspective has certainly helped liberate people from unrealistic and self-destructive feelings of guilt for events over which they may have had no real control or for feelings and thoughts which clearly harmed no one. However, this perspective was of little help when people felt guilty for acts of omission or commission which may have either ignored real debts to another or clearly been unfair or harmful to the other. When actual injury has occurred, guilt is not necessarily pathological or irrational.

The recognition of indebtedness as a real aspect of relationships implies that a distinction must be made between "irrational" and "realistic" guilt (Buber, 1957; Boszormenyi-Nagy, 1973). In those cases in which there is a realistic basis for guilt, the existence of such feelings is anything but pathological. In fact, it was a psychoanalytic thinker, D.W. Winnicott, who first recognized that the *capacity* for guilt reflects a significant developmental accomplishment in terms of the infant's growing ability to maintain relationships (1965). It implies an ability to consider the other person's side and the impact of one's actions on him or her. Bear in mind that guilty feelings are often linked to a fear of or act of betraying another, the ultimate violation of loyalty.

In this sense, guilt is sometimes like the pain which accompanies a wound: it signals that something is wrong and may serve as a spur toward eventual healing if it is tended to. As such, it constitutes a valuable resource rather than pathology for individuals and for the family as a whole.

It should be emphasized that this is not to deny the existence of irrational, pathological guilt, just as the recognition of obligation does not eliminate the existence of cases of excessive, unrealistic demands and obligations. It does suggest the value, both theoretically and practically in treatment, of recognizing loyalty as a resource, without automatically transforming it into a weakness. We find it helpful, and we encourage students when they find themselves thinking about someone's feelings of guilt, to consider the relevance of the concept of loyalty at that point.

Deciding What's Fair

We have discussed obligations and entitlements, acknowledgment and claim, ethical balance, legacy, loyalty, and irrational versus realistic guilt. These concepts raise a host of questions. Who is to say what's fair and what's unfair? When is guilt realistic and when irrational? How do we differentiate between fair and excessive obligation? Between genuine entitlement and martyrlike manipulation of gratitude? The answers to these questions are rarely simple. Nevertheless, there are some guidelines which make the task more manageable.

First, it must be accepted that the final word on what constitutes fairness and unfairness in a particular relationship must come from the persons who are directly involved in it. We are not talking about "objective," external, ethical criteria, but of the search for mutual facing, for the settling of accounts, person to person, between and among the individuals whose relationships are in question. This is not a fixed ethical code, with universal application, like that of certain religious approaches; it is, instead, an intergenerational, interpersonal ethic which members of a relationship work out together in the context of the specifics of that relationship. The therapist (or any third party) can help them in this process by asking questions which encourage them to consider the balance of debts and entitlements. But no outsider can ever impose on them particular solutions to how those debts incurred should be repaid.

The only fixed ethical value which the therapist can introduce into treatment is that attached to *efforts to reassess the balances of fairness* with significant members of one's own context. The process of give and take which this joint examination requires, of individuals considering and asserting claims, trying to see the others' sides and presenting their own, marks the beginning and the most important part of efforts to rebalance. Often, resolution is discovered in ways quite different from what the therapist would have thought best. This is natural since only the participants can gauge the weight and meaning of events and considerations in context and even these assessments may change significantly as new factors are introduced from their ongoing dialogue.

The first principle, then, is that persons outside a particular relationship can encourage participants to examine the degree of balance in their relationships; the particular decisions as to what constitutes fairness, what is owed and how it is to be repaid, can only be arrived at by those directly involved.

Realistic Accountability

A second guideline involves what contextual therapists refer to as "realistic accountability." This suggests that the greatest benefits for all participants derive from the participants' conjoint efforts to repay or balance debts fairly, without either "shortchanging" the other or paying excessively and self-destructively.

The term "realistic accountability" represents a stance which encourages people neither to ignore debts nor to tolerate unfair, unrealistic obligations, but to look for ways to balance their own entitlement with that of another. In this sense, realistic accountability encourages us to face our responsibilities and debts in relationships but puts some ceiling on how much we can ask ourselves and be asked to pay. The "height" of the ceiling will be determined by the partners' consideration of the balance of indebtedness and entitlement in context.

This is a particularly helpful concept in therapy, whether individual, marital, or family. It allows the therapist to acknowledge the individual's obligation to others but gives people the tools to steer away from pathological repayments or evasion of debts. By confirming the individual's loyalties and redirecting them to less self-destructive forms of expression, the therapist: (1) helps the individual avoid guilt feelings that accompany a sense of betrayal, (2) allows the individual to continue to derive entitlement that is linked to caring for others, (3) works to reduce or eliminate symptomatic expressions of negative loyalty, (4) side-steps a potent source of resistance in treatment, and (5) acknowledges the presence of loyalty and trustworthiness in a relationship.

Like the majority of concepts associated with the ethical dimension of relationships, realistic accountability cuts both ways. It applies equally to all parties in a relationship. The most important implication of this is that a ceiling also exists on the extent to which the other can be held accountable in a relationship. We may have wished for perfect or total accountability from a parent, for example, but we need to consider the limitations, lack of resources, and exploitation suffered in their own lives. In other words, we need to judge their actions towards us by the same standard of realistic accountability by which we try to judge our own.

Trust and Trustworthiness

We have already introduced the notion of conjunctive forces in close relationships. One of the most vital of these forces, and one which runs through virtually all individual and relational theories, is trust. Trust is generally recognized as a necessary basis for lasting, healthy relationships and as a cornerstone of individual psychological development. While granting its importance, however, therapists and theorists often feel they can do little but mourn its absence or its violation in people's lives. Our feeling is that often (although by no means always), this sense of helplessness in the face of mistrust reflects the limitations of both internal individual and system theories. We feel, with Boszormenyi-Nagy, that without consideration of the ethical dimension of relationships, trust remains unnecessarily mysterious and abstract as well as resistant to therapeutic change.

If we only look at the internal experience of one person, it is impossible to appreciate the *relational context* of trust. And if we limit ourselves to questions of communication, function, and structure, we operate in the middle of that context but without access to the dynamics of trust—somewhat like a person who can perceive shapes but not color and fragrance studying the pollination of flowers by insects.

We can begin to demystify trust by asking where it comes from. Does it fall from the sky? Is it inborn? Is it a response to early parenting, essentially fixed by the age of 3? Or is it an act of will, susceptible to structured exercises in groups with strangers? Fundamentally, trust is a response to *trustworthiness.* Trust is the *readiness to depend* on someone who we have *reason to know* is *dependable.* And each element of this definition sheds some light on the dynamics of trust and trustworthiness.

The "readiness to depend" highlights the riskiness and the vulnerability which often make trust so frightening and brittle a prospect. The person who trusts allows him or herself to be put in a position in which (s)he can be harmed or betrayed by another person. If the person "counts on" the other for functional help or relational security, (s)he may not get it and may be hurt, disappointed, cheated, betrayed, embittered.

The importance of the "dependability" of the other points up the critical significance of *trustworthiness* in the dynamics of trust. Trust makes no sense outside the context of a trustworthy relationship and is not merited in the context of an untrustworthy relationship. Our own clinical experience suggests that, regardless of the complexities of early infant experience and the possible indirect benefits of positive experiences in groups, the most salient factor affecting an individual's level of trust (and potentially the most accessible and powerful avenue of therapeutic change) lies in the trustworthiness of his or her most important close relationships.

The basis of trustworthiness is a capacity for fairness. And even when this capacity for fairness is limited in an individual, either by their own life circumstances, by their own victimization in past relationships, or by physical or cognitive factors, their willingness and their effort to do their best for the other constitutes a critical component of trustworthiness.

While these limitations may be more striking in some cases than in others, they exist to some extent in all cases.

Realistically, we cannot expect of others that they always succeed perfectly in meeting our needs but rather that they do the best they can. Again, we are talking about realistic accountability. And again, this cuts both ways. The degree to which a person can be trusted is measured by the extent of his or her efforts to consider the other's side and to be as fair and as responsible as possible in an effort to balance what both (or all) parties deserve.

Actualized Trustworthiness

References above to "efforts" by one party or the other relate to the last element of the definition of trustworthiness given earlier—that we trust when we have "reason to know" that the other is dependable. Both of these concepts highlight the essential importance of *action* in the dynamics of trust and trustworthiness. If trust derives, in large part, from the experience of trustworthiness, it does not derive from the other's claims to trustworthiness or from their promises of trustworthiness. It emerges from their demonstrated or, in the words of contextual therapy, *actualized trustworthiness.*

Actualized trustworthiness refers to the fact that trust fundamentally depends on trustworthiness which is demonstrated in action and can be tested in action. If you take a risk to help me and I promise to be available when you need help, what do I actually do when you need me to take a risk for you? If you assure me that I can depend on you, how do you actually react when I do so?

This does not necessarily mean a physical action. In some cases, what a person says may contribute to trustworthiness in a relationship. For example, someone who has refused to admit any fault in a relationship in which (s)he has wronged another finally is able to acknowledge his or her failure. In doing so, (s)he may be taking a first step towards actualizing trustworthiness by facing the ledger of that relationship. Similarly, sometimes even a statement which reveals a feeling may contribute to actualizing trustworthiness.

Two grown sisters discuss their childhood together with an abusive father. One learns that, at one point when father gave her a brutal beating and she thought her sister was indifferent, the sister in fact was trying to think of a way to stop it without breaking up the family.

Purely verbal expressions of trustworthiness, however, are not likely to sustain trust if the person's actions contradict them. In the realm of trustworthiness, "actions speak louder than words." The following examples, taken from ongoing family therapy cases, illustrate particular efforts to actualize trustworthiness by family members:

A 17-year-old man is in prison for breaking and entering. He is the third of five children to serve time in prison. His mother, who lives in the same state, travels regularly to visit his older brother who is in jail in another state but does not visit, call, or write to him. In addition, he is not given her present telephone number. He understands that his mother is upset over his wild and disruptive behavior when he lived with her and her second husband for a short period between jail terms but is hurt and angry at the persistence of her rejection. The young man is depressed and somewhat suicidal. His therapist contacts the mother who agrees to come in for one session with her son and the therapist. At that meeting, she shares her fears that her son will somehow endanger her current marriage which she considers the first dependable relationship she has ever had. Her willingness to attend this meeting represents one step towards actualizing trustworthiness. She adds to this effort by giving her new telephone number to her son and by offering to have him visit occasionally when he is released from prison, although she draws the line at letting him return to live with her.

A husband and wife are reunited after a one-year separation following the wife's disclosure of a previously secret affair. The husband continues to suspect his wife of seeing or being in contact with the other man, which she denies. She responds to the therapist's questions by voicing her fear that if she were to make even a fairly innocuous admission, her husband would interrogate her endlessly afterwards. After much discussion, the wife is able to admit that the man has called her twice in recent months but that no further contact has ensued. Her husband reports that he now believes her, promises to ask no further questions, but requests to be informed if the man calls again.

The concept of actualized trustworthiness serves to demystify abstract concepts of trust and trustworthiness and provides specific, concrete steps toward building or restoring these resources in people's lives. In addition, it demonstrates the importance of *action* for the ethical dimension of relationships. If long-term unfairness occurs in a relationship, it occurs in the realm of action, not merely feeling or thought. And therefore, if it is to be corrected, this also must occur in the realm of action.

Finally, these relationships between trust, trustworthiness, and action provide a final example of the interlocking of intrapsychic and interpersonal dynamics. Trust, which refers to the *internal experience* of one person, is based on past *actions* and predicts future *actions* by the other person (actualized trustworthiness); it encourages trust-building *actions* by the person, which contribute to the *internal experience* of trust in the other.

This chapter has presented a theoretical framework for the analysis of family structure. But family structure is not static. Families change over time, particularly as they move through predictable stages of family life. Together with family structure, the family life cycle is an essential element in the therapist's understanding of families. It is, therefore, the subject of the next chapter.

2

The Family Life Cycle

An analysis of family structure, even one which includes each of the dimensions described in the previous chapter, reveals only part of the picture. Such an analysis addresses the predictability of pattern but not the predictability of change; it informs us about typical relationships and configurations within the family at a given time but not about how families change over time.

Fortunately, this aspect of family life has begun to be explored and described within the framework of the family life cycle. Just as the life cycle of the individual has come under increasing scrutiny over the past two decades (Erikson, 1959; Neugarten, 1976; Levinson, 1978), family theorists and therapists have developed a framework for the life cycle of families and postulated a number of predictable stages within that cycle

(Rogers, 1960; Hill, 1970; Haley, 1973; Solomon, 1973; Duvall, 1977).*
The reader who wishes to study this area more extensively is referred to
these sources and especially to Carter and McGoldrick's excellent book
(1980) on the subject.

We referred earlier to the predictability of change. Those who study
the family life cycle assume that all families go through *predictable stages*
of family life. They may differ in how they go through them and in when
they go through them, but there is no skipping them, just as no individual
can skip infancy or adolescence.

Each stage is precipitated by a particular *life event,* a new fact which
demands changes and adjustments on the parts of all family members. In
this sense, each stage presents the family with a *crisis* and brings with it
some increased pressure and disorganization. This is because many of the
patterns and regularities which have developed up to that point are disrupted by this new fact of family life; they must be reorganized if the
family is to be able to move on with its development. In the broadest
possible sense, one of the fundamental tasks of all family life is to integrate
stability and change so that the family as a whole and its individual
members can grow, without either becoming "stuck" or being overwhelmed by sudden, drastic changes.

Each stage presents the family with specific *tasks* which must be
mastered. And there are *typical problematic patterns* which indicate that
the new changes are not being well handled by the family. Theorists of
family development assume, as do those who study individual psychological development, that there are consequences to how well or how
poorly the family manages these stages. They assume that a poor resolution of any one stage makes the resolution of subsequent stages that
much more difficult.

Before proceeding to the stages themselves, two points should be made
concerning the family life cycle framework. One concerns its utility; the
other its limitations. In terms of clinical utility, the family life cycle
framework allows the interviewer to understand the presenting problem
and the family as a whole in its historical and developmental context. Just
as the therapist asks him or herself how the presenting problem fits into
the overall structure of the family, (s)he asks how the presenting problem
is related to the stage (or stages) with which the family is currently struggling. We will have more to say at the conclusion of this chapter on the

* The discussion which follows is largely derived from Solomon's (1973) work on family
development which impressed us in our early reading in this area. Our own additions or
revisions of this scheme involve (1) a greater emphasis on the ethical dimension in each stage,
(2) the division of his "Individuation of Family Members" stage into two stages, "Individuation of the Children" and "Individuation of the Adolescents," and (3) minor changes in
the names of the stages for somewhat greater stylistic consistency.

use of the life cycle framework as a diagnostic baseline in evaluation. For now, we simply want to highlight the fact that many common marital, family, and individual problems are often strongly related to pressures which accompany specific stages of family development. Examples of these typical expressions of stage-related problems will be presented as each stage is discussed.

Finally, while schema such as these are not necessarily limited to traditional nuclear families, they are certainly derived from and most neatly applicable to such families. In view of the significant increase in single-parent and remarried families in the United States, theorists are beginning to examine the impact of these phenomena on family development. The reader is referred to McGoldrick and Carter's chapter in their book (1980), which presents an analysis of developmental stages in the formation of remarried families. If the life cycle of the traditional nuclear family is not universal, it is nevertheless the norm from which other types of families depart. Having said this, we can move to an examination of the stages of the family life cycle.

MARRIAGE

In a technical sense, the family begins with the birth of the first child. But from the perspective of the family life cycle, it begins earlier in the future spouses' individual struggles to separate from their own families of origin and in the formation and consolidation of the marital relationship. Because the young adult's separation from family is explored later in this chapter, we will pass over that stage here and move directly to the formation of the couple's relationship. Precisely because the child is born into an already existing relational context and because that context is fundamentally changed by the inclusion of the child, we will better understand the family if we understand the couple's relationship from which the family grows.

And while the couple's relationship obviously begins earlier, the wedding constitutes the life event which sets significant relational changes into motion. In unmarried couples, the analogous event is usually the point at which the couple set up housekeeping together. In both cases, these concrete life events optimally will reflect a deepening mutual commitment between the partners and a potentially major step toward the consolidation of the relationship.

The major tasks of this stage are related to both partners' moves (in both literal and emotional senses) away from their families of origin and towards one another. This movement requires changes on a number of different levels.

At the level of individual psychology, both partners need to look less to their families of origin and more to each other for meeting basic emotional needs—for caring, comfort, company, and support—and for a variety of practical services as well. It follows that they are also called upon to respond to the needs of the other, a task which is often more difficult than it appears at first, since the kinds of needs expressed as well as the level of needs expressed may be very different from what each partner has experienced in their families of origin.

At the systemic level, the partners need to establish a series of ground rules and patterns which allow them to function well as a couple. These include ground rules for meeting one another's needs, for negotiating differences and disagreements, and for coordinating the activities necessary for the daily life of the marriage (income, shopping, house cleaning). They need to establish boundaries which work well for them, both within and around the marital relationship. Ideally, the boundary *between* them should be flexible yet firm enough to allow both partners to feel that they are part of a "We," without having to sacrifice a sense of themselves as a separate person, an "I." Boundaries *around* the couple ideally are those which allow them intimacy and privacy without disrupting their connections to the wider community of social relationships and to each of their families of origin.

At the level of relational ethics, the central task of this stage involves both partners' efforts to balance loyalties to their families of origin, their new spouses, and themselves. They are now faced with multiple (and sometimes competing) relational obligations, and with the task of trying to balance all these claims without seriously shortchanging any of the parties involved.

In terms of their families of origin, this means trying to restructure relationships so as to allow for greater mutual independence without disrupting ongoing mutual loyalty and availability. In terms of the marital relationship, it means trying to establish a relational structure of fairness and trustworthiness, so that neither partner is fundamentally shortchanged or mistreated by the other.

These efforts to establish mutual fairness and trustworthiness are often complicated by the colliding legacies and entitlements of both partners. Individuals who have been seriously shortchanged in their own families often feel entitled to extensive unilateral availability and caretaking by the other and are dismayed when the other not only fails to meet these expectations, but places identical (and often it seems to them unjustified) demands on them. Similarly, legacies which call for extraordinary levels of professional achievement and success in one partner may conflict with the other's needs for intimacy and close family life.

Common Problems

There are a number of fairly typical presenting problems among young couples which suggest that they are having difficulty with the basic tasks of this stage. They may complain of chronic, ongoing conflicts in which a host of previously unresolved issues are raised. Or, there may be little or no explicit conflict, but a high degree of tension or irritability and a general feeling of "walking on eggshells." Both patterns suggest difficulties developing ground rules for integrating differences and resolving conflicts. Mutual complaints of the selfishness, unavailability, or relentlessly excessive demands of the other indicate probable difficulties in developing ways of meeting one another's needs, in the regulation of distance and boundaries within the marital relationship, and possibly in the replication in the marital relationship of partners' "unfinished business" with their families of origin.

Other patterns point more clearly to difficulties in balancing loyalties and establishing boundaries between families of origin and the marital relationship. One common pattern involves a rigid alliance of one spouse with his or her family of origin against the other spouse (the "I'm going home to mother" syndrome). A variant of this pattern involves protracted conflicts between the spouses, each of them closely allied with their own families of origin. Another pattern is marked by the assumption of major responsibilities for the couple's daily life by one or both sets of parents, with the couple in a submissive, irresponsible role. Lastly, one or both partners' "cutting off" or renouncing all ties with their families of origin constitutes another indication of difficulty in balancing loyalties and integrating multiple relational claims.

As will be true for each stage we discuss, this is not meant to suggest that these common problems are always caused by these stage-related stresses. In some cases, similar patterns may develop from quite different issues. And even when such difficulties are present, there can be significant variation in the degree to which these are situational, stage-specific problems, or to which they reflect more serious and long-term problems, as will be discussed at the end of this chapter. For the most part, however, the therapist is wise at least to consider the significance of stage-related pressures and demands in the kinds of common problems found during each stage.

Regardless of the quality of resolution of the tasks of this stage, the couple is catapulted into a new stage, with new tasks, by the birth of the first child. The decision to have a child sometimes represents a natural next step after a reasonably good resolution of the first stage. Other times, it represents a desperate attempt to "solve" the lingering problems of that stage. In still other cases, the child is conceived without either partner explicitly deciding to have a baby; (s)he may have been conceived before the marriage, in fact, and may even have been a major reason for the marriage. While these different situations have significant bearing on the resources and pressures which will exist in later stages, the fact of the child's birth moves the family in all of these cases into a new stage of family life.

BIRTH OF THE CHILDREN

Rarely, if ever, does a normal life event have so sweeping an impact as the birth of the first child. The twosome becomes a threesome (and then some, with the births of other children). Persons are transformed into mothers and fathers; spouses suddenly become parents. Virtually all patterns of time, schedule, expenditures, leisure, use of space in the home, even (and especially) relationships with in-laws and friends are shaken up and reorganized around the needs of the child.

At the level of individual psychology, this means first of all an increased level of physical and emotional demands being placed on both parents. They are confronted with the responsibility of caring for the infant, which brings with it a host of fairly constant worries (about correct feeding, health, and safety) and requires new skills (such as changing, pacifying, and feeding the infant). Their reserves of patience are likely to be sorely tested, while their physical and emotional needs for rest and "recharging" are being denied or disrupted. At one and the same time, they are faced with complicated questions of judgment regarding the infant and with repetitive and largely boring chores imposed by the infant's needs.

The birth of the child can have a significant impact on each parent's sense of individual identity. It may give meaning and a positive identity or it may trigger feelings of inadequacy and resentment and constitute a negative identity (especially where other areas of positive identity, such as career success, are disrupted by the arrival of the infant).

The major task of this stage involves both parents' attempts to integrate their new relationships to the child with the relationship that already exists between the two of them. At the systemic level, this involves the creation of new boundaries, subsystems, and roles. Specifically, the marital subsystem must make room for a parental subsystem. The task is for the spouses to participate in both subsystems without seriously short-changing either. The boundaries they create (whether the child has a room of its own, whether the parents spend any time together without the child, etc.) will regulate the coexistence of these subsystems within the new family. The parents also need to develop ground rules for sharing and coordinating the new chores and responsibilities imposed by the infant.

At the ethical level, the basic task of this stage involves both spouses' efforts to balance their increasingly complex networks of obligation and entitlement—at this point, obligations to one's child, one's spouse, one's family of origin and one's self. And this is made even more difficult by the fact that this stage calls for an extended period of essentially *unilateral devotion* by the parents towards the child since the latter cannot actively help or thank the parents in any way at this point. This places a major stress on both parents' reserves of availability to the claims of others.

If the potential exists for colliding entitlements when the couple marry, it is increased by the arrival of the child, whose natural entitlement to caretaking, devotion, and protection may come into conflict with the parents' own needs to be cared for and with the depletion of their reserves for giving and caring. The question arises in these situations as to how the resources for the child's care can be mobilized. The answer often involves the extended family or, in some cases, the institutions of the larger society.

Common Problems

Couples who are having difficulty dealing with the tasks of this stage often present with fairly typical complaints and problems. Perhaps most common are complaints by one parent (usually but not always the father) that the other is overinvolved with the child and by the other parent that his or her spouse is underinvolved with both of them. Another typical complaint is of decreased marital satisfaction, often with a prolonged decrease in almost everything associated with the marriage (communication, intimacy, sexual relations, social activities). Both complaints indicate parental involvement with the child to such an extent that the marital relationship is neglected and thereby endangered. Other typical complaints revolve around one (usually but not always the mother) or both parents feeling depressed and overwhelmed by the stresses of parenthood.

Other patterns may suggest the opposite of the above patterns—that is, both parents' insufficient attention and accountability to the child. This may occur in the context of a stormy, enmeshed marital relationship in which partners are so intensely focused on one another that there is little room for investment in the child. Or, it may reflect the exhaustion and depletion of the parents. Typically, this pattern presents with evidence of neglect or rejection of the infant (either subtle or overt) by the parents. It may also be seen when a member of the extended family (typically grandmother) has absorbed major caretaking responsibility for the child.

In many families, the first child will be followed by a second and perhaps more children. Depending on the number of years between children, then, as the family moves into subsequent stages they may have several children at the same stage or experience different stages at the same time, or both. Again, regardless of how well or poorly the tasks of this stage are resolved, the natural physical and psychological development of the infant into a young child moves the family into a new stage of the family life cycle.

INDIVIDUATION OF THE CHILDREN

This stage is marked by the growing definition of the child's individuality within the family and by the consequent reorganization of parent-child expectations and reciprocity. In one sense, the stage could be said to begin when the child reaches the "terrible twos." At about this age, (s)he discovers the power of the word "no" and begins to use it with relish to assert a newly discovered will. The major tasks of this stage, however, become most sharply defined when the child becomes old enough for two major new developments, developments which inevitably follow from the child's natural psychological and relational growth.

One involves the beginning of social activity outside the home, with peers and adults, whether at school or in neighborhood play. The other involves the natural evolution of parental expectations regarding the child, which coincides with the child's developing readiness for such expectations. This second development includes changes on a number of different levels. It may involve such mundane matters as whether or not the child begins to be expected to dress him or herself or to clean up his or her room. At increasingly profound levels, it may involve expectations of caring for younger children or for one or both parents, as in excessive parentification of children.

The major tasks, then, of this stage are twofold. One involves trying to balance the growing autonomy of the child with his or her sense of belonging and loyalty to the family, without either "binding" or "expelling" the child, to use Stierlin's (1974) vocabulary. The second involves trying to maintain a reasonable and fair balance of accountability between parents and child, without either overburdening the child with expectations and missions or expecting too little or nothing of the child.

At the level of individual psychology, the parents must face what may be their first sense of real psychological separation from the child. They may experience increased fears concerning the child's welfare out of the home and out of their sight, as well as concern over the kinds of influences to which the child will be exposed.

The child may face fears associated with the world outside the home—fears of being separated from his or her parents, of unfamiliar surroundings, of other children or adults. (S)he faces new expectations for performance, at home, at school, and with peers at play. The child has to begin to consider how to balance his or her own needs and desires with those of other children as well as with the demands of parents and other adults.

At the same time that the child faces these new risks and complexities, (s)he stands to benefit by grappling successfully with them. (S)he can reap the positive growth which results from friendships, learning, and beginning to feel useful and helpful to others, especially to the family. This points to the other major factor developing in the child at this stage—what Boszormenyi-Nagy (1973) describes as the child's "capacity for meaningful contribution." The child begins to develop a need and a capacity to contribute, to be of help in some way, especially to his or her parents and other family members.

The ways in which a particular child's capacity for contribution meets and coevolves with the parents' needs and expectations for him or her will set the direction for much of his or her sense of identity and role in the family. We have already indicated how these expectations, communicated first and foremost by the parents, may involve more than just the personal needs of the parents. They may reflect transgenerational legacies from both parents' families of origin as well as from the religious, ethnic, racial, or national groupings into which the child is born.

At the systemic level, the boundaries between and around the child and the parents are significantly changed in this stage. As the boundaries of the child's world expand outside the home and as the child begins, for the first time, to spend significant blocks of time away from the parents, boundaries between the parents and child necessarily become firmer than they have previously been. Simultaneously, the child becomes involved in systems outside the family, such as friendships, peer groups, and school. And the clarity and flexibility of boundaries between these systems become increasingly important as the child grows older.

When two or more children are born into the family, a sibling subsystem is created. As the child grows older, he or she may begin to be
included in a male or female subsystem as well as in subsystems organized
around certain activities (those who clean house, those who do yard work,
those who go shopping and so on). All of these developments require
boundary changes between and around the parents as well. As children
become included in more activities with one or both parents, those areas
in which the parents spend time alone or alone together are reduced. The
necessity of maintaining boundaries between the generations and of balancing marital and parental obligations or investments continues. However, the particular areas or activities which parents and children share
together or engage in separately do change significantly in this stage.

As stated earlier, the child's growing capacity for meaningful contribution combines with the parents' functional and emotional needs in ways
which radically redefine the child's position in the family. This results
in profound changes in the family at the level of relational ethics. At this
stage, the child may begin to take on missions (and with them, roles)
which can exert a major influence on his or her future life. Missions to
care for one or both parents, for their marriage, or for the family as a
whole, or to achieve and reflect pride on the family may become noticeable
at this stage.

These missions may or may not be harmful to the child, depending
largely on the fairness of give and take between parent and child, the
degree of parental acknowledgment for the child's earned merit, and the
degree to which these missions take into account the needs of the child.
For, as the child first begins to make a contribution to the family, the
previous structure of accountability, largely unilateral until now, begins
to be redefined. As the child becomes more available to help out, (s)he
can be asked to give too little or too much and the parents can give too
much or too little in return.

Several questions should now be raised in considering the parents'
management of the tasks of this stage. Is too much being asked of the
child? Is (s)he being expected to sacrifice too many of his or her own
needs in order to help others in the family? Is the merit of the child's
contribution being acknowledged? If circumstances lead to the child's
temporarily being asked to give too much, do the parents take steps later
to repair or to correct for this? Is too little being expected of the child?
Is (s)he being encouraged to think only of his or her own needs and
unrealistically to expect that they will be met by others without the child's
concern for fairness in return?

We can raise similar questions on the child's side. Does (s)he contribute
anything? Does (s)he give enough, too much or too little, considering the

context and needs of the family, the contributions of the parents and of any other children? It should be remembered, however, that in view of the still enormous influence of the parents in the child's development at this stage, what the child actually does is largely a matter of what the parents encourage, allow, and hold him or her accountable to do.

Common Problems

Families that are having difficulties with the tasks of this stage typically present a child as the Identified Patient. The most common exception to this rule involves the parent in the home (usually the mother) presenting with individual complaints, for example, anxiety, depression, loneliness, and self-doubt, following the child's starting school. These feelings usually occur when the youngest child goes to school since any younger children in the home can most likely postpone the parents' feelings of "unemployment."

Sometimes, in fact, these feelings are postponed by having more children or by bringing foster or adoptive children into the home. Often the parents' feelings of loss when the children go to school are quite manageable; they may even be accompanied by feelings of relief. The parent may seek work outside the home. When these feelings are more severe, however, and a substitute daily focus is neither sought nor found, the parent may present for treatment with one or more of the described symptoms.

More commonly, families that are having difficulty with this stage present with a child-focused problem. Occasionally (and perhaps increasingly, as family therapy becomes better known), the family presents the problem as relational—that is, they define it as between parents and child. But more often, the child is presented as the Identified Patient and the problem may take several different forms.

One typical presenting problem involves what is described as a "school phobia." Literally, this means that the child is afraid of school but this may or may not in fact be the case. Often what is called a fear reflects loyalty and responsibility on the part of the child for a parent in the home. Whatever the particular mixture of the parents' and child's anxiety, the problem does reflect the difficulty of family members tolerating the child's absence from the home and his or her participation in social life outside the home which is required by school. The child may instead present as regressed in some way—enuretic or encopretic, for example, or refusing to be separated from some transitional object, such as a doll. He or she may present with a psychosomatic disorder, such as asthma or vague gastrointestinal complaints.

Finally, parents frequently present with a child whom they describe as stubborn, rebellious, or selfish, a child who may have temper tantrums or who mistreats siblings or other children. Often, this picture reflects a child who is not held accountable enough by the parents, a child for whom little is expected, much is allowed and discipline is inconsistent or nonexistent. These children are, paradoxically, deprived. They are deprived of learning about those aspects of reality, such as the needs, feelings, and rights of others, which force and allow all of us to put limits on our own needs and expectations. Without any effective counterbalance, their needs and expectations may grow largely unchecked. The result is that reasonable natural limitations may begin to feel genuinely unfair to these children. And while this may be evident to some extent in childhood, like many of the other patterns discussed here, it is likely to become much more dramatically so in the next stage of the family life cycle—the individuation of the adolescents.

INDIVIDUATION OF THE ADOLESCENTS

At the risk of oversimplification, the fact which precipitates the family into this next stage of development is puberty. The physical changes which the child undergoes at puberty, together with the psychological and relational changes which they trigger, disrupt the structural patterns which have evolved in the family between parents and child. All family members are forced to accommodate to these changes and to evolve family patterns which take them into account.

The central task for the family at this stage is to redefine the terms of the parent-child relationship, primarily regarding issues of autonomy, responsibility, and control, without fundamentally violating their basic trustworthiness. Part of what makes adolescence so confusing for all involved is the extent to which it is a sort of "limbo" between childhood and adulthood. The person who was a child is clearly no longer one, but (s)he is just as clearly not yet an adult.

At the level of individual psychology, the parents face, in most cases, a loss of control over the now-adolescent son or daughter. They may, for the first time, be faced with overt rebellion. As the teenager begins to exert more control over the definition of his or her own identity, the parents may face threats to aspects of their identities which interlock with the adolescent's. They are confronted with the development of sexual maturity in the adolescent and, when their own past sexual development or current functioning is problematic to them, this can be especially difficult.

In spite of the validity and importance of these issues of control and sexuality, in our own clinical experience, by far the most common and the most significant issue presented to the parents by the advent of adolescence is the loss of the child. To the extent to which parents have actively participated in and derived enjoyment from the childhood of their children, they may sharply feel the loss of that period and its gratifications—participating in the child's discoveries and feeling needed and "looked up to" by the child. Often parents become more aware of the imminence of the child's actual departure from the home and of their own aging in this stage.

The teenager faces similar losses—a loss of the special exemptions of childhood, a loss of the world of play. (S)he begins to face increased responsibilities, in the home, in school, and in the community. (S)he is confronted with the tests of adulthood, e.g., part-time work in a family business or taking a test for a driver's license. (S)he faces in a very immediate way the issues of sexuality, identity, and peer-group relations, which can be so unsettling for the parents who are one step removed. Last, (s)he faces decisions with increasingly important implications for the future—which cliques (if any), to join, whether to spend a summer away from home, whether to work part time and if so at what, which skills and interests to pursue, and, eventually, what to do after high school.

The fundamental change at the systemic level during this stage involves the strengthening of boundaries between the parents and the adolescent, a change which affects virtually every area of daily life. Adolescents normally develop a greater sense of privacy in certain areas, areas in which they now say to the parents in effect, "It's none of your business." There may be changes in rules concerning nakedness, for example, with the teenager becoming more self-conscious or with one or both parents becoming more uncomfortable, even in a strictly medical context such as visiting the doctor.

Typically, these changes in boundaries are expressed nowhere more clearly than in the adolescent's room (when the adolescent has a room of his or her own). For the first time, parents may be asked to knock before they enter or they may be forbidden entrance altogether. Changes in boundaries within the sibling subsystem may be signaled when, if space allows, a teenager is moved out of the "children's room" and given one of his or her own. Sometimes, a new room is created for this purpose in a basement or attic.

This change in boundaries is significantly felt in the adolescent's life outside the home as well. His or her participation in the system of the family begins to be more evenly balanced by participation in the system of peers outside the home. Changes may take place in the amount of time spent away (how often (s)he goes out and how late (s)he stays out), in the amount of distance (s)he can go from the home and in the amount of indirect parental supervision (s)he receives (from other adults or older siblings, for example).

The radical changes which accompany adolescence put a significant strain on whatever trustworthiness has been established at the level of relational ethics. As the adolescent begins to develop a more separate, autonomous self apart from the family, as (s)he necessarily becomes more involved in developing his or her identity as a separate, individual person, the effort to balance loyalties to self and to others in the family necessarily becomes more complex. His or her entitlement to greater freedom and greater privacy necessarily cuts into the parents' entitlement to the adolescent's availability.

From the parental side, some variant of the complaint that the adolescent is not home enough is often heard. Parents are vulnerable to feeling underappreciated or shortchanged, especially "after all we've done for you." Similarly, as the adolescent's life outside the home and his or her sense of privacy expand and as a youngster pursues his or her own interests and priorities without informing his or her parents, the parents may experience doubts about trusting the adolescent. This is especially true if they still expect the adolescent to perform as if (s)he were a child and to earn trust by those rules.

From the adolescent's side, trust in the parents is often endangered by the imposition of parental decisions or rules which make no allowance for his or her own private interests and growing capacity for thoughtful decision making. Often, as much as anything else, this reflects the parents' difficulty in letting go of the child or in managing the now more complex equation of reciprocity themselves.

In a sense, the standard of trustworthiness changes somewhat in this stage just as what is considered fair between the adolescent and the parents has changed. In adolescence, the child is in fact entitled to a greater measure of freedom and independence from the family and yet the interdependence remains. And so the trustworthiness of the parents now includes the degree to which they can be expected to try to renegotiate the balance of give and take. Mistrust can develop when the parents' desire to renegotiate these terms collides with their need to hold on to the child, when they have difficulty adapting to the demands of this stage or, as sometimes happens, when they make a deliberate effort not to allow the adolescent greater freedom.

One final point should be made concerning this struggle over the adolescent's growing separation and freedom from the family. While it often appears as though the struggle is between adolescent and parent, with the adolescent wanting freedom and the parent resisting it, a closer look suggests that this is only part of the picture. Not surprisingly, if considered at a deeper level, both parties are often considerably more ambivalent. Parents may be torn between their urges to hold onto the child and to see him or her grow up and away, just as the adolescent may be torn between urges to grow out of the family and to remain in it as a child.

Finally, during this stage, familial (as well as broader cultural, racial, and religious) legacies become, if not more important in the life of the child, certainly more visibly prominent in shaping identity, choices, and goals. In Stierlin's terms, the adolescent begins to be assigned and to accept certain "missions" (1974). These missions play a significant role in the separation process of the adolescent or young adult from the home and will be discussed further in the following stage. At this point, we simply wish to point out that these missions or legacies, whether overt or covert, have a profound influence on the adolescent's sense of who (s)he is and on his or her decisions about the future.

The adolescent's inherent concern for and obligation to his or her parents and wider loyalty group constitute major factors in his or her willingness to accept these missions or legacies along with the burdens they often entail. The fact that attitudes of concern and obligation are often unconscious (hence, "invisible" loyalties) does not lessen their impact. They often dovetail with the adolescent's own need for a model, a guide, for directions and values worth pursuing in his or her struggle to create an adult self. These missions and legacies constitute powerful influences (at the level of intergenerational patterns of merit and ethics) in what Erikson has called the adolescent's "search for identity" (1959).

The specific forms of missions and legacies are innumerable. The adolescent may be expected by the family as well as him or herself to continue a family tradition, perhaps in the choice of a career, in the fulfillment of civic responsibilities, or in the choice of a spouse. (S)he may bear a strong legacy to achieve or succeed in some way in order to reflect pride on the family or, just the opposite, to fail so as not to surpass a parent's level of achievement.

The adolescent may be expected to stay at home in order to care for a needy parent or to put life into a stagnant marriage. (S)he may need to prove something about the family—that they can be as great as they once were or that they are not as bad (as poor, as uneducated) as they once were. The adolescent may be responsible for "living up to" the image of a revered parent, a deceased sibling, or a national hero, or (s)he may be charged to "make up for" the sins of a parent or others. And, the adolescent may feel called to help or defend his or her national, ethnic, or religious loyalty group. (S)he may bear more than one of these missions or legacies, which may or may not be in direct conflict with one another. In all of these cases, the call of relational, often transgenerational, obligations exercises a decisive impact on the actions and the future of the adolescent.

Common Problems

Probably the most common picture presented by families seeking treatment at this stage involves a rebellious, acting-out adolescent. The parents typically request treatment, with the adolescent often loudly resisting or sullenly complying. Usually, the parents point to one or more of the following as the focus of their concern: poor grades in school or truancy, experimentation with sex or drugs, and running away from the home. The adolescent complains that the parents are too restrictive or treat him or her like a child; the parents complain that the adolescent is hurting him or herself and (harkening to our earlier discussion) cannot be trusted.

We need not look very deeply to see how this type of presenting problem expresses the struggle in the family over greater independence and autonomy for the adolescent. More interesting are the particular patterns to which this often leads and what they suggest about the nature of the struggle. Quite frequently, the teenager's actions are, on one level, remarkably self-defeating in that they almost inevitably result in longer and longer periods of being "grounded" in the home. Therapists may try to reason with the adolescent about how all they have to do if they want to have more freedom is to be a little more careful about how late they stay out, etc. These efforts are usually remarkably unsuccessful. It is almost as though the adolescent were trying to be kept home; this is precisely the point.

These repetitive patterns of adolescent acting out and being grounded often reflect the teenager's own ambivalence about greater freedom and independence from the family. His or her actions and their predictable consequences express both the urge to grow up and get away and the desires to remain a child and to be loyal to and available to the family. Hoffman (1981) has brilliantly analyzed the dynamics of such problems at the systemic level. Seeing the family as unable to make a leap to the next stage, she interprets symptoms as "a primary irritant that both monitors the options for change, lest too rapid movement imperil someone in the family, and also keeps the necessity for change constantly alive" (p. 166).

Parents in this stage may be so unsettled by the changes in their children that they experience them as "strangers." Laing and Esterson (1964) have documented some rather extreme examples of this pattern.

Often, these are situations in which the child was, previous to adolescence, especially docile and cooperative. Parents may complain that there has been a "change in personality."

Often, these mysterious changes are vaguely related to a specific precipitant, such as a trip away from home, what the parents think or know to be some experimentation with drugs, or a minor illness or accident. Therapists in these cases need to consider the possibility that the adolescent has in fact experienced a major change, possibly related to serious psychological factors (depression, anxiety, psychosis) or physical changes (infection or injury). Nonetheless, it pays to be alert to the possibility that such a description may simply express the normal changes which accompany this stage of family life.

The second most common presenting problem for families at this stage involves not the adolescent who is struggling to be more free from the home but the one who is all too tied to it. These teenagers may present with any or all of a host of problems—with peers, school, and family as well as psychiatric and somatic symptomatology.

Often they have some difficulty relating to peers. They may describe themselves as shy and self-conscious, feeling like "an outsider" socially. They may have difficulty in school academically or in terms of attendance. But while the adolescents discussed earlier are likely to skip school without their parents' permission and to spend time away from school with friends, these teenagers more often avoid school with parental approval for vague medical complaints and spend their time by themselves at home.

Somatic complaints are not uncommon, usually of a vague nature, such as stomachaches, headaches, or weakness. Occasionally, this pattern may coexist with a bona fide, even serious, medical problem, such as seizures or diabetes. In these cases, the physical problem provides a convenient focus for the family's difficulty with the tasks of this stage. Unlike cases in which the medical problem exists without these more significant family problems, in these families, medical symptomatology and its interfering impact on the adolescent's life are often remarkably responsive to therapeutic intervention.

These teenagers can also become highly preoccupied with aspects of their appearance which have some bearing on their social life such as complexion and weight. The increasingly visible eating disorders in adolescents, such as anorexia and bulimia, are essentially more extreme variants of this presenting picture with quite similar underlying family structural patterns.

These are families in which the teenager is again caught between an urge to be more independent and a need to remain a child, both for his or her own needs and for the parents. These adolescents, while they may be hostile or sullen in the home, document their loyalty to the family by their continuing availability to them in the home. Often the only area in which they resist the parents is that of their symptomatology—not eating, overeating, missing school, failing courses. One of the hallmarks of this pattern is how neatly the presenting problem serves both to keep the adolescent in the home (thus expressing loyalty to the family) and to drive the parents wild with frustration (thus expressing some form of rebellion).

What the family accomplishes in this stage (and what they do not) usually becomes apparent during the next stage of family development—the departure of the children from the home.

DEPARTURE OF THE CHILDREN

The family enters a new stage in its developmental history when the child becomes old enough to leave home. This stage is initiated then by the child's reaching late adolescence and early adulthood—the ages normally associated with moves toward independent living. When there is more than one child, this stage usually begins with the coming of age of the oldest child and reaches its climax during and after the last child's leaving home.

The basic task for the family at this stage is to separate without breaking ties. Family members must be able to tolerate the losses associated with separation without rupturing or cutting off relationships. From a slightly different angle, we can say that the basic challenge of this stage involves family members being able to balance a dual commitment. They need to be able to invest in independent lives, households, relationships, and/or work of their own, as well as to maintain their investment in one another in spite of physical and sometimes significant geographic distance.

The family's resolution of this stage is problematic if either of these investments is prohibited or ignored. If the child is not permitted or is unable to develop some kind of independent life of his or her own, if the parents are unable to find a new life focus (whether it be in one another, in work, or in other activities or relationships), or if the physical separation is accomplished but continuity of contact, availability, and concern is disrupted, symptomatology of some type is likely to develop and the tasks of subsequent stages are likely to be more problematic.

At the individual level, the parents are faced with the loss of the child as a focus in their daily lives. This has aptly been described as the "empty-nest" syndrome. When the family's growth has proceeded without major obstacles or setbacks, there is some preparation for this in that the child has most likely been growing increasingly independent within the home and has been away from the home more often, following his or her own hours and requiring less daily supervision from the parents. Often there is a period of time preceding the child's actual departure when family members describe the child as "only coming home to eat and sleep." But even with reasonable preparation, this separation can be wrenching for all concerned. Parents may experience feelings of sadness, loneliness, sudden awareness of aging, and lack of purpose. And, with the sudden absence of the child, they are often brought face to face with each other. As the child leaves, the parents are left increasingly alone together.

Thus, the parents are forced to identify the resources and limitations of their marital relationship and of their own individual lives. To the extent to which they have been predominantly involved in parenting, they must find a new focus, a new purpose, for their lives. They may find this in one another, in work, in grandchildren, new activities, and relationships. Or they may not. They may choose to cling to their primary identification as "parents" and try to place the young adult back in the role of "child."

The young adult may be only too happy to comply with this attempt to stop the clock because of the difficulty of the challenges (s)he is beginning to confront at this stage of development. (S)he faces either the prospect or the reality of life away from home, a prospect which is fraught with potentially stressful and unpleasant experiences as well as with exciting and rewarding possibilities.

First and foremost, the young adult faces unfamiliarity, living alone or among people who are at least initially strangers. (S)he may experience loneliness, "homesickness," a sense of not fitting in. (S)he is usually forced to accept a much greater level of responsibility for his or her own life—finding an apartment, paying bills, getting medical care, car insurance, and the like. Those with whom the young adult interacts may be much less tolerant and indulgent than family members had been. Above and beyond these concerns, the young adult is inevitably struggling with issues of identity and direction, sexuality, and social integration.

The very name of this stage suggests the relevance of the systemic level, since the departure of the child involves a major change in boundaries within the family. The question is: what kind of change? When the young adult and his or her family manage to make the separation, a major change in physical boundaries occurs: the child is now outside the home. While this marks a change in the systemic level of the family, it does not in itself significantly change the deeper ethical dimension of structure, as will be discussed below.

When the child leaves home to be married or, soon after leaving, develops a couples relationship, family structure is again significantly altered. The family is presented with a new member, an "in-law," one who occupies a special position simultaneously within and outside of the family's intimate circle. Issues in defining the boundaries between the new marital subsystem and the families of origin have already been discussed in the context of the first stage of family development.

When there are younger children left in the home, they are often informally "promoted" to the rank of "oldest" (child, son, or daughter) in the home. A prized room or other possession may accompany this promotion. When there is only one child, or when the last one leaves, the generational boundary dissolves transactionally, leaving the marital subsystem, perhaps, in something of a vacuum.

The child may or may not actually leave home during this stage, and even when (s)he does, the question of how (s)he leaves has significant bearing on how (s)he and the rest of the family will fare afterwards. Helm Stierlin (1974) has described three basic modes of separation between parents and adolescents, in the context of studying runaways. These modes are well suited to the separation process for young adults as well.

In the "binding" mode, the child is unable to leave home. These "bound" young adults remain in the home, often out of a mixture of concern for and attachment to the family and fears of facing stressful aspects of independent living. In the "delegating" mode, the child is sent out of the family but with some kind of "mission" to accomplish. These "delegated" children are permitted to leave home but are held responsible (often covertly) by themselves as well as others in the family to pursue the missions called for by the family structure and history. Examples of such missions were described in the previous section. Finally, in the "expelling" mode, the young adult is, as it were, spit out of the family with no missions to fulfill. "Expelled" children are permitted to leave, often even forced to leave, with little sense that they are either wanted or needed in any way by the family.

Stierlin's framework addresses changes at the ethical as well as systemic and individual level of family structure. And the concepts of delegation and mission lead directly to the ethical dimension of relationships at this stage.

As the discussion of the "bound" child suggests, this stage raises the question of whether the young adult has the right to leave home, whether (s)he is entitled to a life of his or her own. If the answer is yes and (s)he does move out, the young adult begins in earnest what will be a life's work of balancing the dual commitment which we described earlier and which will often be complicated by new commitments—to lovers or spouses, children, groups, organizations, and vocations. We emphasize the original dual commitment to oneself and one's family because in our experience it operates as a critical foundation for efforts to balance later commitments. When this original balance is attained with relative success, it makes balancing later commitments easier. When it is not, it often takes an appreciable toll on the person in question.

The young adult has to balance loyalties and obligations to his or her family of origin with his or her obligations to him or herself. If (s)he is involved in a committed relationship, the generational wheel has come full circle and (s)he must now find ways to balance loyalties to family and to the new partner as in the first developmental stage we discussed. While this is sometimes a matter of balancing visible, practical, and limited demands (e.g., whether to spend a Sunday with one's parents or with one's spouse), the issues at stake are often less obvious and carry much greater weight. For example, consider the young man who carries a life-long legacy to achieve excellence in his profession but whose efforts to do this render him effectively unavailable to his wife. Or the woman who has unconsciously "promised" to a neglected mother that she will not give aid and comfort to the enemy (that is, men) and who cannot understand herself when she is so critical and distant with her boyfriend.

Like the young adult, the parents are trying to balance their dual commitments to the grown child, to themselves, and to each other. The fact that the young adult is out of the house does not mean that (s)he is in no further need of the parents. And it is not uncommon for the child's emotional, financial, and practical needs for the parents to conflict with their own needs. Probably one of the most common examples of this occurs when a young couple's entitlement to ask for babysitting services from one set of parents conflicts with the parents' entitlement to well-earned peace and quiet.

A process which typically develops gradually in families becomes clearest in this developmental stage. It involves a more even balance in responsibility and reciprocity between adult parent and adult child. During early childhood, this equation is clearly imbalanced, with the parents being responsible for essentially unilateral caring and responsibility. It becomes gradually less so during the child's adolescence, and it is when the child reaches adulthood that the parent-child relationship truly becomes more of a "two-way street." In this sense, the standard of trustworthiness changes again and family members must again try to evolve an understanding of what they feel they owe and can expect from one another. An understanding needs to be reached which takes all sides into consideration and tries not to shortchange anyone.

Common Problems

With the young adult's departure from the home, it becomes more common for the parents and the young adult to present separately for treatment. Typically, the young adult presents for treatment individually (and is most often seen individually) for what usually appear to be individual problems. Similarly, the parents, either individually or as a couple, may seek treatment in response to the child's leaving home. While these are the most common, they are not the only ways in which family members present for treatment at this stage.

The relationship between presenting problem and stage-related difficulties is most obvious when either the primary complaint or an obvious feature of the family structure involves an exaggeration of some aspect of the separation process. Examples might include the family in which several adult children remain in the home indefinitely, where they are "kicked out of" the home, or where repeated attempts to leave end in failure with the young adult returning home with an ever-decreasing sense of confidence. In these cases, family members may themselves describe the problem in terms of one or more members' difficulties leaving home or letting go. A common scenario is that which involves the youngest and last child remaining in the home, especially in the context of either a conflictual or stagnant parental marriage or a single-parent family.

In other cases which present for treatment at this stage, the context of stage-related problems is less obvious. This is often true when the young adult presents individually for treatment. The primary problem often involves difficulties adjusting to a new context, such as college, the military, or a new job in a strange place. The individual may complain of feelings of social isolation, "not fitting in," with related symptoms of anxiety and/or depression. (S)he may complain of problems which are developing in a committed relationship with a boyfriend or girlfriend. When the young adult has married, marital problems may be prominent, especially those which involve in-laws as an area of contention.

As we have emphasized earlier, while it may not always be the case, it pays the therapist to consider the possibility that these different symptomatic presentations may reflect the individual's difficulty with the tasks of this stage—letting go of the family of origin and facing the challenges of independent living, and balancing needs for family relationships and personal identity and development. This is obvious when the person can acknowledge "homesickness" (the child's complement to the parents' "empty-nest" feeling). But when this issue is not recognized or acknowledged by the patient, the therapist should always establish for him or herself whether stage-related issues are part of the picture. The difficulties of the young adult in these cases very frequently involve a mixture of genuine life stresses, identity and social issues, separation anxiety, and loyalty to family of origin.

Sometimes it will be not the child but one or both parents who present for treatment. Usually, if one parent seeks treatment individually or is presented as the Identified Patient by both, it is that parent who has been most deeply affected by the newly "empty nest." This is often the parent who has been especially close to the child or most closely involved in the daily life of the child by virtue of being in the home. Obviously, this problem is somewhat more likely in the case of a single parent. These parents often present symptoms of depression, anxiety, or somatic complaints.

Parents may present with marital complaints at this stage of the life cycle. When the parents have avoided facing one another by facing the children, their departure creates a very different marital context. Needs which have been at least partially met by the children may now be directed at one another. Problems which have been long neglected may emerge or erupt in the silence which follows the departure of the children.

As with each of these stages, the poorer the resolution of an earlier stage, the more difficult the tasks of following stages will become. The better the resolution of this particular stage, the better prepared the family will be for the last stage in this sequence.

AGING AND DEATH OF THE PARENTS

The title of this stage clearly signals the facts which precipitate it—the aging and eventual death of parents. The basic task of this stage for all family members involves facing and accepting a variety of losses. These include, most importantly, relational losses: the parents' loss of friends and siblings, the survivor's loss of a spouse, and the children's eventual loss of both parents. In addition, the parents face physical, vocational, and possibly financial losses. The family's task is to face and accept these losses without significantly damaging the basic level of trustworthiness which has been built up in these relationships.

At the individual level, parents face the losses mentioned above. Those who have worked lose the benefits as well as the burdens of steady work. They may feel some decrease in self-esteem and self-worth without the sense of positive identity, "carrying one's load," and making a contribution which may have accompanied work. They may miss the activity, the social life, and the daily structure which work provided. They may feel unwanted, "put out to pasture," no longer useful.

As old age progresses, they must cope with a gradual diminishing of physical strength. They may have greater difficulty seeing, hearing, or walking. And they may experience greater difficulty with memory, concentration, and mood. They may have to deal with serious medical problems, perhaps for the first time. And as they grow more frail, they are likely to become more susceptible to injury as well as illness. Aside from the physical stress this greater vulnerability imposes, it may also affect the person's sense of ego integrity and wholeness. It can become particularly difficult for people who have prided themselves in their self-sufficiency for years to need to depend now on the caretaking of others, such as their children.

The parents grow old with their generation—that is, with each other, their siblings, and their friends. They are likely, therefore, to experience the death of others of their generation before their own. In many cases, this represents an equally if not more significant experience of loss than those already discussed. They may see brothers, sisters, and old friends taken from them or they may experience the death of a spouse. These losses, especially in the aged, are often so total that what we consider recovery in a younger person is essentially impossible.

Finally, each parent individually faces his or her own death and, in doing so, faces his or her life—his or her accomplishments, failures, satisfactions, and regrets; what (s)he feels (s)he was given, what was withheld or taken away, and what (s)he made of what (s)he was dealt.

It is impossible to overestimate the stress which these losses impose on the aged—stress which may be expressed in increased irritability, complaining, regression, demandingness, stubbornness, anxiety, or depression. These reactions may then contribute to increased strains in close relationships—for example, with spouses, children, friends, and siblings.

The now-grown child must cope as best (s)he can with these stresses and with the increased burden of care required by the parent. (S)he may in the process experience a significant disruption of his or her psychological world as the once strong parent becomes weak, the once dependable parent becomes more dependent. And even when the parent lives long and dies naturally in old age, the adult child is faced with the loss and grief which accompany this final separation. Above and beyond all else, the death of the parent means an irrevocable loss for the child of an irreplaceable person and (ideally) relational resource. In addition, the child often becomes more acutely aware of his or her own mortality at this stage. People often describe feeling that with parents alive it is as though they were two steps away from death, and the death of a parent seems to move them one step closer.

At a psychological level, the child may be faced with the need to make a shift from being the cared-for to the caretaker and (s)he needs to be able to see him or herself this way. (S)he may have to become more like a parent to the parent who, as (s)he becomes more infirm and dependent, may become more like a child. At the material level, the child may be faced with increasing demands (by the *fact* of the parent's aging, whether the parent actually makes demands or not): for time, money, transportation to doctors, help with errands and chores related to daily living, and possibly residence in the child's home.

At the systemic level, there are always changes in subsystems and boundaries and usually changes in roles at this stage. Changes in boundaries and subsystems occur when first one parent and then the other dies. More concrete boundary changes take place when one or both parents move either to a child's home or to a nursing facility. Such changes in boundaries and subsystems may be especially marked when the aged parent moves in with one of two or more siblings, although the particular realignment of subsystems may vary considerably. In some cases, sharing the same roof leads to a greater closeness between parent and child, with other siblings moved to more peripheral positions. In others, alliances may form between the parent and the other sibling, often centered in the felt mistreatment of the parent by the child with whom (s)he now lives (and sometimes his or her spouse or children). Changes in roles primarily involve a reversal in "parent" and "child"—i.e., caretaker and cared-for—roles, as has already been discussed.

Changes at the ethical level are highly significant during this stage of family life. For many, the finality of death defines these issues more sharply perhaps than at any other time in life. In the limited time left, both the dying and the survivor may ask themselves if they have "done enough" for the other. They may wish they had done more or that they could undo things they have done. They may try to "make up for" things that have happened, to get the other to admit to or apologize for things they have done. They may wish for or ask for or offer forgiveness.

In this sense, even in the context of regret over wasted years, there is at least some potential resource for the family in a parent's dying in that it may provide the spur needed for attempts to balance the ledger of relationships more fairly. However, when family members are unable or unwilling to face such imbalances where they exist, the survivors may be left with a stuck ethical imbalance—an assessment of having been significantly and unfairly shortchanged or of having shortchanged the other—which will certainly be more difficult, if not in some cases impossible, to rework. This has serious implications for the future of the survivor's own family since the potential for destructively transferring this imbalance to another relationship (the revolving slate) is increased.

Another hallmark of this stage, as suggested earlier, is that as the parent ages, the balance of active devotion and caretaking is likely to shift again, from the unilateral devotion of parent to small child through the more balanced mutual devotion of adult parent and adult child to the more imbalanced devotion of adult child to aging and weakening parent. While at the individual level, this involves the psychological changes we have already described and at the systemic level, the changes in roles and boundaries, it is at the ethical level that the basic trustworthiness of relationships is most sorely tested.

The adult child's ability to extend greater caretaking for the parent will depend heavily on the devotion and care (s)he has experienced from the parents. What (s)he has received constitutes a critical component of the care (s)he can give back at this point. And this highlights the challenge at the ethical level in this stage of family development. How well can the trustworthiness of relationships be maintained? Especially, in the face of diminishing reciprocity from the parent, increased stresses and demands, and perhaps an intensification of the parents' own "unfinished business" (regrets, guilt, resentments, and disappointment) at the end of his or her life. How well can the children repay the life and the care the parents have given them (however small or great such care has been)? What legacy of trustworthiness can the parent leave the children, as a resource for their own lives and for their own newly created families?

In this stage, it is especially important that adult children be guided by some notion of realistic accountability in weighing how much they can give, and in what ways. Faced with the enormously difficult decision, for example, of whether an aging, perhaps bedridden or senile, parent can be cared for in the adult child's home or must instead be placed in a nursing home, the child must consider the extent and the limits of his or her responsibility to the parent, in the context of commitments to his or her own marriage, family, and him or herself. Such decisions are never easy but they are likely to be most helpful for all parties when they are approached from this standpoint.

Common Problems

Families that are having difficulty with this stage present for treatment in a variety of ways. If one parent becomes seriously ill, the spouse may present with symptoms of anxiety or depression; if one parent dies, the surviving spouse or one of the children may present individually with a grief reaction.

When the parent or parents are living with one of the children, the latter may present individually or with a spouse, complaining that the parent is too demanding and asking for help coping with the situation. Or the parent may complain that the child or other members of the household are uncaring and neglectful. In these cases, the aging parent rarely comes self-referred for help but is often referred either by a physician or by a home health aide who is involved in the parent's care.

When a parent dies who has been especially closely involved (however positively or negatively) with the child's family, the event may disrupt patterns which have been established over an extended period of time. In these cases, any or all surviving members may present for treatment, often unaware of how the presenting problem relates to the loss of the parent. For example, a grown child who has remained heavily dependent on the parent may feel anxious and overwhelmed at facing adult life without the parent. The grandchild who received attention and affection from the grandparent when these had been less available from parents may become depressed or more demanding. A couple who have regulated distance in the marriage by "triangling in" (Bowen, 1978) the parent may need to substitute a different third party (a child, a lover, a bottle, a therapist).

As with each of the previous stages, the therapist needs to consider the possibility that the presenting complaint may have other and perhaps more serious origins than the stage-related issues we have discussed here. For example, an aging parent who stays up nights, wanders around the house, and cries easily may be trying to manipulate others into giving greater attention. Or (s)he may be severely depressed or experiencing neurological impairment. The family life-cycle framework allows the therapist to appreciate the natural developmental issues of family life which may underlie various presenting problems. It is still the job of the therapist, however, to assess, either personally or by referral to the appropriate professional, other possible sources of the problem.

CONCLUSION

The value of the family life-cycle framework derives, first of all, from its usefulness as a developmental context within which to understand all families. In this sense, it is like the physical, behavioral, and psychosocial norms which pediatricians and others use to evaluate the relative progress and difficulties of infants and children. The life-cycle framework allows the therapist to relate specific symptoms and problems to stage-related pressures and tasks. Beyond this, it serves as a diagnostic baseline which allows the therapist to distinguish between different kinds of stage-related problems. The most common clusters of such problems are: (1) normal acute stage-specific difficulties, (2) maladaptive responses to the specific pressures of a given stage, and (3) chronic problems related to unresolved issues from a prior developmental stage or stages.

For example, a newly married couple is concerned over the fact that they have had several disagreements on matters such as where to look for a house and how to budget their finances. Unless more serious problems are uncovered, this couple is most likely experiencing normal problems associated with establishing ground rules for resolving disagreements at this stage. However, another couple whose disagreements have led to a repetitive pattern of the husband's walking out of the house and the wife's then rushing to her friends for support and justification, is more clearly developing a maladaptive response to the demands of this stage. Lastly, a couple in which one or both partners' attachments to family of origin are so strong as to preclude their consolidating the marriage and living independently together may well be experiencing problems related to "unfinished business" from earlier stages of development in their own families of origin.

The value of the family life-cycle framework is increased by the correlation between symptomatology and life crises in family life. Several theorists (Haley, 1973; Hadley et al., 1974; Hoffman, 1980) have observed that symptom onset often coincides with normal crises of family development when stress within the family is highest. One dividend, incidentally, of the life-cycle framework is this view of symptoms as signals that the family is having difficulty with normal life issues. This deemphasizes the notion of pathology in such situations.

Carter and McGoldrick (1980) have gone further in addressing this correlation between symptoms and life crises, postulating two different types of "stressors" in families. "Horizontal stressors" correspond to the crises associated with the family's movement through the life cycle. These include predictable events such as the birth of children, and unpredictable events such as the accidental death of a young child. "Vertical stressors" include "patterns of relating and functioning" which are transmitted across generations in families. These would appear to correspond to the legacies and other intergenerational patterns (e.g., the revolving slate) discussed in the previous chapter. The authors assert that "the degree of anxiety engendered by the stress on the vertical and horizontal axes at the points where they converge is the key determinant of how well the family will manage its transitions through life" (p. 10).

For example:

A husband and wife, both of whom had strong relationships with now-deceased fathers, have two children, a boy and a girl. Both parents are clearly more involved with their son who becomes the focus of much of their unresolved relationships with their fathers. The boy dies accidentally, leaving the daughter with feelings of guilt for having survived him and inadequacy at being unable to replace him. She marries and, after long and vocal anticipation of a grandson by her parents, delivers a girl.

In this case, the normal horizontal stresses of having a first child are compounded by the vertical stresses of having once again "failed" her parents. In our minds, Carter and McGoldrick's hypothesis that many families present for treatment not simply when they are experiencing horizontal stressors but when horizontal and vertical stressors interact suggests a promising area for research as well as a useful guide for therapists evaluating families.

This concludes two chapters which present what we consider to be the basic concepts necessary for family evaluation. The next chapter introduces and examines one particular family in detail. We hope, in this way, to concretize some of these concepts, to underscore their validity and significance, and to convey the unified relational whole which together they comprise.

3

The Turner Family

The Turners* are a family of four. William Turner, 46 years old, has been a Lutheran minister for eight years, before which he worked as an insurance salesman for twenty years. Mary Turner, 44 years old, is a homemaker. Before their marriage twenty-two years ago, she did clerical work for several years. This is the only marriage for both partners and there have been no separations.

There are two living children. The couple's first child was stillborn at six months of pregnancy. One year later, their daughter, Ann, was born two and one-half months premature with an extremely low birth weight. Now 20 years old, Ann began but dropped out of her father's alma mater two years ago. She has worked part time as a salesperson since that time. Her younger sister, Wendy, is 15 years old and attends a local high school. Both daughters live in the home. Mary's mother is the only living grandparent. Residing about one hundred miles away from the family, she visits often, staying for several days at a time. A genogram for the family is provided in Figure 1.

* Names and other identifying data have been changed for reasons of confidentiality.

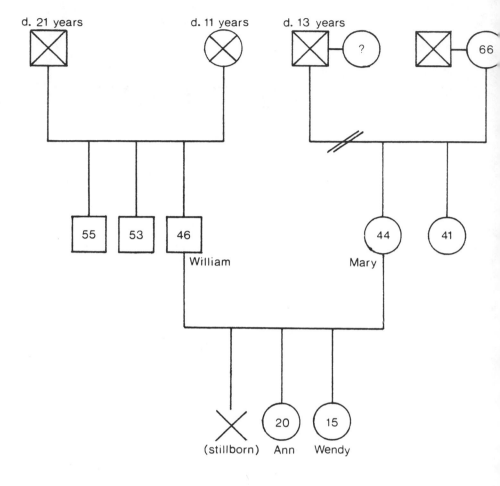

Figure 1. The Turner Family.

The Turners were referred for family evaluation by a psychiatrist who had seen Mary for several meetings. Her primary complaint involved a germ phobia and related compulsive rituals. Her fear of contamination led her to wash her hands "100 to 150" times a day, and to go through long, arduous cleaning procedures in order to use shared household conveniences, such as the bathtub and washing machine. She found physical contact with all persons, including family members, painful and so restrained herself from hugging or touching them. As a consequence, husband and wife had drastically limited their sexual relationship.

While Mary describes herself as having been a very neat child, all family members agreed that she had never displayed symptoms such as these until five years earlier. At that time, after finishing seminary training, William and the family moved into the parsonage of his first church assignment. They reported that the problem had continued at about the same level since it began, but was, in Mary's words, "80 percent improved" when she left the parsonage for several days, for example, on family visits.

Mary had been involved in individual and marital treatment, but felt that these were of little help. She had also received trials of a minor tranquilizer and an antidepressant with similar results.

In view of the timing involved in the development of symptomatology, it was not surprising to find out that Mary was extremely unhappy with William's decision to become a clergyman. This information was not volunteered, however, and was in no way connected in her own mind to the symptomatology. She described bitter resentment of the emotional and material sacrifices this decision had cost her and the family as a whole, and referred to the parsonage in which they now lived as her "prison." She described having had to leave their old home and sell the family car. More importantly, she reported feeling that she had "lost my husband to God."

When first seen in a full family evaluation, Mary's phobic and compulsive symptomatology was the most striking problem presented, but it was not the only one. In fact, the family presented multiple individual and relational problems. William and Mary described serious marital problems, including poor communication, frequent arguments, and lack of intimacy. Mary reported feeling isolated in the family, in her own words, "Up against the Big Three." Ann described feelings of loneliness and depression, poor social relationships, and a sense of inadequacy and failure, especially after dropping out of college. Wendy described similar problems with peers, feeling she was often excluded socially and had few close friends. In addition, she had a long history of poor attendance at school, usually with vague, unconfirmed somatic complaints. Ann had evidenced a similar pattern as a child.

From their description of life at home, it seemed as though Mary gave very little to either daughter. They were especially hurt that she could not bear physical contact with them. Consequently, both were admittedly closer to William who, at least at this stage, functioned somewhat as both mother and father. William presented no clear symptomatology, but reported feeling needy and neglected by his wife. Finally, as is common when one family member has severe obsessive-compulsive symptomatology, William and both daughters described weariness and resentment at the limitations and complications introduced into the family's life by Mary's symptoms.

It should be noted that both William and Mary are recovered alcoholics. William reports drinking heavily in the service before the marriage and continuing into the marriage. Mary's drinking is said to have started when, in response to her complaint of "extreme nervousness" about the impending marriage, her family doctor recommended one glass of wine before bed. She states that the drinking grew worse after the loss of the first child, and even more so after the other children were born. At the worst point, both were drinking heavily daily and the drinking interfered with William's work. Ten years ago, Mary admitted herself to an inpatient alcohol-treatment program, and afterwards insisted that William join her in Alcoholics Anonymous. They are extremely proud that neither has returned to drinking again since that time.

THE FACTUAL DIMENSION

There are several facts which stand out in the history of the Turner family—in the early lives of each of the parents, in their lives together after the marriage, and in the lives of their children. Most noteworthy in Mary's early individual and family history is her father's abandonment of the family when she was 6 years old. Her mother remarried only ten years ago, so that as children, Mary and her sister were raised without a father. While it is impossible to grasp and enumerate all the possible consequences of this event, a few probable repercussions do stand out. Mary's mother had to go to work. Already deprived of a father, this left Mary with the now added deprivation of her mother's absence for long periods of time and considerable parental responsibilities for her younger sister.

She does remember that her mother "tried to make up" in the evening what her absence took away during the day. Still, overall, Mary remembers a lonely and unhappy childhood. She also remembers that this made her even closer with, and more dependent on her mother "because of what we'd been through together." Even as a young adult, she remembers needing her mother's approval before she felt comfortable buying clothes for herself. This dependency made the separation when Mary left home even more difficult and increased her anxiety about marriage.

She remembers feeling deprived of things which others had, such as nice clothes, because of the family's limited income. Although she was bright and wanted to go to college, because of the financial situation she was able to attend only one year of a business college instead. Interestingly, she describes these disappointments with very little affect; that is, with none of the bitter resentment which surfaces concerning her current situation.

Certainly, we can see how these early material deprivations might have made the financial sacrifices resulting from William's career shift more difficult for Mary to accept. Moreover, it takes little speculation to wonder whether the early loss of her father may have made her more likely to experience her husband's dedication to the church as "losing him to God."

The fact which appears to have had the greatest impact on William's early life is the Second World War. His father, a military officer, was stationed away from the family. His two older brothers enlisted in the army and were away for the duration, either in combat or, in one case, as a prisoner of war. William had an uncle to whom he was extremely attached, who appears to have provided some of the warmth which his own father could not. This man was killed in action during the war. William himself was rarely able to visit his father. Often, his mother would go to visit by herself, leaving William, now a young teenager, by himself with occasional supervision from a neighbor. What stands out in this description of the war's impact on one family are the multiple losses of various kinds and the loneliness and neediness they generated in this teenage boy. Having experienced this abandonment in his own life, albeit a different kind from that experienced by Mary, William seems especially susceptible to feelings of neglect and abandonment. This makes him especially vulnerable to Mary's current physical and emotional withdrawal from him and the girls.

After their marriage, the most salient facts in the lives of the Turners involved the vicissitudes of pregnancy and childbirth. As noted, their first child was stillborn after six months of pregnancy. Again, we can only guess at the impact of this event. We know that Mary's drinking soon became worse and that her anxiety about subsequent childbearing was intensified. We see a different effect of this event, and perhaps get an indirect clue as to the intensity of its impact, when we are told of a grandparent's reaction. William reports that his father was "devastated" by this and was never really able to accept either Ann or Wendy when they were born.

Finally, we know that Ann was born prematurely, also at six months into pregnancy and with an extremely low birth weight. The combination of this fact with the fate of the previous child clearly influenced both parents' reactions to, and eventual relationships with, Ann. Both report being terrified of her dying after she left the hospital. Both parents report that these two facts made them terribly overprotective with Ann, a pattern which appears highly related to: the overall enmeshment of the family, Ann's excessive dependency on her parents, her poor social relationships outside the home, and ultimately, her having been unable to complete her first year in college.

THE INDIVIDUAL DIMENSION

What stands out most in this family is each individual member's neediness and sense of deprivation. Using the terms we introduced in the previous chapter, we are struck by the strength and the frustration of each of their needs to belong.

The particular facts and family configurations which seem to have contributed to this for each of the parents individually were described in the previous section—the impact of World War II on William's family and of the abandonment by Mary's father on hers. Both spouses' long histories of alcoholism add weight to this impression of their neediness.

Furthermore, it helps us understand the neediness of the children. They were, after all, raised by two alcoholic parents, with William described as having been on the road often during those years. To make matters worse, with the onset of Mary's symptomatology, the daughters were faced with a mother who literally could not be close to them and who had given up most aspects of active parenting, and a father who felt great responsibility to be available to his parish as well as to his family. What is so unfortunate in this case is that their individual senses of loneliness, deprivation, and abandonment are compounded by their significant difficulty in giving to and receiving from one another.

Why did William choose to become a minister—a decision which is, at the very least, temporally related to the development of Mary's symptoms? The answer must lie, at least in part, in William himself. While we cannot pretend a full understanding of this decision, several factors seem relevant. There is no question but that William was dissatisfied with his industrial career and felt a need to achieve something which was to him more meaningful. This is primarily an individual issue of identity and life accomplishment. In addition, he tells us that his decision also reflected his gratitude at having survived and come out of his long period of alcoholism. This gratitude and the religious faith with which it is intertwined are also very personal individual matters. And while their impact on the system (in the form of his actual decision) is enormous, their primary focus is not systemic but individual.

What is Mary's contribution to the family's current problems? What do we know of her individually which might help us understand the patterns presented to us in evaluation? One factor which has considerable significance is her remarkable difficulty expressing anger and her general lack of assertiveness. Appearing timid and highly uncertain in evaluation, she describes endless situations in which her own needs are ignored by others and she is unfairly burdened by theirs. But such descriptions do not come openly and forthrightly. They must be slowly and painstakingly elicited from her by the therapist, who is responding to powerful but indirect, nonverbal messages. And in each of the incidents, her failure to have complained, protested, or stood up for herself is prominent. Mary strikes us, in fact, as a very angry woman whose anger is rarely, if ever, expressed directly. We wonder then if her symptomatology, which takes so much from and imposes so much on her family, may represent just such an indirect expression of anger, especially engendered by her husband's decision to join the ministry.

What of Mary's desires to achieve? Of this, we can only guess. We know that she had hoped to go to college but could not afford to do so. She also tells us that she resented the sacrifices it took to finance William's seminary training and what she saw as Ann's assumption that financial support for a good education was owed to her.

Finally, we know of Mary's significant attachment to her own mother and her difficulty leaving her. This attachment, which is again very much an individual matter in terms of Mary's contribution to this family, reflects a lack of individuation which she confirms when she describes herself as an adult needing her mother to help choose her clothes. The intense anxiety which Mary experienced concerning her wedding and marriage and the wine she began to drink, perhaps in order to medicate that anxiety, suggest the probable significance of this lack of individuation for the future of the family.

We should not underestimate the importance of both daughters' fears regarding the outside world and growing up as factors in the current family situation. Both Ann and Wendy are, as it were, standing at the doorway and refusing to budge. And while there are systemic factors (enmeshment) and ethical dynamics (loyalty and obligation) in their remaining so tightly bound to the home, there is also an element of fearfulness at facing the challenges and risks of independent living. This individual dynamic in both daughters' lives helps to perpetuate the family's overall enmeshment and in their efforts to cling to William (who is currently more available than Mary) serves to compound Mary's sense of isolation and deprivation in the home.

THE SYSTEMIC DIMENSION

We can begin an analysis of this family in systemic terms with the configuration of subsystems and boundaries. The family as a whole is characterized by a fair degree of enmeshment. The collective and some-what undifferentiated "We" of the group is much stronger than any of its separate "I"s. All family members cling to the home, hoping to have virtually all their needs met by one another and reluctant to form close relationships outside the family. They are, in Hoffman's (1975) words, "too richly crossed" as indicated by the consistency with which any dis-cussion or argument between two people pulls in a third or fourth until a sort of free-for-all ensues. Ann cannot bear to be separated from the family at college, and Wendy follows in her footsteps, albeit more fitfully.

Within the family, there is a weak boundary around the marital sub-system, with William in alliance with both daughters and Mary isolated, in her words, "against the Big Three." This implies a weak generational boundary and is reflected in the role structure of the family. Both daugh-ters have taken on either parental or marital roles as Mary has withdrawn from (and felt pushed out of) both.

Ann clearly functions in a parental role in relation to Wendy. It is Ann who expresses concern over Wendy's numerous absences from school and who keeps after her on issues of diet, hygiene, and household chores. Ann also absorbs a large share of the housework herself. It is not merely that she talks to Wendy about these things, but she seems genuinely concerned and upset, in a strikingly parental way, when Wendy shrugs off her responsibilities in these areas.

Wendy's role is much more wifely. It is Wendy who listens to William complain about the trials of his work, Wendy who makes special treats for him (a cup of tea in the evening, for instance), who comforts him and, literally, cools his brow when he is ill.

William often functions as what some family therapists refer to as "the switchboard" between mother and daughters. Instead of speaking directly to Mary, the girls will approach William who will then convey the specific request or complaint to Mary. Similarly, Mary is more likely to complain to William about something involving the girls than she is to complain to them directly. As with most "switchboards," William pays a price in the time and energy this role demands as well as the constant risks of getting caught in the middle. He also reaps the benefit of having somewhat greater access to both Mary and the girls than they have to one another. He verbally reinforces Mary's isolation, during the evaluation session, by constantly couching his comments in a "we" versus "you" framework: "We need you"; "We don't know what we've done wrong"; "We hope you get better."

Mary is, to some extent, in the role of Identified Patient and scapegoat. Numerous and serious problems may exist in the family and Mary's symptoms may be partly an expression of other relational problems. However, in the face of the severity and real inconvenience caused by Mary's symptomatology, these other aspects of context seem less significant to the members of the family. The focus of the problem, then, before and at the point of evaluation is Mary's symptomatology.

In the language of common family structural patterns, the Turners are characterized by a "stable coalition" (Minuchin, 1974)—father and daughters against mother. Like many such coalitions, however, there are indications that it is a potentially fluid pattern, with shifts possible in who takes the role of "outsider" at any particular time. For example, when, in the course of treatment, the family was able to modify this pattern so that William and Mary became closer, first one and then the other daughter experienced periods marked by acute feelings of being left out, uncomfortable in the family group, not fitting in. These patterns may well reflect attempts by family members to gain some relational security in the face of diminished resources and tenuous trust by forming alliances against a third party.

Finally, since issues of communication and power are often associated with the systemic dimension of relationships, one last observation and hypothesis can be raised here which explicitly addresses the primary presenting problem—that is, Mary's phobic and compulsive symptomatology. There is a perfect symmetry between Mary's symptoms and William's decision to join the clergy. These things, both of which have caused such pain for the other, are as it were out of their hands.

Mary feels she is the helpless victim of her symptoms. Far from seeing herself as inflicting them on others, she experiences herself as being at their mercy. They are out of her control. Asked how he decided to become a minister, William says that he was called. The facial expressions and comments of Mary and the daughters at this point make clear that, in this family which was always religious and church-going even before William's decision, this is reason enough. It is not to be questioned or debated, and certainly not challenged. It is essentially beyond him and therefore out of his control. His calling and her compulsions are like mirror images, both having enormous and largely negative impact on the other (at least up to this point), both uncalled for and unclaimed.

This leads us to wonder whether both the calling and the compulsions might represent, at least in part, facets of a covert competitive struggle. Are they like exchanges in an unspoken battle? William's decision serves to deprive Mary of himself (and much more) and his efforts to meet needs for intimacy and confirmation outside the marriage are cloaked in the mantle of the church. Mary's symptoms might, in part, represent an act of revenge, depriving William of herself emotionally and sexually in turn. Are her symptoms a sort of silent protest, especially in the absence of any clear overt dissatisfaction? Having established in the evaluation that, in fact, Mary was not in favor of William's decision and did not feel adequately consulted regarding it, it is noteworthy that in eleven years (three years of seminary training and eight years as a minister), both partners admit that they have never really discussed and settled the issue. And this is precisely the point. The conflict cannot be settled in this context. He can no more negotiate with a sickness than she can challenge the terms of his calling.

THE ETHICAL DIMENSION

We can begin an analysis of the ethical dimension in the Turner family with a consideration of the entitlements—in a sense, the "colliding entitlements"—of all members. William grew up lonely and neglected, losing his father and brothers, in a way his whole family, for years to the war. On top of this, he lost the uncle who seems to have provided some closeness and support for him. He wants the attention and affection of his wife and a career which gives him a sense of competence, worth, and meaning.

Mary lost her father and then had to watch him come back to visit the family with his new children, to see him flaunt what he had given them when he seemed to have given nothing to her. She spent much of her time looking after her younger sister while their mother worked, was unable to attend college, and generally remembers a pervasive sense of having had little materially. Mary wants the attention and affection of her husband and resents having to share so much of him with God, the church, and his parishioners. She certainly feels she had the right to retain whatever they had been able to build up materially and is deeply resentful of having had to give up their home and car for William's new life in the church.

Ann and Wendy grew up in a home in which both parents were alcoholic. William and Mary make clear that during these years the girls experienced a significant degree of neglect, parental unavailability, disorganization in the home, and bitter quarreling between the parents. We can sympathize with their claim for two actively involved parents. We can understand their frustration and resentment, in this context, over Mary's withdrawal from them and, to a lesser extent, of William's intensive involvement with his parish.

Each of these four people feels shortchanged, deprived of what they deserve, and each holds one or more of the others to blame for this. This is one facet of the bind they are all in. How can they give when they feel they need so much and get so little? How can the cycle, of giving less in retaliation for getting less, be reversed? Can resources be identified and activated which might allow each to give and therefore to receive more?

The issue of blaming the other suggests another facet of the relational structure which relates to both parents' experiences in their own families of origin. It sheds light on the longstanding conflict in the marriage and helps to explain the more recent intensification of that conflict in connection with Mary's symptomatology.

We know something of Mary's deprivation as a child, of her father's abandonment and unwillingness to provide for her, intensified by his flaunting what he gave his other children. We know that while Mary was extremely dependent on her own mother, she virtually never opposed her in any way—never protested what she considered her mother's excessive criticism, and manipulation through guilt and intrusiveness. Even in therapy, when she presented interactions in which she felt her mother had treated her unfairly, the idea of actually standing up for herself or talking back was unthinkable.

With William, however, while she rarely protests or complains overtly, her whole life—symptoms, depression, and all—has become a sort of silent protest and reproach: "Look what you've done to me. It's not fair." Unable to hold her mother or father directly accountable in any way for what she has suffered, it's as though she can't help but hold William accountable for everything—that is, for his own legitimate share of her unhappiness as well as theirs. This then is an example of what we have referred to as the "revolving slate."

William seems to have his own version of this same pattern. He describes his father as a stern, hypercritical man who was only able to acknowledge his feelings for William when he, the father, was on his death bed. The words he uses to describe his father, "cold, silent, inaccessible, behind a wall," are exactly the words he uses to describe Mary, both before the onset of her current symptomatology and even more vividly following it. In our view, there is little doubt that William's extreme sensitivity to Mary's inaccessibility is directly related to his experience of his father. And that much of his effort to hurt her (even when cloaked in the mantle of the church) expresses an attempt to punish her for her own crimes in his eyes, as well as those of his father. Since he was unable or unwilling to hold his father accountable, it's as though he expects Mary to make up for what he suffered—that is, to repair it and to pay for it.

This mirror pattern of unsettled revolving accounts makes it tremendously difficult for the couple to address, let alone resolve, the real problems which exist between them. Each is trying to settle two accounts at once, one of which involves an absent and unavailable third party. What is more, this unrecognized saddling of the other with the accounts of a third party merely serves to fuel both spouses' sense of unfairness and outrage. Each knows on some level that he or she is being blamed for far more than his or her share.

As complex and difficult as this pattern appears, it would at least be one step closer to a possible resolution if both parties were willing and able to stand up for what they, in their view, feel they deserve from one another and willing to let the other do the same. This willingness to make claims and to consider the claims of the other provides the essential ground from which multilaterally fair solutions could evolve. For this reason, at the ethical level, Mary's enormous difficulty both making and accepting claims constitutes a critical aspect of the structural pattern in the family.

We have described how Mary appears very angry and yet unable or unwilling to be direct about the reasons for her anger, how her bitterness and resentment are almost palpable nonverbally but can only be elicited verbally with enormous effort. We should remember that, as a child, it was almost literally impossible for Mary to make claims. Her father was gone and certainly appears to have been unreceptive to claims when he was present. Her mother had little left to give and Mary grew up feeling unentitled to complain or make demands on her.

It is important to view Mary's failure to make claims in this historical context since it provides a possible source of leverage for therapeutic change. Nevertheless, it still constitutes a major obstacle to the possibility of building trust and support in the family. Unable to make claims, Mary becomes unable to accept the claims of her husband and daughters.

This leads us to a brief consideration, from the ethical dimension, of the event which seems to have precipitated Mary's symptoms. What stands out from this perspective is that the covert power struggle we have hypothesized (William's calling versus Mary's crippling compulsions and phobias) emerged in the context of a breakdown of trust and fairness. Both partners agree that William's decision to join the clergy was essentially unilateral. It is not that he callously informed Mary of his inflexible plans but that its importance to him seemed so great and her claim on him was so insignificant that both allowed the decision to be made and enacted.

It was not multilateral; it did not represent an attempt to balance the indebtedness and entitlements of all parties fairly. It was, in a word, unfair—an act of unfairness in which Mary was, at least initially, the most shortchanged but for which William was to pay significantly later through the agency of her symptomatology. Significantly, it was also an act of unfairness for which Mary herself was partly responsible by not having stood up more clearly and more firmly for her own side. It is in the context then of a breakdown of trust that the power struggle intensified and symptomatology flourished. The significance of this point lies in its therapeutic utility, which involves the possibility that the process of building trust may eliminate the need for symptoms.

We have discussed the concept of "conjunctive forces" in close relationships—those forces which hold relationships together and which balance disjunctive, competitive forces in relationships. We can conclude this examination of the ethical dimension in the Turner family by noting the presence and power of these forces in the family. In spite of the conflict, the withholding and the unsettled accounts of fairness in this family, the evaluation suggested a certain baseline of loyalty, concern, and even trustworthiness.

The daughters' avoidance of school may have involved fears of the outside world and excessive dependency on the family, but (as is often the case with so-called "school phobias"), it also expressed their sense of loyalty to Mary who was, in those years, left largely by herself at home while William traveled extensively. The family's "enmeshment" has a positive side as well—a high degree of commitment to and investment in each other. Without detracting from its existence as a resource in the family, however, it would be better if this intrafamily commitment were more evenly balanced by commitments and involvements outside the home. It is documented by the fact that following the evaluation all members of the family made commitments to family treatment which they maintained faithfully in family therapy sessions for many months.

Their willingness to participate in treatment and the quality of their participation revealed one other critical resource in the family. This was a willingness to examine patterns in their relationships, and most importantly, to consider issues of entitlement and indebtedness in a multilateral context. This willingness, one of the most valuable resources in relationships, constituted the first step towards trust building, reworking conflict, and dissipating the need for symptomatology in the family. It is worth noting that in this case, the family's long-term investment in their religion and church constituted another resource for positive change in that many of their religious values, such as strong family ties, mutual caring, and fairness, were congruent with those of treatment and therapeutic change.

THE FAMILY LIFE CYCLE

In order to round out this analysis of the Turner family, we will briefly address what we can learn about them by considering the stage framework for family development presented earlier.

At the point at which they present for family evaluation, the Turners are experiencing an overlap of issues and processes related to two stages of family development—the individuation of the adolescent and the departure of children from the home. This overlapping of stages is often the case, especially for families with more than one child. In a sense, the Turners are snagged at this point. That they are having difficulty with the tasks of this stage is suggested by Wendy's erratic attendance at school, Ann's having gone off to college and come back to the home feeling defeated, and both daughters' serious difficulties forming peer relationships outside the family.

The family history suggests that, in this case, we are dealing less with normal, acute, stage-specific problems and maladaptive responses to these particular stages than with chronic problems related to significant difficulty in the resolution of previous stages. The extent of Mary's dependency on her mother even as an adult and her severe anxiety in the face of the marriage indicate a lack of preparation and readiness for leaving her own home as a young adult. While there is much that we don't know about the early years of the marriage, both partners' rapid development of significant alcohol dependence suggests appreciable difficulty with and a poor resolution of the challenges posed by the stages of forming the marriage and the birth of children.

It is in the next stage, individuation of the children, that both parents were able, successfully, to overcome their alcohol dependence, efforts which had a direct, powerful, and positive impact on the state of the family as a whole. However, there is little question but that the facts which impinged on this family—the stillbirth of the first child and the premature birth of Ann—contributed to the difficulties that all of them faced with issues of separation and independence raised in this stage and even more powerfully in the stages they currently confront.

SUMMARY

In summary, this is a two-parent family with two daughters, ages 15 and 20, both living at home. It is, therefore, a family dealing with the overlapping tasks of two stages of family development—the individuation of the adolescent and the departure of the children. The family presents a history of chronic individual and relational problems as well as a more recent intensification of these problems, leading to an acute state of distress for all family members.

The primary presenting problem—Mary's phobias and compulsive rituals—appear to be directly related to William's decision to be a clergyman, as suggested by the timing of the development of symptomatology as well as the fact that the symptoms are "80 percent improved" simply by Mary's leaving "her prison," the church parsonage in which they now live. Related current problems include Mary's sense of isolation in the family and her withdrawal from her marital and parental roles, leaving both William and the daughters feeling neglected and resentful and obliged to absorb a good part of those roles themselves (William and Ann as "mothers," Wendy as "wife"). The intensified conflict within the marriage and between mother and both daughters reflects and fuels these problems.

In a sense, the factors which pave the way for the famly's current problems can be traced to both parents' experiences before the marriage and to developments in the earlier life of the family as well. Specifically, both parents' deprivation growing up in their own families and the unsettled accounts of fairness which developed in the face of that deprivation contributed to an intense neediness on both their parts and intense retributive behavior when their needs went unmet. Unconsciously, both appear to have transferred unsettled accounts from parent to spouse and to have tried to get the other to make up for what he or she lost earlier.

This intense neediness, compounded by the loss of one child in utero and the near loss of another in premature birth, contributed to a fairly enmeshed structure in the family, with both parents' own fears of the outside world reflected in their overprotectiveness toward their daughters and in the daughters' fears and insecurities about life outside the home. The parents' lack of preparation for marriage and family appears to have subjected them to a high degree of stress at each new stage of family development, making each succeeding stage more difficult and leading both of them to a long period of serious alcoholism. Their difficulty resolving the tasks of these earlier stages contributes all the more to the difficulties all are experiencing at the family's current stage of development.

Mary's childhood experiences appear to have led to a relational stance in which she is highly sensitive to unfairness and deprivation but unwilling to stand up for what she wants or deserves. While this does not eliminate her anger and resentment—if anything it compounds and perpetuates them—it does put her grievances effectively out of reach. Her inability to voice them assures that they cannot be considered or repaired. Unable to make claims for herself, she finds it nearly impossible to respond to the claims of the others.

If these facts provide the context for the Turners' current problems, it is William's decision to enter the clergy which provides the spark. While we cannot understand completely what led to this event, we can presume a typically human mixture of generous and self-serving motives. There is no reason to negate the validity of William's gratitude for having been able to attain sobriety and his own experience of having been called to the ministry, as well as a genuine wish to be of help to others and to improve his own self-image. However, we can certainly speculate on the less admirable benefits of this move, such as punishing Mary by depriving her of himself and getting needs for intimacy and confirmation met in other relationships, in this case with parishioners.

Both partners acknowledge that the decision was made essentially unilaterally. It was not a case in which one or both of them deluded themselves into thinking Mary was pleased by the decision. Instead, it was one in which her protests were apparently so muted and indirect that William could go ahead with his plans and hope for the best. But while Mary did not protest vocally, she clearly felt bitterly betrayed by this development. One added problem seems to have been that her own religious faith made her feel guilty about such feelings and therefore even less entitled to take a stand on them.

Whatever the level of mutual trust in the marriage before William's decision, it is clear that it was significantly shaken by that decision and its aftermath. In this trust-demolishing context, competition intensified. Unable to protest directly, Mary's life became an eloquent if silent protest. Unable to say "No" herself, her symptoms said it for her, but not in a way which could be addressed or resolved. This was essentially the stand-off which existed at the point of evaluation.

This is not meant to imply that Mary was "faking" her symptomatology or that she consciously desired or planned these effects, but simply that, in a most likely quite unconscious process (no doubt very much like William's turn towards the ministry) she found a certain solution to her predicament. Her symptoms functioned as an expression of the misery she could not express in other ways and served to limit what more could be asked of her as well as to punish those she considered responsible for her misery.

At an individual psychological level, we see Mary's symptomatology as the result of her repressed and unexpressed anger and resentment at William. At the systemic level, we see her symptoms as a weapon in a covert power struggle. At the ethical level, we see the symptomatology as an expression of entitlement and experienced unfairness developing in the context of unsettled accounts from previous relationships, an unwillingness to make and accept claims of fairness and a breakdown of trust and mutual care.

While there is no question of the chronicity and severity of problems in this family, there are considerable resources as well. It is the responsibility of the therapist to assess resources as well as pathology. This task is made more difficult when the therapist's conceptual framework stresses pathology and neglects resources. For example, most family therapists would agree on there being a considerable degree of enmeshment (that is, negative overinvolvement) in this family. What they might overlook is the flip side of this enmeshment—a high degree of mutual concern and attachment (that is, a positive involvement with one another). In their dependency on one another, there is a good deal of devotion and, within the limits of current problems, availability for one another.

Both parents carry guilt over their long period of alcoholism. This guilt reflects their acknowledgment of their responsibilities as parents and contributes to their actualizing their commitment to parenting by becoming and remaining sober for over ten years. We can presume that Ann and Wendy may have felt loyalty-bound as children (and currently) in going to school or forming relationships outside the family. And while this reflects a negative expression of loyalty, an overpayment of a debt, nevertheless, it expresses a sense of loyalty as well, loyalty which can potentially be rechanneled in more constructive ways.

The family's religious values may serve competitive needs, as in William's decision, and may hamper Mary's standing up for her own entitlement (or simply be used as a justification for not doing so). However, these values constitute a powerful potential resource for the family in their emphasis on positive family harmony, fairness, and mututal consideration.

In the final analysis, this was a family whose members cared enough about themselves and each other to be willing to face a stressful and painful consideration of each of their contributions to the family's problems, of their own and each others' merits and mistakes, debts and entitlements, real wrongs committed and sacrifices made. They were willing to take action to rebuild trust and fairness in the family and to face the challenges of their own individual lives more courageously.

Part II
CONDUCTING
THE EVALUATION

4
Setting Up the Session

THE INITIAL PHONE CALL

Only a small percentage of families call asking specifically for family evaluation or therapy. Although this may be changing because of greater public awareness of the family therapy field, most typically one family member calls to arrange an appointment either for him or herself or for another family member. The therapist's relationship to the family begins with this initial phone call, and this "presession" contact is surprisingly critical to the management of the evaluation.

Deciding Who Should Attend

The therapist should plan to spend some time on the phone with the caller, gathering preliminary information about the nature of the problem. He or she will then make a decision regarding how to proceed with the evaluation. This method of scheduling first appointments requires that the therapist handle the initial phone call from the family, and so both time and energy may be expended on cases the therapist ends up not seeing. But the "minievaluation" that takes place during this call is essential for the therapist to decide whom to see in the first session and to present this plan successfully to the caller. The phone conversation also allows the caller and the therapist to make some personal contact and learn something about each other, and as a result it can be useful in building rapport and trust between the family member and therapist.

The therapist will be likely to try to schedule the first appointment as a whole family evaluation session when the presenting problem is said to involve (1) the behavior of a child in the family, (2) relational difficulties among siblings, or (3) relational difficulties between parent(s) and one or more children. Seeing the "nuclear family," or more narrowly, "nuclear family members currently living in the home," may not be sufficient for a thorough evaluation. Separated and divorced parents, grandparents or other relatives, and children who live out of the home may all be crucial to the evaluation and should in such instances be invited to attend. The therapist, therefore, should ask for the attendance of any significant persons in the family's life, even if they are not in the nuclear family or in the home.

Presenting the Evaluation Format to the Caller

There is no value in using this first phone contact with the family to explain the interrelatedness of behavior or the concept of the family system and its role in symptom formation. Such explanations are simply not necessary in order to justify the request for a meeting with the whole family. Instead, the therapist should tell the family member that the goal of the session is to gather as much information as possible about the presenting problem. The therapist can add that the family session is a routinely used method of obtaining a complete picture of the problem, a method that draws on the ideas and observations of everyone involved in the problem and/or everyone who is close to and cares for the Identified Patient.

There are several risks associated with going beyond a variant of the "information-gathering" rationale for the family evaluation. First, any general connection made between family life and a particular problem may lead the caller (usually a parent) to feel that he or she is being blamed for the family's troubles. Or it may cause the caller to become angry and defensive over someone implying that there is something wrong with his or her family. As we will discuss in detail later, a prime therapeutic task in these early encounters with family members is to obtain their trust and confidence and to build therapeutic alliances. Raising potentially threatening or confusing issues in the first phone contact with the family has to be considered an unwise and highly risky approach.

A second difficulty inherent in early theoretical discussions with the family is the fact that the therapist does not know enough about the case at that stage to offer a thoughtful formulation. If and when the family should take exception to a general statement about families' involvement in emotional problems, the therapist would likely be backed into the corner of having to "sell" his or her theory. Because (s)he possessed limited information about the family, the "selling" would remain vague and unconvincing and would likely sound pressured and defensive. Not a good beginning for a procedure built on a therapist's supposed competence, understanding, and expertise.

Many of the above-mentioned complications could be avoided by maintaining the clear distinction between family evaluation and family therapy. The early meetings *are* evaluative, aimed at understanding the problem better, whether it be an individual disorder, a relational disturbance, a sociocultural-based crisis (e.g., poverty, legal difficulties), or, most likely, some combination of ills. The goal is to get to know the family so that the therapist can get to understand the problem, not to discover how the family system is really at the root of all difficulties.

RESISTANCE TO FAMILY EVALUATION

If the therapist presents the evaluation in "information-gathering" terms, then (s)he can expect a fair number of families to understand this and to cooperate easily. Some families may not be so cooperative, however, and will continue to raise objections to coming in as a group. Dealing with such a challenge is a critical and demanding point in the assessment. The therapist needs to walk a tightrope between trying to maintain control of the evaluation and trying to establish a working alliance with the family member on the phone.

Perhaps the most common forms this challenge takes are the parents' reluctance to include siblings of a child or adolescent Identified Patient (often a younger brother or sister and frequently one sibling in particular) or the refusal of a divorced parent who lives with the children to include the other parent in the evaluation.

Reluctance of a Divorced Parent
to Include Ex-Spouse

There are a number of reasons why family members might want to prevent other members from attending. In the case of a divorced or separated spouse, the parent living with the children may be actively trying to exclude the spouse from the family's life and will do so in treatment as just one more expression of this. (S)he may be jealous, competitive, and resentful of any attention, consideration, and sympathy the spouse might receive from the therapist. (S)he may try to prevent the therapist from hearing the spouse's side of things. It should be pointed out that the inclusion of a separated parent does not necessarily imply inclusion in a conjoint session with spouse, children, or both. Especially when parents are involved in a painful and angry separation process or when they have been separated or divorced (and perhaps even remarried) for years, the spouse might best be seen individually on a different date.

Reluctance to Include Siblings of Child
or Adolescent Identified Patient

Perhaps the most common form of resistance for full family attendance involves the parents' reluctance to involve siblings of a child or adolescent Identified Patient. There are several possible explanations for such feelings on the parents' part. Their reluctance may reflect a genuine and healthy effort to protect either the Identified Patient or the other siblings. This could be the case if the Identified Patient's behavior has aroused a great deal of hostility in the other siblings, or if the problem has involved hostile, provocative, bizarre, or hurtful behavior on the part of the Identified Patient. Parents may feel that a full family meeting violates the privacy of the Identified Patient. Or they may be quite innocently responding to connotations of shame, otherness, and even contagion which have been associated with mental illness in the past. They may be trying to protect the still "uncontaminated" child or children from the already "ill" child.

The confusion and bewilderment which accompany a serious psychological disturbance (such as psychosis or severe depression) and their devastating effect on even the best intentioned family members cannot be overemphasized. What sometimes looks like malice or poor judgment on the part of family members must be considered in light of the pervasive helplessness and uncertainty that such problems engender in those who are closely involved with the patient.

Sometimes, however, the parents' reluctance to include one or more siblings of the Identified Patient reflects less generous motives than those described above. Children may be withheld from the evaluation session precisely because they are most likely to support or defend the Identified Patient. There may be parental concern that one or more of the children might "blow the whistle" on other problems in the family. Finally, the presence of other children might expose the parents' own problems which they want either to deny or to conceal. What all these situations share is that, to the extent that the Identified Patient's problems may be related to a scapegoating process in the family, the parents' refusal to include other family members both expresses and perpetuates the scapegoating. The parents are insisting on a definition of the problem which places all the blame, or "sickness," on one family member and drastically reduces the therapist's ability to redefine the problem in more accurate systems terms.

STRATEGIES FOR NEGOTIATING FULL ATTENDANCE

The therapist's evaluation of just how important it is in specific cases to push for full attendance—that is, attendance in some form, whether conjointly or separately, of all those members who appear from the initial phone contact to be significantly involved in, and/or potentially helpful in assessing the problem and its context—will depend on the consequences and considerations of both insisting and capitulating on the requests.

One consequence of allowing the family to withhold certain members from the evaluation involves the potential loss of a valuable (possibly the most valuable) therapeutic ally. This is especially true in those structural patterns which have been described in the family literature as "rigid triads." These often involve the two parents and one child (although other variations are possible) in a particularly rigid interactional pattern which is the immediate relational context to the presenting problem. In these cases, the participation in the evaluation session of a family member who is familiar with the problem and the relationships involved, but uninvolved enough to see things somewhat objectively, is invaluable. Often, fifteen minutes spent with such a person can do much to clarify a confusing picture gathered from an hour or two spent with the principals involved. Even in more ambiguous situations, the participation of additional family members is rarely regretted and almost always quite helpful.

There are other possible consequences of the therapist's letting the family withhold certain members from the assessment. The therapist runs the risk of overlooking significant (and perhaps dangerous) problems in and between other family members who are likely to be under a greater than usual degree of stress in view of the current problems in the family. There is a consequent reduction in the therapist's leverage and overall control of the treatment. From the opposite perspective, the most serious consequence of insisting on full attendance is that the family may back out altogether, thereby eliminating even the chance of getting other members in later.

In addition to the potential consequences of one approach or the other, the therapist's decision on how hard to push for full attendance will also depend on a number of other considerations. These include his or her (and the agency's) philosophy of outreach—that is, the extent to which they expect the patient to be ready for and to accept treatment as offered or to which they are willing to modify guidelines for treatment in an effort to reach and treat a wider population. A related factor is the overall staff/patient ratio at an agency, with the more understaffed program probably needing to be more stringent in its criteria for treatment in an effort to put its limited resources where they will do the most good. The therapist's assessment of prognosis, even before meeting the family, although necessarily more speculative, may nevertheless influence his or her decision. For example, in the case of a chronic problem with a history of multiple requests for treatment and consistently poor follow-through, and where no new acute crisis exists, the therapist may feel the prognosis is so poor that little is to be lost by insisting on a full evaluation as a condition for even considering treatment.

Presession Approach: Postponing Final Decisions

The vast majority of cases call for some variety of a "bargaining" approach. It simply is much more difficult to assess the reasons for the family's reluctance and to resolve such an issue over the telephone than it is to explore and negotiate such a matter in person. After the therapist has met, evaluated, and at least tried to ally with the family members who do attend the session, it may be easier to negotiate a settlement. Bargaining implies dealing with attendance in person as a therapeutic issue and in a therapeutic manner, as opposed to taking a rigid stand one way or another on the phone. For these reasons, it is often best in the initial phone contact for the therapist to respond with a remark that postpones the decision such as "Why don't we start out then with the two of you [the parents] and Sue [the Identified Patient] and talk a bit more at the end of the session about the other kids," or "I'd be willing to see what we can accomplish in a first meeting this way and then discuss it further if it still seems necessary." If, for example, a parent objects to coming in with their family prior to their having a separate meeting time with the therapist, it would be advisable for the evaluation to begin with a meeting with the parents.

Often, at the end of such a first session, even without further discussion (or with only minimal urging), the family will be much more agreeable to the therapist's suggestion. The therapist will have, one hopes, demonstrated by his or her conduct of the session that treatment is neither destructive, accusatory, overly intrusive, explosive, nor ineffectual. In this sense, whatever trust is established between family and therapist in the process of the session can either eliminate the family's resistance or make its resolution much easier.

In-Session Approaches

When further discussion and persuasion is needed in the first session for the family to be willing to include other members, one of the following approaches may be helpful.

Surfacing hidden obstacles. Novice therapists quickly learn that a patient's questions, requests, or refusal on one topic may reflect fears or concerns of a very different nature which (s)he is either unaware of or reluctant to discuss openly. An individual therapy patient's request for fewer sessions may in fact derive from a fear of intimacy with the therapist; a question about the therapist's opinion about certain medications might involve a circuitous effort to test his or her feelings about schizophrenia which the patient feels he may "have"; an individual therapy patient's refusal to accept the therapist's recommendation that he try concurrent group therapy may reflect the mistaken suspicion that the therapist is trying to "dump" him. In each of these cases, the working through of these issues is facilitated by surfacing the unspoken but potent fears and anxieties and is at best impeded by taking the initial statements at their face value. Similarly, sensitive clinical interviewing, in an effort to identify and surface unspoken obstacles, will often eliminate resistance to including certain family members. For example, parents may fear that one of their children, a non-Identified Patient, will become overly upset by the session. In this case, they may respond well to reassurance, clarifications, and other attempts to decrease anxiety by the therapist.

Appeals to caring and concern. The therapist can appeal to the family members' concern over the problem presented for treatment and make clear that the exclusion of certain members for at least the evaluation is likely to impair his or her ability to understand fully and so to help with the problem. Such an appeal attempts to mobilize a family member's conscience or superego (in intrapsychic terms), his or her sense of loyalty, commitment, and concern for the Identified Patient (in relational terms), as therapeutic leverage.

Using family members' observations and comments as leverage. The therapist's case for including other members is strengthened if it can be framed within and supported by the family's own comments and concerns about the presenting problem. For example, if in the course of the session, it is revealed that the 16-year-old Identified Patient's condition deteriorated when she and her 17-year-old sister were separated from a previously shared bedroom, that she still confides in this sister alone, and that her tantrums are paradoxically always worse when the sister is in the house, the family members themselves have offered the most powerful demonstration of this sibling's involvement in the presenting problem. The therapist can then reflect these specifics back to the family instead of attempting a more abstract and less compelling assertion of "all members being in the system," or the like.

Using family members' values and beliefs as leverage. It is always easiest to convince people of something when it can be presented in terms of their own beliefs and values. A typical first evaluation session should reveal enough of these beliefs to the therapist for him or her to be able to frame the request for fuller attendance in similar terms. For example, if resistance is primarily from a rather obsessive father whose self-image rests on the role of the perfectionistic professional, the therapist can stress his or her own emphasis on thoroughness and demanding standards and his or her distaste for shoddy or half-hearted efforts, which in this case leads to a need for a thorough, competent, complete professional evaluation. In a family which places a high premium on caring, concern, and mutual support, the therapist can stress that siblings will want to help the Identified Patient, will feel badly if they cannot do so, and will be grateful and relieved if they are allowed to try to help by participating in the session.

Offering objective predictions. Often, especially when patients seem to be involved in an oppositional struggle with the therapist, the most helpful tack on the therapist's part is to remove him or herself from the position of opponent (that is, advocate for the alternative), thereby removing what the patient opposes and substituting instead a "cold" factual statement from a more neutral position. So, for example, instead of trying to convince, persuade, or cajole the patient into accepting the need to include other family members (s)he can merely inform the patient of the likely consequences of the refusal. Such predictions are best offered from the stance of a sympathetic, concerned, but not overly involved party who can give good advice, but can do no more.

These predictions usually involve percentages or time figures, or both.

For example: "Well, I suppose we could try to go ahead as is [tonally implying that such is at best a dubious proposition] but I feel that it is my professional responsibility to tell you that the chances of success go down by 80 percent if we do," or, "I can't guarantee that we'll get nowhere but, based on experience, it will take about twice as long to accomplish what you want, if we can." Naturally, the therapist should only imply that (s)he is willing to continue on this basis if this is in fact true. Such assertions need not be defended or proven on any basis other than a reference to professional experience. These are honest estimates, but this is secondary to their use as leverage to assure a thorough evaluation which will benefit the family.

Analogies often further clarify these assertions. The therapist can, for example, compare him or herself to a surgeon who is being asked to undertake a crucial operation but being made to work "in the dark," "with his hands tied," or "without the proper instruments." Such appeals are similar to appeals to caring and concern but speak more directly to ego than superego forces and stand a better chance of sidestepping oppositional dynamics.

These examples of therapeutic strategies to enhance the family's compliance underscore that one guiding principle for the therapist working with families is that (s)he must be flexible. The family evaluation is a multilevel assessment. The whole family should be seen together at some point, but the therapist will also likely want to meet with individuals or other subgroupings of family members. The sequencing of these various meetings is generally not crucial, and can be used by the therapist to help ease the family into the evaluation. Avoiding pitched battles over initially scheduling appointments is an important goal because the attitudes of trust and confidence do not flourish in an adversarial situation. Being flexible about the sequencing of different parts of the evaluation and accommodating to the family in ways which do not compromise the therapist's ability to conduct the assessment represent diplomatic responses which occur most naturally when the therapist has confidence in his or her fundamental control of the evaluation. If the therapist is confident of this authority, compromises with the family do not represent defeats. The therapist can say, "Okay, let's hold off on the whole family meeting for now, and discuss it further when we get together next week." And, as we have examined, the therapist has a great deal more "bargaining" power, understanding of the family, and leverage after a first session of some type has occurred.

Irreconcilable Differences: When the Therapist Cannot Compromise

While "bending" to the family's needs represents sophisticated professional judgment, "breaking" in response to pressure from the family is inadvisable and must be avoided. A family may present with a problem child, and refuse to allow anyone but that child to be interviewed. "Fix him or her!" is the message to the therapist. If the family refuses to alter their position after discussion, it would be best for the therapist not to accept the case. In general, in cases with a child or adolescent Identified Patient, both parents will have to agree to be seen in some context for the evaluation to take place. In these cases, the parents are the crucial family members in terms of providing information, managing their "problem" child, and hopefully running their family. The therapist could perhaps make do without meeting one or more of the Identified Patient's siblings in the early evaluation, but could not proceed without the parents' co-operation. As we have noted, the therapist may alter the timing of sessions, but he or she must not be put in a position where permanent decisions' concerning how the evaluation is conducted are made by the family.

WHEN NOT TO SEE THE WHOLE FAMILY FIRST

While careful strategy is often required in scheduling whole-family evaluation sessions, there are instances where the therapist is not likely to want to see the whole family in the first evaluation meeting.

When the Caller Requests Help with a Marital Problem

In these cases, the initial evaluation needs to be focused on the marital relationship and on the individual spouses. It is important to maintain the appropriate boundary around the married couple, and that the children should not be involved in the early discussions of marital conflicts. Such conflicts or problems (sexual disturbances, for example) are frequently not suitable for whole-family discussion. It may be important to obtain the children's perspective on the marital problems they are aware of (e.g., chronic arguments regarding money or relatives) in the evaluation process. Our usual approach is to begin with an evaluation of the couple together and both spouses individually, and then in additional sessions to meet perhaps with the children as a group and/or with the whole family. Children would be likely to be invited in if: (1) they were clearly implicated in the presenting marital problem (e.g., when one spouse feels his or her child[ren] and spouse are united against him or her); (2) if eventual child custody is an issue; (3) if the spouses' descriptions of the problem and the home situation are confusing and/or conflicting; and (4) if the children are older (around 10 or above). If conducted, the family session would not be focused primarily on the marital problem, but would be aimed at better understanding day-to-day life in the family.

As in all whole-family sessions, the clinician should work to avoid or prevent the occurrence of any "boundary breeches" in these meetings. Discussion of parents' personal lives (e.g., their sexual relationship, mutual resentments, etc.) or private aspects of the children's lives should not be encouraged or permitted in the whole family meeting. The therapist's active interventions are frequently required to protect family members from the embarrassment, confusion, and often intense discomfort inherent in the breakdown of the boundary of privacy around an individual's personal life or around the life of a subgroup of the family (e.g., parents or siblings). For example, the therapist can intervene by changing the subject, or by postponing discussion of a given area to a later time and moving on to another topic.

At the outset, then, the clinician may choose to schedule a marital evaluation session, to which an individual evaluation session with each spouse would soon be added. Just as no marriage can be adequately understood without meeting both spouses together, it is also frequently helpful to evaluate each partner individually in order more clearly to understand their perspectives and form an impression of their styles and personalities. The marital session places a premium on the therapist's ability to form a therapeutic alliance simultaneously with two, frequently bitterly opposed, individuals. Because of the difficulty of this task, and because marital conflicts often lead to heated, intense conjoint sessions, the therapist may choose to shift temporarily from the conjoint format and to conduct individual interviews with each partner. This allows the clinician to get to know and form an alliance with each spouse as well as to learn more about the presenting problem, and puts the therapist in a better position to manage the discussion of sensitive issues in the subsequent marital sessions.

During individual meetings, both spouses have an opportunity to come to know and feel more comfortable with the therapist, thereby reducing their anxiety and potential for feeling misunderstood in the marital sessions. It is important that the therapist clearly define these sessions as part of the marital evaluation as opposed to private individual consultations. As we will examine in some detail later in the book, the therapist does not want to have the evaluation compromised by being drawn into sharing a secret with one spouse. This would prevent equal alliances to be formed with each spouse during the evaluation, and can generally be avoided by telling the couple that confidentiality does not apply to those individual meetings. The therapist should state that anything discussed in the individual meetings could be brought into future marital sessions.

When an Adult Caller Requests Help
with a Personal Problem

The therapist is presented with another category of initial phone contact when the caller is an adult (either spouse, parent, or adult child living with his or her family of origin) requesting help for an individual problem. In these instances, the therapist should begin the evaluation process by meeting with the caller individually. A patient who calls with a personal problem generally wants an opportunity to discuss this privately with the clinician. Even when the individual problem appears clearly to relate to family factors, the patient's request for a "solo" session should be respected.

For example, a married, childless woman in her early 20s calls asking to see a therapist and complains primarily of depression. She states that she is not sure why she has felt depressed over the past year, and mentions, but minimizes, marital tensions and problems with her parents as possible factors. It would likely be difficult for this patient to discuss her feelings initially in the presence of her husband or family, and that plan would make little sense to her or to her family. After meeting individually with the patient one or more times, the therapist will have a better understanding of the problem and a firmer relationship and alliance with the patient. The therapist will then have a more accurate idea of whom in the patient's family he or she might like or need to meet, and can more confidently count on the patient's cooperation with the evaluative plan of action.

In many cases which begin with individual evaluations, the therapist will choose to invite selected family members (seen individually or in subgroups) to contribute their perspectives on the problem situation. The patient need not be living with these family members. If the patient considers a family member a significant person to him or her, then that family member might well be invited in at some point for a meeting. At some later stage in the evaluation process a whole-family evaluation session may be held.

It is our belief that more often than not there is a value in expanding the individual evaluation to include an understanding of the patient's family and his or her role in it. This whole system assessment can be used either for the added information it brings to bear on decisions and directions in the Identified Patient's individual treatment, or to determine the potential benefits of family treatment as a concurrent or alternative mode of treatment for the patient.

A 23-year-old man complained of chronic anxiety and multiple physical symptoms, and lived with his parents and 20-year-old sister. The evaluation began with several individual interviews, and then the patient's parents and his sister were seen in separate sessions. A whole-family evaluative session was conducted next, followed by several individual meetings to discuss the assessment and treatment recommendations with the patient.

In this example, recommendations were for concurrent individual and family therapy. The patient's symptomatology was viewed as both characterologic and as an aspect of ongoing family patterns of relationship.

CRISIS INTERVENTION: THE NEED FOR IMMEDIATE FAMILY INVOLVEMENT

It becomes especially important to meet with one or more of an individual patient's family members at the *first* clinical contact if the patient is in acute crisis and/or experiencing acute psychiatric symptomatology. In these cases, the individual patient may not be capable of presenting a clear, or complete, or even an accurate account of recent events. Family members can help the therapist "fill in the blanks" regarding past history, precipitants, recent symptomatology, and may be met with individually, in small groups, or even with the patient in the first session. Arranging the format of a first session involving an Identified Patient and several family members will largely be a matter of the therapist's style and personal preference, and the specific case dynamics. The crucial point is that both the patient and other family members need to be interviewed in order to obtain an adequate perspective on the problem situation, to make recommendations for managing the patient's symptoms, and to arrange subsequent evaluation sessions.

A 45-year-old, married mother of three children called the Psychiatric Outpatient Clinic because of acute symptoms of anxiety and depression dating back several weeks. On the phone, she could think of no precipitants or recent stresses, and sounded agitated, tearful, and frantic. An appointment was arranged for the patient, her husband, her children, and a sister with whom she was quite close. At this first session, the patient was evaluated individually, her husband and sister were each seen individually, and the children were interviewed as a group. A brief attempt was made to see the whole group together, but the patient's agitation and depression increased in that context and quickly became the focus of everyone's attention.

The individual evaluation of the patient allowed her symptoms of anxiety and depression to be assessed, and provided the therapist with some understanding of her life situation and current pressures. It was only from the patient's family, however, that the therapist learned the extent of the patient's dependency on others and desire to be taken care of by her sister at the sister's home. This had occurred the year before, when the patient had a medical illness. The family had returned from a vacation three weeks prior to evaluation, and it was upon resuming her household responsibilities that the patient's anxiety and depression worsened.

It might have taken weeks to get as complete a picture of the problem from meeting with the patient alone, weeks that the therapist most likely would not have had owing to the increasing severity of the patient's only partially understood symptoms. After seeing the family at the first session, the therapist could arrive at a plan for a more extended evaluation. This was aimed at bringing the immediate crisis under control while the more detailed evaluation continued. The patient was given antianxiety medication, and was advised, as a temporary measure only and with the agreement of the whole family, to stay with her sister on weekdays (her wish) and return home on weekends (when her husband was home). The family was asked to return for several more evaluation sessions.

Families of patients experiencing acute psychiatric symptoms (e.g., suicidal ideation, manic behavior, delusions or hallucinations, etc.) are often in the position of having to care for or manage the patient at home, and are in need of professional guidance in this area. The therapist also needs to know that his or her recommendations for the patient's care and treatment will be adhered to, and meeting with the patient's family during the first sessions helps insure this.

Certainly, in any case in which the patient's judgment is seen as impaired or in which there is the potential for destructive behavior (e.g., suicide, assaultiveness), the patient's family has to be seen immediately and thoroughly informed about the patient's condition and how to manage it. This could include giving the patient's medication to the family and advising them on dosage and administration, providing them with guidelines for understanding, monitoring, and controlling the patient's behavior, and informing them of when they need to bring the patient for emergency treatment or inpatient care. Only at a later time, when individual symptomatology was under control, could an exploratory, whole-family evaluation session be conducted.

SUMMARY

In sum, one general principle we have tried to employ in arranging family evaluations has been to place our primary focus initially on what the family has presented as their chief problem or concern. As we have seen, in cases where a parent calls regarding a child's behavior, or the relationship between children, or between parents and one or more children, we will usually arrange a whole-family evaluation to explore the presenting problem. Marital evaluations are scheduled when a patient calls in describing marital problems, and individual sessions (at times along with meetings with family members or the whole family) are initially scheduled for adult patients who call in with personal problems.

Before we turn to a discussion of the evaluation session itself, a brief comment on co-therapy is in order. Our evaluation format can be employed by therapists working alone or by co-therapists, and we have conducted such evaluations in both modes. One advantage of the co-therapy arrangement is that it allows the two therapists to divide up tasks if they like (for example, one could be looking more at process issues while the other centers on content). The therapists can serve to back each other up if one appears to have missed an area or failed to pick up on a cue, and each therapist has the benefit of the other's emotional support during the session. Beginning therapists in particular very often feel more confident sharing the responsibility of conducting the evaluation. By allowing themselves the very useful option of occasionally interrupting the session to step outside and briefly consult about the case, the co-therapists are able to test out ideas and hypotheses in a way that is unavailable to the solo therapist working without live observation.

All of these advantages imply an effective and well-coordinated co-therapy relationship, and such a relationship has to be worked at and developed by the participants. In many clinic settings or private practices it may be difficult or impossible to establish such co-therapy relationships. Also, many therapists prefer to work alone; they keep a clearer focus on the family and the evaluation when they are able to pursue their own direction without any thoughts about a co-therapist's ideas or actions. Overall, it is useful for the beginning therapist to work in both modes, come to some conclusions about his or her own preferences, and then see if these can be accommodated in the setting in which (s)he practices.

Most therapists have had more training in and are more comfortable evaluating individuals or couples than whole families. For this reason, the following chapters will carefully describe a structured format for evaluating family groups. What should the therapist do or say? What should be learned about the family? When and how is the information obtained, and what is done with the accumulated data? How do you manage a group while maintaining a personal contact with each of the family members? What do you do when no-one or everyone is talking? The novice family evaluator typically thinks of these and a host of other anxiety-producing questions before confronting the family. We hope to answer most of these questions, as well as to provide a method of family evaluation that can be learned, employed with confidence, and eventually tailored to the more experienced therapist's personality and theoretical orientation. "How do you begin the session?" is certainly a good, basic question with which to start our presentation, and an answer is provided in the next chapter, on "Opening Moves."

5

Opening Moves

The beginning and the end of the family evaluation are two critical periods for the therapist and the family. The first session's initial intensity is fueled by the family's expectations and anxiety level, and by the fact that the family and therapist are meeting for the first time. As we will examine in more detail later, the closing of the evaluation finds the family wondering what the therapist thinks about the problem and waiting to learn what will happen next. These attitudes provide the therapist with an opportunity to summarize the evaluation and to make specific treatment recommendations, to address unanswered family questions and concerns, and to reassure the family explicitly or implicity that their problems will be attended to.

BUILDING WORKING ALLIANCES

Both the beginning and the end of the family evaluation sessions, however, are perhaps best viewed as the ideal and most critical times for the therapist to devote attention to the building of working alliances with all family members. The family is alert, attentive, and alive as they enter and leave the session. They may remain that way for the majority of the session, but chances are that more than one family member will naturally "settle in" to the session during its middle phase. Being more comfortable, to be sure, is a positive accomplishment for the family member, and shows that the therapist has created an atmosphere for the session that facilitates the family's cooperation and trust. But the moments at which family members are most apprehensive, questioning, and in need occur most consistently at the beginning and end of sessions. Mistakes made at these times are difficult to overcome, while well-chosen moves pay dividends far in excess of the time or energy invested by the therapist. This first critical period occurs as the family members troop into the consulting room.

In that room, the family should find a sufficient number of individual, moderately comfortable chairs grouped in a horseshoe shape facing the chair(s) of the therapist(s). As we shall see, the therapist wants to be free to deal with all family members equally, and so does not want to end up seated within the family group. The family is told to sit anywhere they choose within the horseshoe, and the session begins. There is a more detailed discussion of how to interpret the family's own seating decisions and arrangement later in this chapter.

Obtaining Identifying Data

Once the family is seated, before the therapist has even had time to copy down the seating pattern or formulate hunches about it, the formal evaluation session must begin. At the outset, the therapist needs to know certain basic information about the family's make-up. The therapist should learn the name, age, occupation, and marital status of each family member, including those who are not present at the session. Who lives at home, and who resides away from the parental home? If individuals live away from home, how much contact do they have with the family? Are there other significant persons, family members or not, in the home or in the daily life of the family? For example, a grandparent, either in the home, in an apartment upstairs, or living across town, may play a significant role in the family.

Often the therapist will be aware of much of this information before the family members arrive for their first session, since a good deal of data is usually gathered in the first telephone contact. But regardless of how much the therapist already knows, establishing some basic facts regarding the make-up of the family provides a useful and nonthreatening structure for the opening of the first session.

The therapist should ask each family member for his or her name, age, and occupation/school grade and, where there is a question, his or her marital status and place of residence. Our practice is to start at one end of the horseshoe and work around in a one-by-one fashion. The therapist should avoid starting with the Identified Patient. This would focus all the family's attention on the one member who can be expected to be particularly uncomfortable, and would communicate to the family that the therapist is interested largely in the Identified Patient and not in the family as a whole.

By going around one by one, the therapist has an opportunity to make contact with each family member individually. Everyone is drawn in to provide some minimal information, and the therapist, by casual comments, small jokes, active listening, and interested, brief follow-up questions, begins to demonstrate to all family members that each is viewed as an important and welcome contributor to the session.

If any one family member begins to introduce some or all of the others, the therapist can gently and politely interrupt and state that (s)he will just go around the room one by one. The introductions may be interrupted by a family member's moving on to discuss the presenting problem or some other topic. Here, too, the therapist should return to the one-by-one introductions as gracefully as possible until each member has participated and all information concerning the make-up of the family has been gathered. In this manner, each family member will have made at least a brief contribution to the session. No one will feel talked for or talked about, feel left out, or be allowed to set an undesired tone for the session by dominating its early moments.

Most importantly, the therapist can count on a brief face-to-face encounter with each person in the family during this introductory period. These moments can contribute to the eventual development of therapeutic alliances with family members because they provide opportunities for the therapist and family member to interact directly and to gain impressions of each other.

The major task of the opening minutes of the session is for the therapist and family to begin to get to know one another. The therapist's earliest goal is to relax the family as much as possible, and to start to establish therapeutic alliances with each family member. Inquiring about the make-up of the family can contribute to each of these goals in that it provides an immediate, simple, and comfortable focus for everyone in the room. After these several minutes of introductions and very early impression forming, the therapist should lead the family to a discussion of the presenting problem.

DEVELOPING THE PRESENTING PROBLEM

It is important to remember that the presenting problem is typically the family's only reason for wanting to meet with the therapist. There is a problem, and the request is that it be solved. With this agenda, it is not surprising that any attempt to begin the session with a discussion of other aspects of family life will be resented and resisted by the family. Beginning the session by responding to the family's major focus is a logical step that also helps to build a therapeutic alliance with the family. Once the presenting problem has been explored, the family usually cooperates with the other phases of the formal evaluation.

Phrasing the Initial Question

Prior to the first evaluation session, the therapist will have received a brief description of the problem from the family member who made the initial phone contact and perhaps also from the referring therapist or agency. We usually begin the discussion of the presenting problem by telling the family that:

We know a little bit about the problem that brings you here. We would like to know more about it, and would like the help of all of you in order to better understand the situation.

Instead of letting our statement remain directed at the entire family, we usually single out one member to make the first response.

The reason for this approach is that one basic precept for the first family sessions is to leave as little as possible to chance. The family is a complex group, and much specific information will be generated in the session. Furthermore, the family's anxiety level is likely to be quite high, and the therapist therefore needs to be in firm control of the session. To have the therapist's first major inquiry responded to with anxious silence, for example, would be an unfortunate, although not irreparable, way for the evaluation to begin.

As a rule, the therapist will not choose the Identified Patient to answer first but will select one of the parents. Focusing initially on the "problem person" could precipitate a severe "hot-seat" reaction. This might be evidenced either by the Identified Patient's becoming highly stressed or by his or her becoming more alienated and resistant to the evaluation. The Identified Patient knows that (s)he is the ostensible reason for the family's attendance in the session, and may feel guilty, anxious, confused, or resentful (or any combination thereof) as a result. Putting the spotlight on the Identified Patient accomplishes nothing in the way of building an alliance with that individual, and it contributes to whatever tendency the family has to see the Identified Patient's behavior as the only legitimate topic for the evaluation session.

Beginning with the parents' comments affirms their leadership position in the family, and can help build a working alliance between parents and therapist. If the therapist is aware that one parent is particularly ambivalent about, threatened by, or resistant to the family evaluation, then a special effort would be made to cultivate his or her cooperation. Such a person might be given the "gift" of the therapist's initial request for information about the presenting problem. During the parent's comments, the therapist would work hard to communicate interest and respect, to be supportive, and to establish that (s)he understands the parent's point of view.

The therapist will usually begin with each parent's description of the presenting problem, and will then draw in the other family members for individual comments. If there are other family members who are older or close in age to the Identified Patient, then they should have their say first. The Identified Patient will be asked to comment on the problem somewhat later in the sequence, but before those family members who are significantly younger than him or her. This "age-ordered" sequence generally allows the broadest range of comments before the Identified Patient him or herself takes center stage, and yet has little chance of alienating the Identified Patient since it is a logical system with which to work one's way through the family.

Easing the Family into the Session

All more sophisticated strategies and goals aside, the basic plan for this early portion of the session is to keep it moving along. The therapist does not want to ask any complicated or awkward questions, and does not want to allow any long silences or highly charged exchanges or confrontations. While the therapist will want to observe family interactions during the session, (s)he needs to be careful to prevent any intrafamily discussion from becoming too heated or intense this early in the session. At the beginning of the first session, the therapist does not know the individual family members or the family as a whole well enough to be able to predict where an interaction will lead and how destructive it might be. As a result, the therapist will function more as the "hub of the wheel," directing and controlling the early family discussions, than (s)he might do later in the session or evaluation process. If an interaction begins to escalate or to deteriorate, the participants will be asked to speak to the therapist who can then control the discussion. The family must not be blown out of treatment by too stressful a first session. A therapist who is clear and direct in his or her statements, and who controls the session through his or her information gathering, helps the family to become comfortable in the session and increases the chances that they will remain cooperative through evaluation and treatment.

By asking each family member to talk about how (s)he sees the problem, the therapist also helps to build individual therapeutic alliances since it is made clear that each family member's participation is valued and encouraged by the therapist. No family member gets lost in the discussion because even quiet or younger members are drawn in by the therapist for a brief comment or even a response to a "yes-no" question. Since all family members occupy different positions within the family, their perspectives are necessarily different, and the therapist obtains a multidimensional portrait of the problem by drawing on the ideas and feelings of all present.

This phenomenological portrait will likely include many facets of the presenting problem that are of interest to the therapist. The therapist gathers impressions and facts incrementally, and by asking clarifying questions and bringing up as yet undiscussed areas, (s)he can obtain the understanding of the presenting problem that is necessary for the evaluation. The areas to be listed now are not meant to be seen as a final checklist of questions concerning the presenting problem. They merely represent important aspects of the presenting problem that the therapist should learn about at some point in the evaluation. The order in which they are covered is not crucial.

Important Aspects of the Presenting Problem

Onset. Along with detailed statements from family members regarding the nature of the problem, the therapist will also want to learn when the problem began. What were the family's life circumstances at the time of and since problem onset? What ideas or theories do family members have about possible precipitants for problem onset? Understanding both precipitants and the problem behavior enables the therapist to generate some early formulative leads.

Severity. Other areas or aspects of the problem provide the therapist with information about the nature and severity of the disturbance, and the quality of the family's response to it. What impact has the problem had on individual and family functioning? For example, has mother left her job to stay home and care for her son who has psychotic symptoms? Or has the family become unified around the illness of the Identified Patient? What has been the course of the problem episode from onset to evaluation? Has there been a steady deterioration or a waxing/waning pattern? If the course has been variable, are these changes associated with any other events, actions, or circumstances?

Previous family responses to the problem. Finally, what has the family done in response to the problem? Has the problem been ignored or actively confronted? If confronted, what solutions or approaches have been attempted, and with what results? Has the family received any professional treatment in the recent past? These areas help reveal the family's level of judgment and the success of their own problem-solving or crisis-intervention skills. Information concerning the approaches to the problem that have already been unsuccessfully tried will further highlight family structure and functioning as well as guide the therapist in planning a treatment program.

Apportioning Time for Discussion of the Presenting Problem

The amount of time given to discussion of the presenting problem will depend on the needs of the family and the nature of the problem situation. If the family is overwhelmed by an extremely complex problem, the bulk of the first session might be given over to an exploration of the crisis. This would enable the family to ventilate about their difficulties, and the therapist would be able to gather the information necessary for planning some initial therapeutic intervention. The session would normally end with the therapist making specific recommendations aimed at helping the family regain a sense of control and hopefulness about change. In the average case, however, we have found that approximately fifteen minutes are devoted to the "presenting problem."

THE B. FAMILY: THE INITIAL FIFTEEN MINUTES

What follows is a transcript of the initial fifteen minutes of a first family evaluative session during which identifying data are obtained and the presenting problem is explored. The reader should allow the information received and interactions noted to trigger off his or her own hypotheses concerning the presenting problem and family dynamics. Some background information about the family—as much as the therapist had at the time of evaluation—is in order at this point.

Background Information

The B. family was initially seen in the emergency room of a general hospital because of problems in managing their 12-year-old son, Larry, the second youngest of six children. The family was in great crisis, because of Mr. B.'s unexpected death the week before. Mr. B. was buried in the city where he had lived most of his life, but he, his wife, and their two youngest children had lived for the past year in another state. After the funeral, when it came time to leave for home, Larry got into several altercations with other family members and essentially refused to go. When seen in the emergency room, not only was Larry the problem focus, but Mrs. B. fainted repeatedly in the waiting room and was clearly in much distress. Finally, it should be noted that Larry has petit mal epilepsy.

This family's seating arrangement in the first formal family evaluation session can be seen later in this chapter (Seating Diagram no. 3, p. 129). The specific goal of the session was to evaluate and deal with the family's acute crisis, which was represented by Larry's refusal to return home.

Transcript

Therapist: One place for us to start would be just to go around and get names and ages of everyone.

Mrs. B.: This is Larry . . . (Before the therapist can begin to get information one by one, Mrs. B. volunteers to introduce everyone.)

Therapist: Okay, we'll just go around, okay? (The therapist gently prevents mother from introducing all family members herself.)

Mrs. B.: Okay.

Larry: Larry, I'm 12.

Diana: Diana, 22.

Phil: Phil, 19.

Mrs. B.: Rebecca, 63.

Jim: Jim, 29.

Peggy: Peggy, 10.

Mrs. B.: Maria is 28, she's missing.

(Because of the heavy emotional tone of the session and its distinct crisis nature, the therapist chose not to fill in all the identifying data, e.g., profession, school grade, marital status, at the very outset of the session. Some information had already been obtained in the family's emergency room contact, and the rest was expected to be presented during later parts of the discussion. The evaluation format is designed to be flexible and to allow the therapist to exercise his or her judgment at all times.)

Therapist: Okay, can you tell us a little bit about how you came to be seen at the emergency room yesterday? (The therapist was going to ask mother to respond first, but she quickly volunteered to take charge of the opening discussion.)

Mrs. B.: Larry, you tell the story.

Larry: I don't wanna tell the story. (A characteristic response of an Identified Patient asked to talk first about the presenting problem.)

Mrs. B.: We were all packed, we buried my husband this week, we were all packed, ready to go back to New Jersey, Peggy, Larry, my husband and I have been living in New Jersey since this past June. The other children are home here.

We were ready to go back to New Jersey and Larry decided that he wouldn't go if this one went, he wouldn't go if that one went, and he kicked up his heels real severely. I called our family doctor, and he suggested there was no solution foreseeable in the house in the course of the evening and suggested that we come down to the hospital here and somebody would handle Larry and bring him out of the frame of mind that he had entered into. Larry is an epileptic, uh . . .

Therapist: Okay, Diana, can you fill me in a little on what was going on yesterday from your point of view? (The therapist moved on to Diana next, instead of the oldest child, Jim. This was another intuitive move, based on Diana's sitting next to the Identified Patient and their exchanges of eye contact and whispers during the early minutes of the session. Jim [29] was called on next.)

Diana: Well, it's kind of cloudy, hard to put this together. We've all been running on raw nerves, trying to hold our tempers, it's been kind of rough, yesterday something erupted between Phil and Larry, and at a point it did get physical. Phil restrained Larry, Jim came and removed Larry from the room to keep him away from all the excitement that was in the room at the time, and he just kind of closed up into a corner, didn't want to talk to anybody, hated everybody at the time. Everybody did not know what to do. He does get nervous and very cranky and we know the epilepsy affects his behavior, but we were trying to blame it on something and there was nothing to blame it on last night. It was blind rage, and just everybody blew and then my mother started fainting, and everybody was flipping out. So that's about what happened yesterday.

Therapist: Jim, can you describe that situation?

Jim: I don't know that I could add much to that. Just the straw that broke the camel's back was that he took a poke at my mother yesterday, that started Phil, the natural reaction when someone takes a poke at your mother (sigh), . . . everybody's not ready for it, everybody's mad 'cause my father died, he (referring to Larry) focused himself to the center so everybody's mad at him now. It makes it easier, it makes my father being gone easier, 'cause nobody's worrying about that now, that's gone, that's over with.

Phil: We just let out frustrations in one area and he just happened to get in the center of it.

Jim: That's gone, he's more important now. We've got to worry about him now.

Therapist: You say that everyone's been mad because your father died . . .

Jim: You know it was completely unexpected, he just didn't wake up one morning.

Mrs. B.: They weren't angry because he died, there was no anger because he died. (said loudly) It's uh . . .

Phil: There were three days of hell that we went through and tension building up, we'd been trying to hold it, a lot was building up inside, in every one of us, it just came to a point last night when things started steaming and a lot of people let their tension out.

Mrs. B.: Larry took a poke at me and Phil immediately reacted and I can't criticize Phil for it because if Jim happened to be there I think Larry would have been flat on the ground with a couple of teeth missing. It just happens that Phil happened to be there first, and then Jim removed Larry from the room. He wasn't abused, he was removed from the room. I think he'll corroborate on that. If I'm not telling the truth, Larry, correct me. Because things are a daze.

Larry: I didn't say anything.

Mrs. B.: I know it.

Therapist: Phil, can you tell us about what happened yesterday?

Phil: It was a minor argument. This isn't just yesterday, it's been building up. That's one thing that hasn't been said, it's not something that just happened yesterday. But for two or three days it's been building up to a point where my mother went and gave Larry a slap in the face.

Mrs. B.: I slapped his mouth for mouthing off.

Phil: Me and my mother were having a conversation and Larry sort of nosed in and told me to shut up and started getting loud, and my mother walked over to Larry and slapped him in the mouth trying to shut him up. Larry took a swing at my mother, and I went, well I yelled more than anything at him and held his arms tight, and I hit him once on the top of the head, I didn't hurt him or anything, I held his arms and I yelled at him, and then Jim came along and took him, and I guess through three days of buildup he just, you know, it all just built up at once on him, he figured everyone hated him all of a sudden.

Diana: I'd like to clear something too, this has been, this isn't just the past three days.

Phil: I've been home (from college) for three days, that's all.

Diana: Larry's been having a very hard time dealing with his father's death. They hadn't gotten along for months, and two weeks before he died there was an awful scene. This rage isn't just this weekend, this is going back. Now we realize we have to do something about it and none of us feel that Larry is in any way responsible for my father's death. He is carrying an awful lot of guilt, and that's why we're here.

Therapist: Have you talked with him about that? In the last few days?

Diana: Yes I have, I can take it from any point of view, a religious point of view, anything, there's no way that it was his fault. He doesn't know what to think, there's different reasons, he's rationalizing, why my father died, he wonders if it was because he was mad. This is putting him through hell, just the fact that he had high blood pressure, we all knew not to upset him beyond a point, but there is an awful lot of guilt that he's carrying and none of us want him to carry it, it just doesn't belong. (After this supportive statement by Diana, the therapist chose to draw in Larry for the first time.)

Therapist: Larry, you and Diana have talked about this. What do you think about what she's saying?

Larry: I don't know what to think really. (A little gentle pursuing was indicated.)

Therapist: Can you tell us a little bit about how you were feeling after your father died?

Larry: My mother always told me, after we'd get into a fight she'd say, you see your father, you'll drive him to a heart attack, you'll put him on his deathbed. So what am I supposed to think?

Therapist: So when he did die, you felt responsible.

Jim: (Cuts in, almost as if to rescue his mother and Larry from the impact of his response.) Prior to his death he'd been to the doctor and got a clean bill of health.

Mrs. B.: The day before he died.

Jim: A couple of months ago he had problems with a tightening of the chest, went to a doctor, a week before he died he went to the doctor, his blood pressure wasn't high it was down, he'd lost twenty pounds, he was very pleased with himself. The EKG came back no heart attack, the doctor was very pleased with him, he was following a strict diet, the lightest weight he'd been in twenty-five years. The doctor was happy, my father was pleased with the report, it was kind of ironic there . . .

Therapist: Larry, when you felt that way, when you felt responsible, felt guilty and upset, who did you talk to, what did you do?

Larry: I talked to my doctor and I talked to Diana.

Diana: And you did talk to Mom.

Larry: I talked to her for about five minutes.

Jim: You talked to her for a long time Friday night, Larry. (The other siblings try to present a more positive view of the mother-Larry relationship.)

Mrs. B.: He's rejected me totally, he's rejected me totally.

Jim: You know it's complicated by the epilepsy. He's having a tough time accepting it.

Mrs. B.: I'm getting fainting spells now and he voiced the opinion I was doing it purposely. I'm not doing it purposely, Lord knows. (At this point, the therapist felt the need for some more facts about the family.)

Therapist: Larry, how long ago were you diagnosed as having epilepsy?

Larry: April.

Therapist: This past April?

Larry: Yeah.

Therapist: You mentioned right at the beginning the family kind of split geographically. Could you give us a rundown as to who is where?

Phil: Maria, who's not here, lives in Maryland, works in a hospital in Maryland.

Therapist: Is she married?

Mrs. B.: No, she's single.

Diana: None of us are married. (Laughter by all.)

Mrs. B.: My husband and I are in New Jersey, we had a home for ourselves and our two little ones. Very comfortable, a very nice home.

Therapist: The little ones are Larry and Peggy?

Diana: And Jim and myself have the home here. My mother had planned on maybe in another five years moving back here.

Therapist: What were the reasons for the move?

Mrs. B.: We have a business in New Jersey, a year-round business. My husband retired from active work last year, figuring he was sixty-five, we would eke out a comfortable living for the four of us in New Jersey. He didn't feel equal to hassling full-time work as he did previously. The other four are on their own, we have no financial responsibility for them whatsoever.

Phil: It's almost like having a split family, alright, like having two families in one. Larry and Peggy are younger, all of us have grown up and untied the apron strings. (Diana laughs and shakes her head "no.") They thought that they could give Larry and Peggy a better upbringing, a better life down there, bring them up the same way they brought us up, without having six bosses. It's hard. Larry always had one of us looking over his shoulder, Peggy too.

Mrs. B.: We felt in New Jersey we could give them things by themselves, listen to their stories, enjoy them, which is hard to do when you have four older ones coming into the house. Their lives are far more interesting, and we felt as though in New Jersey we could devote our lives to the two younger ones.

Therapist: And when did you make the move?

Mrs. B.: July.

Therapist: Last July? (One year prior to evaluation.)
Mrs. B.: Yes.

The discussion which followed focused on the family's evaluation of
the move the previous year by parents, Larry, and Peggy. During this
discussion Peggy was drawn in for a number of comments, so everyone
had participated in the session by the twenty-minute point. We will be
presenting additional excerpts from the B. family evaluation session at
other points in the book, but now let us look in more detail at the identifying data-presenting problem section.

As was noted parenthetically in the transcript itself, the therapist could
have gathered more identifying data at the very start of the session. He
felt, however, that the clinical situation called for moving quickly on to
the problem itself. Everyone did introduce themselves by name and told
their ages, yet retrospectively it would appear that little would have been
jeopardized by also gathering information at that time concerning job,
school grade, marital status, and place of residence. The therapist's decision caused this information to appear in fragments, and necessitated
his having to ask directly for information or clarification later in the
session.

The Plot Thickens

It is always fascinating to see how the "story" or presenting problem
develops as each family member makes his or her contribution to it. In
our example, Mrs. B. first states that Larry "kicked up his heels real
severely," and adds that she hopes "somebody could handle Larry and
bring him out of the frame of mind he had entered into." Mrs. B. concludes
by announcing that Larry is epileptic.

Next, Diana broadens the picture by stating that others besides Larry
are involved in the problem. "We've all been running on raw nerves," she
says. The conflict between Phil and Larry is reported, as is Larry's subsequent upset and withdrawal. Diana goes on to describe Larry's moodiness and epileptic condition, Mrs. B.'s fainting during the crisis, and
sums up by saying "everybody was flipping out."

Jim is drawn into the story development next, and immediately adds
a crucial detail. Larry "took a poke" at his mother the day of the emer-
gency-room consultation, and that is what precipitated the brief physical
confrontation between Phil and Larry. But Jim does more than add these
pieces to the puzzle, he goes on to provide an explanation for the crisis
itself: "Everybody's mad 'cause my father died, he [Larry] focused himself
to the center so everybody's mad at him now." It is unusual, but not rare,

for a family member to present such a cogent formulation of a family crisis. Jim clearly states that Larry has been a lightning rod for the family pain, and that having this distraction has made it temporarily easier to cope with their father's death.

Jim's comments appear to lead Phil to go even further in filling in the details of Larry's temper explosion and individual upset and in developing the theme of the family's group-tension level. He reveals that Mrs. B. slapped Larry for talking back to him, and Larry's "poke" at his mother was in response to that attack. Phil describes "three days of hell" prior to evaluation, when "a lot (of tension) was building up inside, in every one of us."

"I'd like to clear something too," says Diana, "this has been, this isn't just the past three days." Diana adds depth to the earlier view of Larry as the lightning rod for family upset by discussing Larry's feelings of guilt regarding his father's death: "He is carrying an awful lot of guilt, and that's why we're here." Larry himself concludes the family's initial group portrait of the problem by stating that he does feel guilty, and revealing that his mother used to tell him he would put his father "on his deathbed" as the result of his arguments with him. "So what am I supposed to think?" he asks.

Working Hypotheses

The therapist, at this early stage of the evaluation, was able to generate some working hypotheses about the B. family. Obviously the family was still in shock over Mr. B.'s death, and appeared to have suppressed much of their grief and sadness and to have expressed more anger and sheer tension in its place. As Jim said, Larry appeared to have become the focus of the family's agitation. He seemed a likely candidate to be focused on owing to his past history of conflict with the family and behavior problems. It would also appear possible that Larry contributed to being placed in the "target" role, or in a sense "volunteered" for that position, because of his feelings of guilt over his father's death. It could be hypothesized that he arranged his own "punishment" by becoming an immediate behavior problem, and that this action on his part served the purpose of distracting the family from their grief.

Larry reportedly had difficulty adjusting to his epilepsy, and had a history of conflict with both his parents. The splitting of the family one year earlier meant that Larry lost close contact with his older siblings, and it was also at this time that his epilepsy was diagnosed. Mrs. B. sounded ambivalent about raising younger children, stating firmly that her adult children's lives were of more interest to her. She and Larry each felt rejected by the other. So it can be speculated that the past year had been a difficult one for the new family of four (parents, Larry, and Peggy), with greater stresses to deal with and fewer resources (family members) to draw on for help.

The family as a group seemed to rely heavily on denial as a defense mechanism. No one was angry at Mr. B. for dying, Mrs. B. stated firmly and repeatedly. No one held Larry responsible for Mr. B.'s death, said several family members. Perhaps Larry's behavior can be explained as a function of his epilepsy, offered Jim. Jim appeared to be assuming the role of father-surrogate, and worked hard at it. His support seemed directed most strongly to his mother, however, as did Diana's to Larry.

Looking at the diagram of the family seating pattern (Seating Diagram No. 3, p. 129), Larry and Mrs. B. are on opposite sides of the room sitting next to their closest allies in the family. The image that comes to mind is of a duel, with each combatant's second standing at the ready. But a piercing sense of hurt, guilt, and loneliness appeared to lie beneath the surface of both mother's and son's words and actions.

All in all, exploring the presenting problem in an organized, controlled manner yielded a rich picture of the family structure and the nature of their current crisis. Early hypotheses would need to be tested by later information and impressions, and other specific areas of family life, as we shall see shortly, would need to be directly assessed. This form of early discussion of the presenting problem tends to limit the amount of family interaction possible, since the therapist is asking questions in turn and is being addressed by individual family members. Some interaction between family members does, of course, occur, and the therapist's observations of these interactions add much to his or her understanding of the family.

OBSERVATIONS

Family Seating Arrangements

The therapist's initial opportunity to observe the family as a whole entity occurs as the family seats itself to begin the session. As we have noted in an earlier chapter, families never seem to seat themselves in a random manner. The several seconds of looking, milling, and finally sitting that begin the session almost always result in a seating arrangement that reflects something significant about the family structure. A chain of interpersonal processes begins as the family seats itself. A diagram of any family's seating arrangement in the evaluation session will provide the therapist with an opportunity to generate hypotheses about family structure. We usually find that one hour of inquiry and observation confirms and amplifies what the seating arrangement has "told" the therapist in the first half-minute of the session. For this reason, we encourage those who are evaluating families to make a note of the seating pattern at the start of the session for future hypothesis testing. Consider the following examples of seating diagrams and generate your own hypotheses about relational structure before reading on to learn some of our ideas.

Seating Diagram No. 1

This most simple example shows a 24-year-old daughter seated between her mother and father. Hypotheses could include: (1) the daughter functioning in a "middle-person" position between her parents, with a potential for divided loyalties, and (2) the parents having a split or strained relationship, with poor direct communication.

Seating Diagram No. 2

This large a group offers a wider range of possible interpretations. Hypotheses could include: (1) the mother possibly viewing herself and being viewed by others as one of the children; (2) the parents' relationship being split and inadequate; (3) the father being largely disengaged from the family; (4) the oldest son also being somewhat removed from the children-mother subgroup; and (5) the two sisters being allies.

Seating Diagram No. 3

<u>Son</u>	<u>Daughter</u>	<u>Son</u>	<u>Empty</u>
(I.P.: 12)	(22)	(19)	Chair

Mother

(29) | S o n

DTR (10)

    This last example is striking in that this family (the B. family) was seen for evaluation several days after the father's sudden death. Hypotheses could include: (1) the empty chair next to mother emotionally signifying the loss of the father; (2) the oldest son's attempting to be a father-substitute in the family by sitting next to his mother; (3) an alliance existing between the Identified Patient and his older sister; and (4) the youngest daughter's also being on the periphery of the family's functioning outside of the session.

Family Interactions

    Once the session has begun, the therapist is called upon to be an accurate observer of the family members' interactions and behaviors. The therapist should learn to look for sequences of behaviors, for patterns, to come into focus. Initial observations may be simple. For instance, some family members may seem very active and verbal while others are more withdrawn and quiet. Or some family members will be observed frequently to attack or criticize other members, while others in the family will defend those same individuals. Or one family member may consistently contradict or consistently confirm another family member's point of view.

    Certain patterns are more difficult to perceive. One family member may be functioning as the family's "switchboard," with all messages going through that individual before reaching the "outside world." Parents may talk to one another indirectly, through their personal messages to one of their children. One family member may repeatedly speak for another, who quietly "allows" this to happen. Clearly, the list of possible interactions or patterns of intrafamily behavior is endless. The main point is that in the session the family will replicate significant aspects of their family structure through their behavior. The therapist needs to develop an "eye" for interactions and patterns, to allow observation to follow observation so that the mosaic of the family's behavior can be revealed.

In the introductory transcript of the B. family, several observations can be made even though the family's opportunities for interaction were limited by the therapist's approach. Mrs. B. initially tried to serve as the family's spokesperson, and it would be helpful to see if this turned out to be a pattern in the family's life together, and if so, what others' reactions were to it. Jim and Diana made several attempts to support and/or rescue others from difficult moments. When the pressure built up on Larry or Mrs. B., Jim or Diana would periodically step in to change the subject or present the subject in question in a more positive light. It might be that they are relied on by the family to perform in this way. These observations are added to the therapist's list of impressions, out of which will eventually come a coherent formulation of the family dynamics.

ONE FINAL QUESTION

We have found it useful frequently to add on one additional question at the close of the discussion of the presenting problem. Very often the family needs to spend some time with the therapist before they become comfortable enough to risk personal or painful disclosures. At other times a family member may not have found an opportunity to make a certain point or raise a new area for discussion. For these reasons, and for the sake of closure, we frequently ask the family as a group if there is anything else we should know about the presenting problem, if, for example, there are any other recent changes, problems, or stresses for the family that they view as significant. This broad question is not directed at member after member, because a positive response does not have to be made to it. If no one responds, the therapist can move right along to the next part of the assessment. Offering the question to the whole family also allows room for freer family interaction, thereby allowing the therapist to sit back somewhat and observe the group process.

As an example of this final phase of the presenting problem discussion, let us consider a few minutes of the M. family's interactions in a family evaluation session. The M. family was seen for an initial evaluation session several days after 17-year-old Ken was treated in a hospital emergency room for signs of an acute psychotic episode. The M. family consists of parents, 17-year-old Ken, and 20-year-old Susan.

Therapist: Let me ask all of you again, in recent weeks, recent months, have there been any other changes for people in the family or the family as a whole or any other problem areas besides the situations you've mentioned so far. Susan, you were nodding before.

Susan: Yes. Um, well, Dad drinks. Okay, and I think it has a lot to do with everything that goes on. Um, he escapes by having a drink when he comes home at night. I don't know how much otherwise he drinks, but to me that is an escape, just as it is to go out and smoke a joint, or uh, for me, some nights, just to go out and have a few drinks. Only I feel for myself that, especially recently, you can't escape it, you can't just go out and have a drink or go out and smoke pot, 'cause it catches up to you. It goes, it's still there the next day, whether you face it or not, and uh, I think, that has a lot to do with a lot of our problems.

Therapist: How does that affect the family, you or other people in the family, from your point of view?

Susan: Um, . . . well we don't really talk. We're hardly together as a family as a whole very often, even for supper. You know, you never know who's gonna be there . . . I think that . . .

Therapist: Okay. Mr. M., any thoughts about what your daughter's been saying?

Mr. M.: She's saying I have a drinking problem. Well, I suppose I do, I've been drinking for thirty years and it's an out. I go to bed at night, and the next morning it's like nothing happened. I'm talking about the problems, and I try to go to work and forget 'em. There was times that I didn't.

Therapist: The problems . . .

Mr. M.: Through the years, like I say, he [Ken] didn't work and we decided that he should work or whatever or help around the house . . . it would bother me, there was times, I worked eighteen years in one job and I think maybe not altogether but I stayed out of work a few days because of him and uh different things related. I left that job after eighteen years.

Therapist: What were the reasons for that?

Mr. M.: I really don't know. I'd get upset, thinking about my problems, and then at work I'd get into an argument or get upset with them, and then one time I just decided to get out.

Susan: But that didn't, it didn't . . .

Mr. M.: Well I say, you say I have a drinking problem, it isn't just drinking, it's uh . . .

Susan: It didn't start just yesterday.

Mr. M.: No it started . . .

Susan: I can remember . . . when you wanted your keys to take a ride . . .

Ken: That's when I remember the first time I saw you drunk. I was only, what, 8 or 9 years old.

Susan: I remember that too . . .

Ken: You know how much that hurts when you're a little kid?

Therapist: Okay, Mrs. M., you seem to be reacting to what was being said.

Mrs. M.: I honestly feel that my husband doesn't think it's so much of a problem. He's a good provider, does his work, does his job, he's a good father, it's that he doesn't realize that this is a problem, being a father also means you're there when I need you, you're not just sleeping because you've drunk too much. He doesn't see this side I guess. I really don't think he thinks it's such a problem.

In this case, the family members generally speak one at a time, with few interruptions and in moderate tones. Susan clearly takes the initiative in disclosing a family problem/secret—i.e., Mr. M.'s drinking. Her comment aligns Mr. M. and Ken as substance absuers and escapists, and she points to their behavior as fragmenting the family. Mr. M. perceives himself as on the "hot seat," and defends his behavior by commenting on how chronic problems with Ken have taken their toll on his own overall well-being and job performance. The blame appears to have been passed from Mr. M. to Ken, but then both Susan and Ken redirect the blame to Mr. M. with emotionally charged statements. Mrs. M. concludes this segment by softly, calmly, and in condescending tones, stating that her husband just does not get the point. This last comment seems both patronizing and hostile, and Mr. M. appears subdued and powerless at this point.

So all family members point to Mr. M. as the "problem bearer" in the group. But Susan and Mrs. M. also are clear in their upset about and criticisms of Ken's "irresponsible" behavior, and his psychiatric symptoms are evident. One possible pattern being uncovered is that the men in this family are seen as helpless, problematic, and incompetent, while the women are competent, sensitive, and long suffering. In this excerpt, the women are decidedly more eloquent and insightful than are the rather depressed looking and sounding men. In later points of the evaluation the therapist would more directly probe the nature of the alliance between Susan and Mrs. M. There also does not appear to be any clear alliance between the spouses for dealing with their family's problems. In that regard, Mrs. M.'s comment about her husband not realizing that "being a father means you're there when I need you" might be interpreted as an indirect statement of her need for Mr. M. to be a husband and be there when she needs him.

In the M. example, the therapist's "wrapping up" question about additional problems leads to the disclosure and discussion of a highly significant fact—Mr. M.'s drinking. Also, the interactions which accompany the discussion offer much material with which to build hypotheses and plan further inquiries.

SUMMARY

In sum, it has been seen that the beginning portion of the first family evaluation session is a time when the therapist attempts both to build alliances with all family members and to obtain a multidimensional view of the presenting problem. This period of introductions and impression forming allows the therapist to develop initial hypotheses regarding family structure by observing the family's seating pattern and interactions in the session itself, and by learning more about the presenting problem in its context of family life. The family's stated reason for coming to the session, its presenting problem, is respected and provides the initial focus for the meeting. The therapist attempts to ease the family's way into the evaluation in these opening minutes, avoiding confrontations and awkward pauses, and maintaining control of a well-modulated, efficient beginning. After this portion of the evaluation, the therapist continues to provide a structure for the evaluation, but the discussion moves away from the presenting problem to a broader consideration of family life. Such "probe" questions are the special concern of the next chapter.

6
Probes

After the initial discussion of the family's presenting problem, the therapist will want to move on to a broader consideration of family life. How is day-to-day life organized in the family? What are the patterns of family relationships? What alliances or coalitions exist? What are some typical points of conflict and how are these managed? How does the family manage discipline? These areas, and other like them, all reflect the relational structure of the family. The presenting problem exists within the context of the family's organization and relationships, and so obtaining a map of this structure is crucial to the evaluative process.

As we have seen, the therapist's observations of the family's seating pattern and interactions and the discussion of the presenting problem offer opportunities for the therapist to learn about the family's system and its style of functioning. Some families spontaneously offer information on key areas of their lives together during discussion of the presenting problem or other issues. They express themselves clearly and well, and the therapist finds that much of his or her work is to clarify and amplify the family's own statements. Most families, however, require more of the clinician's initiative in raising certain aspects of family life for discussion.

GENERAL CHARACTERISTICS OF PROBE QUESTIONS

We have found that it is possible to probe the broad area of family structure in a routine, organized fashion that is both direct and nonthreatening, and that can be adjusted for the clinical situation and level of articulateness of the family. Having such a set of "probe questions" also helps the therapist to organize the evaluation session. The session does not need to slow down or wander after consideration of the presenting problem, but can be led clearly and confidently by the therapist to a discussion of several routine aspects of family life.

One common feature of the probe questions is that they are not problem oriented. The therapist states that (s)he would like to learn more about the normal routine and behavior of the family. The "probes" are neutral stimuli and should not cause the family to feel pressured or confronted. As we shall see, the probe questions cover a number of areas of family life, but the therapist should be selective in choosing how many or what particular probes to use. A very talkative and articulate group might not require any specific probes, but might offer their own leads for the therapist to follow. A less responsive group might require most of the probe questions to tell about their family life or just to settle down and relax in the session. It will not be necessary to ask the probe question about disagreements at home of a family whose chief complaint concerns frequent arguments. The probe questions do not represent a checklist of areas to be covered in precise order, but should be used at the therapist's discretion to help the family provide a statement about its organization and dynamics.

The probes also can represent a type of "time-out" period, a welcome change of pace from the close and direct examination of the family's presenting problem. The therapist should let the family know that (s)he is making this shift to more general questioning, and the first probe we usually turn to concerns the physical layout of the family's home. While there is no fixed order for the probe questions, we generally begin with very neutral questions about family life and then move to a more direct probing of areas which may be more stressful for the family. The probe questions will be presented in such a typical sequence in the rest of this chapter.

Moving from the Presenting Problem to General Probes

Let us turn now to the wording of the therapist's transition statement. As in all instances in this chapter, the therapist's statement that follows has been taken from an actual transcript of a family evaluation session:

I want to take a little bit of time to pull back from discussing the immediate problem, just to get a little better idea about the family. You've mentioned some things already, but maybe one way to start would be for you to give us a description of your home, the layout of the rooms, who's where?

The therapist may choose to ask a particular family member to respond first, especially if (s)he expects the family to be hesitant to respond or if an effort needs to be made to build an alliance with that particular family member. The therapist will try to choose a family member who seems likely to set a cooperative tone for this portion of the session, and will therefore rarely select an overtly truculent or glowering member to field this first question. If a family member has had a moderately difficult time during the preceding discussion of the presenting problem, the therapist can allow that person a chance to regain his or her composure and control by leading off in a response to a neutral probe question. If a parent is singled out first, his or her leadership position in the family is thereby affirmed.

It is really up to the therapist's judgment and discretion whether the probe questions are initially directed to the group or if more specific responses are solicited. If the question is left for the group to respond to, and a number of family members answer at once, then the therapist may need to select one person to lead off and so on. During the course of the discussion of each probe area, most family members should be actively drawn in for at least a brief contribution to the family's response. People seem to enjoy responding to the probe questions. They provide an opportunity to answer a therapist's question without getting caught up in difficult feelings and problems, and without possibly antagonizing or hurting or embarrassing another family member. These questions also allow family members to present their families in a positive way, to tell what is good or humorous or warm about their families, to show what they enjoy or value about family life.

THE PROBES

Layout of the Home

We begin the probes section of the evaluation with a question about the layout of the home because this is a basic, important, yet minimally stressful area for the family to handle. This verbal analog to the home visit helps the therapist appreciate and understand the physical context of family life. Physical surroundings certainly affect how the family lives, and the family's use of space reveals much about their structure. As noted earlier, we begin by inquiring generally about the layout of the home. We want a verbal blueprint of the home, which should include an indication of who sleeps where and a notation of how many bathrooms there are and where these are located. While the family may spontaneously provide much of this information in response to the probe question, the therapist will usually need to ask numerous, brief, follow-up questions in order to obtain an accurate working blueprint of the home.

It will be helpful for the therapist to know that a family of eight lives in a small and cramped home, or that a teenaged son lives largely cut off from others in the family in a basement bedroom. The routine discussion of the family's home may reveal an adolescent who has never had and does not now have a room of his own, but sleeps, fairly publicly, on the living room couch, or it may reveal a husband who, while not stating that he and his wife do not share a bedroom, is said to sleep each night downstairs on the couch. A bedroom may turn out to be shared by two murderously rivalrous brothers. Twin 18-year-old sisters may share a small bedroom, while an extra bedroom, always available, is used as a den. A child or adolescent may usually sleep with a parent or both parents.

Seemingly small details can reveal much about family life. While clarifying the layout of their home with one family, we inquired where they usually spent time together. We learned that this group of six people owned four television sets. These were located in the living room, in two of the children's bedrooms, and in the parents' bedroom. What was revealing in this case was that the only television set that was frequently used was the portable set in the parents' small bedroom. This meant that in the evening anywhere from three to six people would be in the parents' bedroom, most on their bed, watching television. This simple detail said much to us about the family's attitudes towards separation and closeness and about the family's difficulties with boundaries and privacy.

All of this information comes at little cost, in the midst of the family's responses to an innocuous question. The therapist's reaction to all information received is interested and polite, but (s)he does not want to become too problem focused or confrontative, or to deviate greatly from the probe questions. If a probe question elicits the discussion of a conflict, problem, or upset feelings, the therapist should feel free to pursue such a direction briefly. At a point when the discussion is becoming too heated, complicated, or upsetting to one or more members, the therapist should pull out and move to continue the more formal sequence of the evaluation. In the first session, emotionally charged discussions or confrontations which are viewed as potentially difficult to control and manage fully should be sacrificed in favor of completing a wide-ranging and thorough assessment of the family. The pressure should not be on the family in this middle portion of the evaluation session. The family should feel comfortable and relaxed, and the information should just flow.

A Typical Day

After obtaining the family's description of their home, the therapist can turn to a discussion of a "typical day" in the life of the family. Once again, the therapist announces the transition from the previous topic with an introductory statement:

I want to also get a description from all of you of what a typical day consists of for the family. Starting from the first thing in the morning, beginning with who gets up first.

It may be necessary to direct the family back in time somewhat, to avoid hearing about some very untypical days that may have been engendered by the recent crisis. The family can be asked, for example, to describe a typical day several months prior to the onset of problems. The therapist will want to specify whether a typical weekday or weekend day is the day in question. Both types of days are of interest, but for the sake of time we often only inquire about weekdays or working days.

The therapist wants to know about the family's usual style of getting up and beginning the day. Do any family members have breakfast at home? Do they eat together? Which members, if any, are home during the day, or return home from school or work for lunch? At what time do different family members arrive home from school or work? A major focus during the discussion of a typical day concerns the family's managing of dinnertime. Who usually prepares dinner, and who is usually home for dinner? Does the family eat together, and do they have an established seating arrangement around the dining room table? If so, the therapist should make a diagram of it because this seating arrangement, too, can say a great deal about family structure. What is the atmosphere around the table at a typical family meal? Are things quiet or noisy? If noisy, is it the sound of animated conversations and joking, or is it a time of petty arguments or major conflicts? The probing of a typical day for the family usually ends with the discussion of how the different family members spend the evening.

Again, these innocent questions can elicit crucial aspects of family life. They may reveal a friend of the father's who, although not a member of the nuclear family, is quite frequently in the home and involved in family matters. The therapist may learn that a mother and her son and daughter, ages 18 and 20, typically walk around the house nude when preparing for work in the morning and often share the bathroom with one another. A mother and adolescent Identified Patient may be discovered to be home alone together all day, every day.

In one family, the parents may work different shifts, and so rarely see each other. It may be learned that a young adult son who lives at home remains almost totally separate from the rest of the family—eating at odd hours when no one else uses the kitchen, and keeping to his room. A father/husband may state that he is besieged with problems by the rest of the family as soon as he arrives home from work. This causes him to become anxious and withdraw from the family and, he states, leads to his angry and resentful outbursts later at the dinner table. One family may remain together almost all the time in the evening, while in another family the members may come and go unbeknownst to each other. All information about the family's day and organization, no matter how small or mundane, helps the therapist develop a better feel for the family and a more accurate sense of its special character.

Rules and Regulations

The area of limit setting within the family is also well suited to probe questions, since it is a factual yet revealing issue. The family's ideas about what is necessary in order to live successfully as a group, and how they manage to implement and support these beliefs, tell the therapist a great deal about the family. It is a valuable rule of thumb to try to avoid employing any technical or professional language or potentially stressful words or phrases in the initial inquiry about a probe area. In the present instance, the therapist should normally avoid using the words "limit setting" or "punishment" in his or her first statement. Instead, the therapist low-keys the entry into this area by asking about "rules and regulations":

All families have certain kinds of rules and regulations for people in the family, chores, curfews, and that kind of thing. What are some of the rules and regulations in this family?

When following up this question, the therapist can find out how each child is dealt with in regard to chores and rules, and can ask about what happens if chores are not done or if rules are broken. This can lead to a consideration of how disciplining is managed by the parents. Is there any discipline at all? If there is, do both parents play an active role in disciplining, and if so, do they work together or independently and perhaps at cross-purposes? Does one parent serve as the "enforcer," with the other parent either being supportive of him or her, remaining neutral, or covertly sabotaging the spouse's efforts? How well do the parents adjust their punishments to fit "the crime" and the age of the "offender?"

In one family of parents and four children, both parents stated their discomfort with formal rules or chores. To them, and to the children as well, this seemed a punitive and authoritarian way of running the family. On further inquiry, it appeared that the behavior of the two older children was frequently "out of control" and upsetting to the parents. The only clear consequences of the children's problematic behavior was their seeing their parents' degree of upset and depression over the situation. This led to some guilt, but not to much improvement in their behavior. In this family, rules were very unclear, and therefore could never really be broken, but the children felt they frequently failed to live up to their parents' expectations of them.

Another family of six had very clear and firm rules, but the parents in this case each wanted to have little to do with enforcing them. The children were given numerous chores, up to and including preparing all meals, and this system actually left the parents with little to do at home. This was resented by the children, who, by breaking the rules and avoiding responsibility, appeared to be attempting to draw their parents back into their lives.

A third family with three children had rules for their behavior, and these were easily and pleasantly adhered to by their two older children. When the youngest child reached middle adolescence, his parents were surprised when he stalled and delayed performing all manner of work at home, generally avoided responsibilities, and sidestepped or ignored most of the family rules. Because of their lack of experience with this type of behavior, their philosophy of discussing, and thereby reasoning out, all problems, and their guilt over perhaps being too critical of their son, both parents only lectured him about his behavior and expressed their disappointment with him. There were no more tangible and specific consequences for his actions, and so he continued to manifest an immature and impulsive style in and out of the family.

Alliances and Coalitions

Direct inquiry about the layout of the home, a typical day, and limit setting usually proceeds smoothly, and this factual information is of great help to the therapist. Greater discretion and awareness of the family's sensitivities are required when the therapist moves on to explore the more personal and anxiety-producing topic of alliances and coalitions within the family. This topic, therefore, fits in especially well as part of the series of probe questions.

It can be awkward and difficult to assess closeness patterns too directly. The question, "Who are you closest to in the family?" does not work well in a family evaluation because any response may hurt the feelings of those not mentioned. It is far easier to ask, "I'd like to get a better idea of who spends a good deal of time with whom in the family, whom each of you is most likely to talk to when something is on your mind?" These questions would then be directed at specific family members in turn, and, of course, yield more information in larger families. "Spending time" and "talking" certainly imply closeness, but providing information about these matters does not seem to feel as personal or revealing to the family members as does answering a direct question about closeness or concern.

As is the case with all probe areas, the therapist often gathers impressions about an area even without asking a question about it. These impressions can then be pursued, and the specific probe(s) will not be needed for the assessment. In one family, the therapist noted that the 16-year-old daughter, the Identified Patient, appeared to be the only family member who was tuned into her mother's feelings and difficulties. The therapist said to the mother that her daughter appeared to know a great deal about the mother's feelings, and the Identified Patient's mother answered, "Oh yes, she's the same as I am." The rest of the family supported the point that the mother and daughter were alike in personality, and it became clearer that the daughter was mother's only ally in the family. Subsequent discussion allowed the daughter to describe the bind she was in, being both mother's ally/confidante and wanting to be one of the children in the family. When asked how she reacted when her mother was doing something which was generally ridiculed by the rest of the family (e.g., compulsively cleaning, rambling in conversation), the daughter stated, "Sometimes I laugh at her, sometimes I stick up for her." The stress of this conflict of loyalties was seen as being directly associated with the Identified Patient's serious psychiatric symptomatology.

If a colloquial expression taps into the area of family life being probed, the therapist should attempt to work it into his or her questioning. Colloquialisms are generally benign and normative terms or phrases, and so are useful in efforts to discover relaxed ways of discussing potentially anxiety-producing material. The expression "stick up for" works well in assessing alliances and coalitions. It implies support, but does not immediately convey a type of intense devotion or loyalty. A family member may be more comfortable unveiling those latter qualities while responding to a less pointed question.

When asked, "Who sticks up for whom?" one family's initial response was that they all stuck up for each other. The therapist gently asked the question again, wondering if this always occurred equally among all family members. A few moments of silence brought forth a response from the 23-year-old daughter in the family, who said, "I feel like I want to protect her [mother]." A follow-up from the therapist, "Can you say more about that?" led the daughter to add, "If we don't stick together, we'll go down the drain. We always seem to be the ones who are left." By this, she meant that her father and 19-year-old brother both tended to keep to themselves and both men had experienced serious personal problems that stressed the family. Her comments clearly established the daughter-mother alliance that characterized this family.

One other way of assessing patterns of closeness and concern in the family is to ask, "Who worries about whom in the family? Who do you worry about the most?" When these questions were asked of a large family with two severely disturbed adolescent siblings, several family members stated that they were most worried, not about the Identified Patients, but about their mother. This indicated a good deal about the chronic and more subtle nature of mother's difficulties, and revealed her to be the focus of much concern at home.

Disagreements

One other significant aspect of family life that is usually difficult to tackle head-on is the area of conflicts and arguments. Families tend to be defensive about such matters, normal as these might be, and may read an implied criticism into the therapist's question about arguments in the family. For this reason, the therapist should give careful thought to the timing and wording of a probe question about family conflicts. It is wise to place this question toward the end of the probe portion of the assessment, so that the family will have already become comfortable responding to more benign questions about family life.

With families who are particularly sensitive in this area, a therapist can choose to avoid stronger terms, such as conflict, fight, or argument, and use the milder "disagreement." The therapist's introductory question frequently makes use of "low-risk" terminology, and emphasizes that disagreements are a normal part of every family's life. As is the case with most aspects of the evaluation, once the family has settled into a discussion of a certain issue, such as conflict, the therapist can pursue points more directly and forcefully. There is a virtue in conservatism at the opening moments of discussing an issue, because a more direct or stressful opening comment by the therapist can have a "shock" effect on the family. As a controlled discussion continues, the therapist can adjust his or her degree of directness and confrontation to the family's attitude and comfort level in the session.

Here are two phrasings of an introductory question about disagreements, and, like all quotations in this chapter, each has been taken from the transcript of a family evaluation session:

Every family has certain areas of disagreement, areas they frequently disagree about, but these areas differ from one family to another. I wonder if you could fill us in on the kinds of disagreements your family tends to have most often?

Or:

Most families have some kind of disagreement every once in a while about something, or some gripes about something once in a while. What kinds of gripes have there been from time to time in this family?

Even with these nonconfrontative phrasings, a good number of families are hesitant to respond. They say they cannot think of any areas of disagreement, or they remain silent. In these instances, the therapist should gently and briefly restate the question, emphasizing that (s)he is not looking for huge conflicts or big problems, but is interested in everyday kinds of disagreements or gripes. This is often sufficient to get one or more family members to break the ice and bring up innocuous examples. In one such "conflict-avoidant" family, the example of an everyday argument was of mother's and 22-year-old daughter's extreme upset over the 18-year-old son's changing his hairstyle without first consulting them. This small incident provided the therapist with a succinctly eloquent statement of the family's attitude toward individuation.

Other families can respond directly to the therapist's inquiry, with consistently productive results for the evaluation. One father of a large family stated that his biggest gripe was feeling "left out" of things because of his hours at work and the family's attempts to keep things from him. Mother and children said they kept problems from him to avoid adding to his already considerable work worries, but father clearly stated he would feel less anxious if he actually knew what was going on in the family. The therapist's follow-up questions to these statements revealed more of the emotional split between the parents, and the children's way of coping with this.

When a family brings up a specific disagreement or argument, the therapist should actively pursue a "blow-by-blow" description of the event. What was said or done first, what happened next, what was everyone doing at the time, and so on. Not only does this provide the best understanding of the particular conflict situation, but it helps the therapist prevent the discussion from getting sidetracked in any way or deteriorating into an argument itself. The therapist's high activity level also helps to maintain a controlled and pleasant tone during the discussion. The therapist appears interested and relaxed in the family's eyes, which helps them believe that conflicts are indeed normal and manageable. There can even be an occasional element of fun or humor in the ". . . and then what happened?" joint storytelling.

Additional Probes

There are several other probe questions that we employ less consistently than those already mentioned, but that may come in handy during the course of a particular family evaluation session. The clinician can ask directly about family activities on the weekend or on vacation, or can ask each family member what are their favorite and worst times at home, or what they like most or least about the family. As we have mentioned before, not all families require all the probe questions. Through experience, the therapist learns to judge how many are needed and how far to go with each for a particular family. Having a good number of probe questions at the ready can provide the therapist with a sense of confidence that even if the family is tight-lipped, (s)he will be able to keep the session going by trying out a variety of lead questions. If the therapist gets that "What do I do next?" feeling during the middle of the session, a probe question can be quickly and calmly introduced and may regenerate activity in the session.

Desired Changes

One final probe question which we have found especially useful deals with the family's attitude toward changes in its life:

Can any of you think of any changes you'd like to see made in the family?

If you could change anything you wanted about the family, or about life in the family, what kinds of changes would you make?

[Directed at the children] If you had magic powers, and could change anything you wanted, what would you change about your family?

These questions all fall in the mildly stressful category, since they require the family member to make a personal statement to the rest of the group. The desire for a change implies that things may not be good enough as they are, and so may be taken as a criticism by others in the family. Some families deal with this stress by initially denying that any changes are necessary or desired. Everything is fine, they say, except for the Identified Patient's problem which has brought them all into treatment. If the family holds to this position even after being asked gentle follow-up questions concerning desired changes of any magnitude, the therapist should smoothly move on with the evaluation.

Other families offer a response to the initial question, but state only obvious and impersonal, if understandable, desired changes. More money, a bigger and better home in a nicer neighborhood, the return of a deceased family member, and the symptomatic improvement of the Identified Patient are all examples of logical, sincere, but generally nonrevealing responses.

The probe question about desired changes does offer each family member an opportunity to go beyond the obvious and make a direct, personal statement to the therapist and family, and some individuals do just that. Children and adolescents are generally less likely to censor their responses than are adults, and often provide useful information. An 8-year-old boy in a large, conflict-prone family tearfully said he wished there were fewer fights at home. A 16-year-old girl, youngest of three daughters, said she would like fewer restrictions on her behavior, and said she felt her parents did not understand life for a teenager today.

In making these kinds of personal statements, a family member has the chance to state his or her feelings in a way that cannot be overlooked or misunderstood. These statements may also represent a family member's chance to step out of character, and surprise everyone with their true feelings. For example, a father in a family of five who typically acted in a haughty and aloof manner, and who was treated by the rest of the family as a hostile outsider, said he would like to be part of the family, to have them all spend more time together. The possibility of the surprising, "out of character" response is one major reason for posing a question about desired changes in family life.

Previous Family Crises

Toward the end of the "probe questions" portion of the evaluation, the therapist will also want to inquire about previous family crises. General types of stresses include health crises (a member's illness or injury, a chronic illness), financial crises, or crises involving loss or separation (death of a family member through illness or accident, abandonment by a parent, divorce, psychiatric hospitalization of a family member, departure of an adult child). Past problems, both big and small, normative or unusual, are significant because of what they reveal about family structure, about the nature of the individuals who constitute the family, and about the family's capacity to cope with stress and adversity.

We usually introduce this topic by presenting some variant of the following statement:

It will help us in dealing with the present problem to learn something about any previous problems the family has experienced, or that any members of the family have gone through themselves. Any past situation that has been especially upsetting to the family or put stress on it would be of interest to us, as would any previous problems that required professional help.

A more casual question that can be inserted in the general "probe" would be: "Have there ever been times that have been really rough for the family?" This type of inquiry is made to the family as a whole, and some families may need to be told that even relatively minor, normal, or successfully resolved crises are of interest to the therapist. In certain cases, the family will offer very little in response to this question, and the therapist will usually not push them on this. Family members may be hesitant to bring up a past problem area if one or more members at the session have previously been unaware of it. Or there may be concern that one or more family members may be embarrassed or greatly upset if a particular problem is discussed. Discretion is indicated at such time, since the therapist wishes to avoid boundary violations and moments of unexpected individual upset and embarrassment. As we will discuss in more detail later in this chapter, some information can only be safely and appropriately obtained during individual interviews with family members.

If the family does describe previous crises, the therapist may discover that these are similar in nature to the present crisis. The current problem situation would then be viewed as an acute exacerbation of a chronic family difficulty. For example, a family consisting of parents, ages 50 and 48, and children, ages 23, 19, and 14, presented for evaluation as a result of the 14-year-old's resistance to attending school regularly. In obtaining a history of previous family problems, it was learned that both of the Identified Patient's older siblings also had a history of truancy, and that in fact neither of them had completed high school until a year or more beyond their original graduation date.

This added information helped place the current problem in the proper family context, and it eventually could be seen how the children's truancy reflected a severe and chronic marital split. While ostensibly supporting regular school attendance, the mother in this family also provided tacit support of her children's truancy and sided with them against the "rigid" and "unfeeling" attitude of their father. The extent and rigidity of the current presenting problem could not be adequately understood without an awareness of this pattern, and such an awareness would have been much more difficult to obtain without the benefit of the historical data.

Even if the past problems reported are not earlier incarnations of the current crisis, they help alert the therapist to significant themes or issues in the life history of the family, some of which may still be active for them. In a family with parents and seven children, ages 24 to 8, the Identified Patient was a 19-year-old girl who was experiencing an acute psychotic episode. One pattern that began to emerge from the evaluation was mother's awkward and uncomfortable inclusion as part of the children's subgroup and father's apparent emotional split from his wife and children. When asked about previous family crises, the 19-year-old Identified Patient hesitantly stated, "When the baby was born." By this she meant when the youngest child, a girl now 8, was born. Follow-up questioning led to the family telling the therapist what was known to them all; that mother had "accidentally" become pregnant with her youngest child against father's wishes, and that when she learned of this she confided first in her children before finally telling her husband. He stated clearly that he had never been able to trust her since that time.

The family's organization, judgment, flexibility, mutual trust, and internal resources are also revealed in their manner of coping with past crises. In one family, a 17-year-old daughter's increasing withdrawal from the world and bizarre behavior were tolerated and catered to for over a year before a situational crisis triggered her acute psychotic decompensation and panic. In this case, when the daughter wanted to quit high school and take correspondence courses in the safety of her room, her parents supported the idea and tried to make her as comfortable as possible at home.

Another family presented with a concern over the oldest of four children, a 16-year-old girl who had recently been breaking the rules at home and at school and getting into minor difficulties. The evaluation uncovered information about a previous problem with a younger daughter, then age 11, who had colitis. The parents had actively sought treatment at that time, and were sensitive to the effect of family stresses on the children. They were not comfortable accepting any of their children's individual symptomatology, and were capable of looking beyond the symptom to broader tensions and patterns that might be of importance to them all. This more adaptive response to stress does not indicate, however, that the family was free from or aware of its own specific problem areas. Their constructive responses to family crises constitute a positive prognostic indicator, but more on that later.

The therapist needs to know the nature of the previous family crises, the family's style and success in coping with these, and the individual family member's contributions to the group's adaptive or maladaptive responses. The family has to be understood as a unit, and the individuals who make up that unit have to be recognized in their singularity. Such an appreciation of both "group," "relational," and "individual" dynamics represents the major challenge and advantage of the family evaluation, but it can accurately be stated that while no family-oriented therapist ignores the patterns of family life, many are guilty of undervaluing or even forgetting the significance of understanding the individuals who comprise the family.

Inquiring about previous family crises frequently leads to a description of an individual family member's past problems, since the family's presenting problem is often stated to be the Identified Patient's alone. During a previous crisis, someone other than the current Identified Patient may have been identified as the problem bearer, and as a result, the therapist's understanding of that individual is greatly deepened. This information becomes quite helpful in assessing what approach to take with the current problem, and what the reactions of individual family members will be to specific types of change.

For example, a family presented with a depressed adolescent son as the Identified Patient. Evaluation indicated that the son and mother were overinvolved with each other, and that the boy was underinvolved with his father and with peers. A marital problem was also uncovered. One possible therapeutic approach would be to try to deal with the marital difficulty, and simultaneously increase the boy's contact and time with his father and peers. While it was expected that all family members would be somewhat stressed by this approach, the Identified Patient's mother appeared likely to be under the most pressure.

It was therefore extremely important that the therapist know that this woman had a history of depressive episodes and had made two minor suicide attempts a number of years earlier. The therapist might choose to work more slowly toward the proposed changes, or at the very least would want to keep a close eye on the mother's emotional state as treatment continued to try to provide her with as much support as possible. Knowing this individual's personal history allowed the therapist to anticipate the outcome of the proposed interventions more accurately, and to modify the strategy accordingly.

KEEPING THE INDIVIDUAL IN FOCUS

The therapist comes to know the cast of characters in the family in a gradual, incremental fashion. As we have seen, important information can be obtained by inquiring about previous family crises, but observations of individual family members' current behavior in the evaluation session are also crucial. The therapist must be building impressions of each individual's personality and level of functioning as the evaluation goes on. Neglecting to come to some tentative conclusions regarding the dynamics and "mental status" of each individual family member can lead the therapist and the family to some serious pitfalls.

The most significant error that the therapist can make in this regard is failing to perceive that a family member, not necessarily the Identified

Patient, is experiencing serious emotional difficulties. If the family member's symptoms are not initially debilitating, their problem may go entirely unnoticed and untreated until an explosion occurs. At that point, the family treatment is certainly derailed, the therapist may lose credibility with the family, and the symptom bearer and family have to go through a difficult, discouraging, and perhaps dangerous period. The therapist must be alert to signs of individual symptomatology and distress during the sessions. An adolescent whose statements begin to sound looser and more tangential, a wife/mother who appears pressured and panic stricken in her comments and actions, a husband/father who seems preoccupied, tearful, and depressed, all are individuals who require the therapist's attention and diagnostic skills.

SEEING SUBGROUPS

In each of the above-mentioned examples, the therapist would gently question the family member about their comments, mood, or some aspect of the family evaluation and hopefully reach some clearer conclusions as to what was going on for that individual. But there are times when such an approach is ruled out by the individual's degree of disorganization or upset, and when the therapist is convinced that a more substantial individual evaluation is needed, one that cannot occur in the presence of other family members. At such a time, the therapist can temporarily adjourn the whole family session and meet with individual family members separately or in various subgroupings. Such an approach is not used at a set point in all evaluations, but is dictated by clinical circumstances. Breaking the family down to see subgroups or individuals is, however, a technique employed at some point in most family evaluations, and so deserves additional comment at this time.

It is helpful for the beginning therapist to keep in mind that the family coming for evaluation has few preconceived ideas about how the session should be conducted. They will generally follow the therapist's lead without comment, and the therapist should feel free to vary from the "whole family" format to see whatever combinations of family members (s)he chooses. The therapist should introduce this change of format in a brief, clear fashion, leaving little room for debate and offering little in the way of explanation to the family. A typical way of phrasing this would be:

I'd like to break now from seeing you all together, and meet briefly with you individually and perhaps in smaller groups. So, perhaps I can excuse the rest of you back to the waiting room for a few minutes, and start off meeting with . . .

The therapist must, again, be concerned with building alliances with all family members, and so must have a sense of balance in arranging these individual meetings.

Ideally, the therapist would benefit from seeing each person individually, each significant subgroup (e.g., parents, children), as well as the whole family together. If time does not permit this arrangement, then the therapist should at least insure that no one is completely left out of or singled out by the smaller meetings. There is a particular advantage in talking individually with older (e.g., adolescent) children in the family, but if each adolescent cannot be seen alone, then it is preferable to see them all together rather than seeing only one individually. Of course, the older children could each be seen individually while two or more young (e.g., 10 or under) siblings are seen together. The key is to try to anticipate the impact of such arrangements on the family members, and to determine what is fair, appropriate, and helpful in maintaining therapeutic alliances. For example, if you see one spouse alone, you must also see the other alone. Everyone should be included as at least a part of one subgroup meeting after the whole family session has been adjourned. Nothing will alienate someone more than a twenty-minute wait while all the other members of his or her family are seen in "private." The therapist could also arrange a second family evaluation meeting which will be devoted to subgroup or individual meetings, and the family will, therefore, arrive expecting such a format.

When an individual or subgroup is seen for general evaluative purposes, the therapist can begin by just rephrasing or reoffering one of the major questions from the whole family evaluation. We usually refocus on the presenting problem, and ask the family members whether they have any additional comments to make about it. Individuals can also be asked to give brief personality profiles or descriptions of everyone in the family, a request that could not be made in the whole family session. If subgroups are seen (siblings, parents), they can be asked to comment directly on their relationship with each other.

Also, an open question about whether there are any other current or previous problems or aspects of family life that have not yet been discussed can be asked in these individual or subgroup meetings. There are times when a previous crisis involving a particular "Identified Patient" will not have been mentioned in the whole family evaluation session owing to concern over that previous Identified Patient's or other family members' reactions to such a disclosure. In a smaller or private meeting, such information may be given (either by that Identified Patient him or herself or by another family member). If the former patient him or herself mentions the past problem, the therapist should follow this and learn more about that individual's personal difficulties and the nature of family life at that time. As we have noted earlier, if an individual family member appears in acute distress or is impaired in any way during the whole-family evaluation session, (s)he should be seen and further evaluated in an individual meeting.

By adding these meetings with key subgroups, the therapist obtains a richer portrait of each family member and of their network of relationships. These meetings are usually brief (five to fifteen minutes), but this, of course, can be adjusted as circumstances dictate. While there needs to be equality in "who" is seen, "how long" is purely up to the therapist. Sometimes a family member is seen for five minutes largely for "balancing" purposes. Another family member, for example, one who has a complex history, is currently in crisis, or has a particularly astute "eye" for the family problem, may be seen for fifteen minutes. As we have noted, the assessment of a family may stretch beyond one appointment, and this may be necessitated by the size of the family or the length of the subgroup "minisessions."

SUMMARY

We have, in this chapter, taken a careful look at a method of probing the family and the individuals who comprise it. Employing neutral, routine questions, the therapist gradually learns more and more about the way the family functions. Questions slowly build from the innocuous to the potentially stressful. All the while, the therapist is continuing to work on building and maintaining alliances with all family members. Our hope has been to provide therapists with more "ammunition" than they would ever need in an actual family evaluation session. Very articulate families may require little in the way of step-by-step probing, and may just "tell" the therapist their structure and dynamics in discussing the presenting problem or providing basic history about family life. Most families will require probing in several of the routine areas, and some taciturn groups may require the therapist to exhaust most of the list. The more experience the therapist has with a given question or probe area, the more (s)he takes away from a particular family's response to it. Their responses are compared to many previous families' ways of dealing with the same question, and this enhances the impressions the therapist gathers through the use of the probe.

By the time the "probes" portion of the evaluation (subgroup meetings and all) has been completed, the therapist will have concluded almost all of the family evaluation. Before examining in detail the methods and techniques for "closing" the evaluation session, we turn first to a consideration of an area of importance throughout the whole evaluation—the art of building therapeutic alliances. While we have commented at various points about building alliances, this topic warrants a chapter of its own and a more focused examination.

7
Therapeutic Alliances

Much of the success of any form of psychotherapeutic treatment is dependent upon the quality of the "healing partnership" created between the patient and the therapist. A relationship based on the patient's comfort with and confidence in the therapist can aid tremendously in preparing the patient for positive therapeutic change. The patient's belief in the therapist transfers to a belief in the therapist's skills and treatment approach, and to the patient's expectations for the success of treatment. The patient's positive attitudes and beliefs can enhance his or her sense of well-being and hopefulness, and starts the treatment process well on the way to success. The relationship between patient and therapist is clearly a significant factor in treatment, and this area has been closely examined in the context of different forms of individual treatment.

THERAPIST-FAMILY ALLIANCE PATTERNS

In family evaluation and treatment, the therapist-patient relationship is no less significant, but the relational context is very different. Instead of a person-to-person relationship in isolation, in family therapy the therapist is confronted by a group. The therapist must work to build alliances with each family member, and will typically need to do so while the entire family is present. Furthermore, the particular intensity of the private, one-to-one therapeutic relationship is absent. The therapist is confronting a group that is already in relationship with each other, where all members do not feel the same way about being in the session, where all members do not even see the problem in the same way. Faced with a complicated task, the therapist should try to be alert to the family's particular alliance characteristics and should keep in mind certain key strategies and techniques of alliance building in group situations.

The term "alliance characteristic" refers to the family's pattern of relating to the therapist. This is a shorthand classification, and is helpful because it allows the therapist to organize his or her impressions of the family into one of several therapist-family alliance patterns. The categories themselves do not do justice to any family's complexity, and are only rough guidelines that the therapist can follow. It is also important to note that the nature of the family's alliance pattern is to a certain degree a function of their particular relationship with the therapist. One therapist may enhance most family members' confidence in the treatment process, while another therapist might raise doubts and questions in the minds of several members of the same family. The interaction between therapist and family helps create the alliance-building context with which the therapist will then have to deal. In any event, we have noted three major therapist-family alliance patterns, each of which points to a different alliance-building strategy on the part of the therapist.

ALLIANCE CONSENSUS

The therapist always tries to be aware of each family member's ability and willingness to enter into a therapeutic alliance. Some families demonstrate to the therapist in the first evaluation session that most family members can enter into working alliances with the therapist. There is an alliance consensus in these collaborative families. The therapist tries to make younger children feel comfortable during the session, and hopes for their cooperation, but judgments regarding collaborativeness are more appropriately reserved for teenagers and adults.

In collaborative families, there appear to be no members who are strongly resistant or opposed to the family evaluation, and most family members appear capable of establishing a "good enough" alliance with the therapist. With these families, the therapist feels that (s)he is "in touch" with everyone, (s)he and the family seem to establish an early ease of communication, and the therapist feels a strong connection to and understanding of most family members. As an example, let us examine one such family's pattern of alliance formation.

The C. family was referred for evaluation by the mother's physician because several family members were experiencing anxiety symptoms and were attributing these to family tensions. The family consisted of parents (mother, age 42, father, age 49), and two sons, ages 16 and 17. Both parents and their oldest son had previously made brief individual contacts with therapists, and the whole group entered the evaluation upset about the degree of conflict and lack of "caring" evidenced in their family life.

While the family's upset and concern over their situation was intense and authentic, it soon became evident that each family member could hold his or her own in a discussion and that all could clearly present their views and feelings. No one was incapacitated by symptoms, excessively hostile or provocative with the therapist, or prevented from speaking by the rest of the family. Each person appeared concerned about the family and seemed initially motivated to take part in the family evaluation. Through the routine series of questions concerning identifying data, the presenting problem, and daily family life, the therapist established contact with each family member. In listening to their responses, the therapist also obtained a preliminary reading of each family member's personality and style.

The therapist attempted to make a personal connection with each family member by listening carefully to their comments and demonstrating understanding and respect for their opinions and feelings. The therapist must, however, attempt to build these individual alliances without antagonizing or alienating the other family members in the room. For example, the therapist must not support those statements of a particular family member which reflect negatively on another. The therapist can remain polite and neutral while hearing potentially controversial material, and carefully pick his or her opportunity for a more direct supportive statement so that no other family alliances are threatened. One family member's description of his or her own feelings, problems, or concerns for another are examples of safe opportunities for brief yet direct therapeutic support. Individual alliance building in a "public" context is a challenge to the therapist's timing and tact, drawing on the skills of both a juggler and a diplomat.

In the C. family described above, early comments by each family member and the therapist's preliminary impressions gave indications that: (1) father had a strong need for a sense of family closeness and possessed the most authority in the group; (2) mother was a highly self-critical and insecure woman, who felt she was a failure in her relationships with her husband and children; (3) the older son was viewed by all as the "explosive, uncontrollable" one and was usually at the center of family conflicts; and that (4) the younger son felt somewhat lost in the shadow of his more exuberant and dramatic sibling and was quiet and well behaved, but mildly depressed.

These observations allowed the therapist to develop an early alliance-building strategy for this particular family. Even with a family which seems collaborative in nature for a given therapist, the therapist must make an active effort to connect with each family member. Taking the alliance issue for granted can easily turn an initially cooperative group into a second-session cancellation. The use of the term "collaborative" indicates more about a family's potential attitude than about already accomplished alliance formation.

With the C. family, the therapist made a point of verbalizing in an understanding way Mr. C.'s desire for the family to be close and "friendly" (his word), and made a point of avoiding any challenges to the father's authority in the family. The approach to Mrs. C. called for the therapist to be sympathetic and to demonstrate understanding of her self-doubts and upset. The younger son was appreciative that the therapist allowed him an opportunity to express himself without being interrupted, and was also helped by the therapist's sensitively drawing him out verbally on a few occasions.

The therapist began to develop an alliance with the older son by simply blocking the sequence of family interactions that usually resulted in his being blamed and losing control of himself. When another family member made a "triggering" remark to this young man, the therapist quickly stepped in and deflected it by raising another question altogether. If the older son began to get too animated, the therapist politely took center stage and directed an altogether different question to him or even to another family member. By such active questioning and cordial interruption, the therapist prevented the older son from assuming or being placed in an unpleasant spotlight. Additionally, the therapist made several brief comments to the son that implied an understanding of his feelings and a recognition of his own upset and concern about the family's well-being.

The therapist serves as an editor of the family's verbal and nonverbal statements and interactions. (S)he attempts to encourage and underline the statements or experiences that help build alliances, create a positive atmosphere, and generally help the evaluation along. Conflict and difficult feelings or statements are an important part of the family evaluation, but as we have noted in earlier chapters, must be managed carefully. Editing does not imply strict and total censorship. Stress or confrontation is permissable during the family evaluation, but only up to a certain limit, and the therapist must remain aware of the family's tolerance for stress and the need for them to have a positive experience in the evaluation. The therapist can edit out, most often indirectly, particularly destructive statements or interactions by redirecting the discussion. The family should not be allowed simply to replay their most distressing moments in the family evaluation session. Those moments should be described to the therapist, but in a way that leaves the family feeling more hopeful than before, and leaves the individual family members feeling less abused, upset, misunderstood, confused, or discouraged. The therapist's active participation in the session, with an eye on alliance building, insures that the family's experience in the family evaluation will be different from their usual problematic interactions.

Because of the delicate nature of alliance formation in a group context, and because of the varying degrees of difficulty in allying with each family member, the therapist will frequently want to spend some time with several or all family members in individual meetings within the course of the evaluation sequence. This is another advantage or dividend of meeting with subgroups or individuals. Without everyone present, the therapist can more forcefully and directly attempt to make a connection with an individual family member. These meetings, brief as they may be, carry some of the special force of the patient-therapist, one-to-one encounter. Although the approach can be more direct in a solo meeting, the same general family alliance-building considerations apply. The therapist wants to ally with everyone and does not want the individual being "courted" to feel either "x-rayed" or like a "traitor."

In the C. family, the parents and the younger son seemed receptive and motivated to attend the family sessions. The older son, however, filled the role of the family "troublemaker" and so might be expected to bail out of the evaluation and once again disappoint the family. It was difficult in the first whole-family session to comment too directly on this hypothetical pattern, and it was also harder in that context for the older son to vary from his angry, sullen, and demanding style. Brief individual meetings were held with all family members after the "probes" section of the evaluation was concluded, and the individual meeting with the older son was devoted almost exclusively to alliance building.

After some preliminary ice breaking, this young man was told, in a sympathetic manner, that the therapist saw him as continually taking the family's bait and blowing up in some way. This was interpreted as a loyal action on his part, something that ended up focusing the family's attention on some important issues and tensions. It was regrettable, said the therapist, that part of the price for this act of family loyalty was that the young man himself often felt like "the villain" and was denied the opportunity to express more caring or sensitive feelings about his family. The therapist then predicted a possible family scenario over the next week. An argument at home would culminate in the older son's refusing to attend further sessions. The rest of the family would say this was just what they feared would happen. The therapist added that he just wanted the young man not to worry if all this did indeed occur. The therapist understood that the older son was concerned about the family. If he blew up and missed the next session, this would represent only a temporary setback, attributable to the force and rigidity of the old family patterns.

This individual meeting had a very powerful effect on the young man. An interpretation or process comment made in a supportive manner without an invitation for debate or discussion can often have a dramatic impact on the family member in question. The statement is based on the therapist's having a good sense of that member's situation and perspective, and is grounded in the therapist's confidence in his or her assessment being largely on target. Such a crisp and clear miniformulation, aimed at demonstrating respect, good faith, and an accurate understanding of the family dynamics, resulted in the case of the C. family not only in the older son's avoiding an explosion, but in his actually being remarkably cooperative. Eventually, he was able to disclose to his family needs and feelings that they had long considered to be alien to him.

The therapist's alliance building with all family members is of prime concern early in the evaluation, but must remain a consideration throughout the therapist's contact with the family. Different members may be more in need of being drawn in by the therapist at different times, and the value of the brief, individual meeting as a "booster shot" during later meetings must not be underestimated. Ideally, every family member should see a personal reason for continuing to attend the sessions and should view his or her own attendance as a sign of concern and consideration for their family group.

THE THERAPEUTIC ALLY

In many families, certain family members initially appear unable or unwilling to enter into an alliance with the therapist. Individuals experiencing acute symptoms (for example, major depression, psychosis, alcohol abuse) enter the session as the focus of the family's concern, and their disorganization and symptomatology can impair their own perspective on the family evaluation. Their degree of cognitive and emotional disorganization places them in the position of being talked about by the family, and may prevent them from communicating clearly and allying with the therapist. While such Identified Patients can often cooperate and even ally successfully with the therapist, in many cases the therapist will have to deal with their resistance to treatment and serve in a "case-management" capacity with the family. In these instances, the therapist's need for a particularly sensitive and reliable ally within the family increases.

There are also cases in which no family member is compromised by acute symptomatology, but where one or several members appear moderately to strongly resistant to the evaluation process. Here also, the therapist's task is aided by being able to count on the cooperation of at least one family member. This person can often be instrumental in helping to ease the family group into the evaluation. In both of the above-mentioned family situations the existence of a "therapeutic ally" within the family is a promising sign for general alliance-building, and we turn now to a consideration of this role within the family and its management in these two different family situations.

The Therapeutic Ally in Families with an Acutely Disturbed Identified Patient

In these families the Identified Patient's symptoms are or have recently been quite severe. Patients with a major thought disorder, manic excitement or profound clinical depression, suicidal or homicidal ideas or intent, or alcohol/drug abuse, for example, are the logical focus of the family's concern.

In such cases, the therapist's primary task is to evaluate and manage the crisis effectively. The therapist will, of course, still attempt to make a personal connection with all family members, including the Identified Patient. But by focusing on the Identified Patient's symptoms and behavior and trying to "manage" the case successfully at the earliest moment, the therapist has at least temporarily spotlighted the Identified Patient's special status in the family. The severely disturbed Identified Patient is often not immediately capable of entering into a full, responsible alliance with the therapist that is equal to other family members' potential therapeutic alliances. In these cases, the therapist's "case-management" responsibilities are superimposed on and slightly alter the basic alliance-building efforts.

When one family member is compromised in his or her ability to function in and out of the evaluation session, then the therapist must look to other family members to take up the slack. The most descriptive term for this type of individual is the "therapeutic ally." The Identified Patient will usually need to be sensitively monitored at home, and the initial treatment plan worked out by the therapist will have to be implemented accurately and reliably. In the evaluation session with a family that presents with this type of problem, the therapist should be looking for family members who appear capable of both clearly reporting on the current situation and successfully taking on the responsibility of supervising the Identified Patient's management at home.

In gathering information during the family evaluation, the therapist should continually develop impressions of each family member. Sometimes a certain individual stands out in a session as a result of his or her insight, sound judgment, and common sense; these are the prime characteristics of a "therapeutic ally." These individuals appear to be respected and well liked within the family and are clearly invested in helping the Identified Patient and the rest of the family group. They demonstrate a willingness to be realistically accountable within the family, but are not prone to feelings of martyrdom. The therapist finds that (s)he can easily direct questions to such a therapeutic ally and can rely on his or her having the perspective and ego skills to respond in a useful manner. The therapist comes to feel that (s)he can deal directly and collaboratively with the therapeutic ally, which can be of great help in a crisis-torn family.

A family with an acutely disturbed member may have more than one member who is capable of being a therapeutic ally, but more typically one person appears most able to function in such a role. If the Identified Patient is a child, it is ideal for the therapeutic ally to be a parent. But a sibling (at least of adolescent age) can also adequately assume such a position. The presence of one therapeutic ally is a very significant positive prognostic sign, and bodes well for the successful management of the crisis situation. By identifying the therapeutic ally and relying on his or her information, the therapist can feel confident of understanding the presenting problem well enough so that treatment recommendations can be made. If medications are prescribed, these can be monitored and supervised by the therapeutic ally, who can be counted upon to cooperate. The therapist can also count on follow-up reports from the therapeutic ally on the Identified Patient's progress over the next several days or weeks.

In focusing on the special characteristics of the therapeutic ally, it is possible to lose sight of the alliance-forming process that must continue with all other family members throughout evaluation and treatment. The therapist will try to create a space for each member's comments, and attempt to gain an impression of each person's particular style and needs. (S)he will tailor comments to each family member along lines which will hopefully communicate the therapist's respect and understanding of the family members' position and feelings. Once again, brief individual meetings with family members may aid the alliance-building process. These meetings are often especially useful in establishing a working relationship with a potential therapeutic ally.

The therapist can use an individual meeting with the therapeutic ally to describe the treatment plan directly and clearly, to state what the therapeutic ally should be looking for in the way of symptomatic improvement or regression, and to gather more information from the therapeutic ally about the Identified Patient and the family. It is essential, however, that the therapist not get carried away and come to view the therapeutic ally as an actual co-therapist. The therapeutic ally is part of the family, involved in the family's history and daily life, and is not totally objective or outside the influence of family patterns and pathology. The therapeutic ally serves in a certain capacity because of his or her own abilities and the nature of the family crisis, and the role is a temporary and limited one. When the crisis is under control, the special status of the therapeutic ally no longer exists. If the therapist loses sight of this, it will be hard to involve the therapeutic ally as a more equal part of the family evaluation or any family treatment at a later date.

Also, if the therapeutic ally becomes the therapist's confidant or is given too great a responsibility for managing the family, the therapeutic ally may become alienated from the rest of the family. The therapeutic ally may initially appreciate being singled out and may enjoy the status of the new role, but it is the therapist's ethical obligation to remember that each family member's primary loyalty is to the family and not to the therapist. The therapeutic ally must not be allowed to feel as though (s)he has left the family behind by working with the therapist. Instead, all the therapist's statements to the therapeutic ally should be presented in terms of the ally's interest and concern for the family, and the temporary nature of the more special, "ally" status. When speaking with the therapeutic ally, the therapist must communicate an attitude of respect toward all other family members.

The P. family represents an example of a case presenting with an acutely disturbed Identified Patient and a potential therapeutic ally. They were first seen for a family evaluation shortly after the Identified Patient, a 20-year-old girl, was treated in a general hospital emergency room for acute anxiety symptoms. The family consisted of parents (father, age 45, mother, age 44), the Identified Patient, and a 22-year-old brother, all living in the family home. The Identified Patient's symptoms of anxiety were associated with an extremely severe set of obsessive-compulsive concerns and rituals which were paralyzing the lives of the Identified Patient and her family.

In gathering the preliminary information about the family members and the presenting problem, the therapist was sensitive to the parents' exasperation over their daughter's condition and behavior, and the Identified Patient's apparent lack of any strong motivation to be treated. The 22-year-old son, however, appeared to be well thought of by all and to be sensitive to the concerns and needs of the other family members. Because of his personal qualities and his central position in the family, this young man was an excellent candidate for therapeutic ally status.

The therapist actively attempted to ally with the mother in this family. Recognizing her worry and concern for the Identified Patient, and hearing from others in the family how the mother was dominated by the Identified Patient, the therapist listened supportively to mother's anxieties about her daughter's condition. He commented on how hard the mother was trying to help her daughter get better or at least to prevent her from getting worse. The father impressed the therapist as being exasperated by the whole situation, frustrated with both his daughter and wife, and feeling hopeless about the future. The therapist made it known that he could understand the father's feelings, and used the word "powerless" to describe the father's sense of himself in the family. Father responded immediately to this, and described how he was kept out of situations that involved his daughter because his wife felt he was "too tough" on the Identified Patient. The therapist then made a brief comment (brief to avoid excessively threatening the therapist's alliance with the mother) about how the father, like any normal parent, would like to be helpful to his children and counted on in a crisis.

These moments of alliance building took place in the whole-family evaluation format, but it was difficult to draw out the Identified Patient in that context. She remained downcast and quiet, and gave minimal responses to the therapist's questions. In an individual meeting, it was possible for the therapist to be more directly understanding of the Identified Patient's concerns and perceptions, and to avoid appearing overly eager to get the Identified Patient to stop the "bad" behaviors. The beginning of a possible therapeutic connection was made in an individual meeting.

An individual meeting was also quite useful in dealing with the son, the potential therapeutic ally in this family. This meeting allowed the therapist to obtain a more detailed account of the presenting problem and the home situation from what was probably the most reliable source. The therapeutic ally was aware of his mother's overinvolvement and feelings of guilt regarding the Identified Patient, his father's withdrawal from the situation, the existing marital tensions, and the Identified Patient's degree of regression and disturbance. The son demonstrated clear concern for the family, appeared to have good common sense and judgment, and felt unable to change things in the family on his own.

One benefit of working with a therapeutic ally is that it enables the therapist to capitalize on and strengthen a positive resource within the family itself. By helping the therapeutic ally, a "natural" family resource, to work more effectively on the family problems, the therapist has helped increase the family's internal strength. Similarly, by building upon family resources the therapist also prevents him or herself from being put in the position of trying to change the family totally on his or her own. A very significant component of the therapist's repertoire is the use that (s)he makes of the family's own potential or actualized resources.

Moving back to the P. family, the therapist acknowledged the therapeutic ally's prior attempts to help the family and noted his concern and caring for his parents and sister. The therapeutic ally was then told directly what the initial evaluation/treatment plan was going to be. Because he was seen as having influence over his sister, he was to encourage her to attend the family and individual sessions which were to be scheduled. The therapist had some concerns that the Identified Patient would refuse to attend future meetings, and become embroiled with her parents over that issue. It was clear from the history that the Identified Patient's parents were rarely successful in forcing their daughter to do as they said. The therapist hoped that the brother, the therapeutic ally, because of his less conflicted relationship with his sister, could prevent the Identified Patient-parent clash and be successful in inducing his sister to attend the sessions.

The therapeutic ally was told that the therapist was going to schedule a meeting with both parents together, in which a plan to set more effective limits on the Identified Patient would be discussed. The therapist would, in a sense, coach the parents on how to begin to create changes in the home environment. The therapeutic ally was asked to be on the lookout for how his parents handled this assignment (whether mother did it, whether father participated as well), and to be sensitive to the pressure this change would place on them and the Identified Patient. The therapeutic ally was asked to be supportive to the Identified Patient during this period in a way that did not sabotage his parents' efforts (e.g., by offering to spend some time with the Identified Patient at or away from home). The therapeutic ally was finally asked to keep the therapist up to date on all developments, either by phone or in the next session.

The parents' account of how they managed the therapeutic task would certainly be solicited and would be of value to the therapist. But because both parents were so caught up with the Identified Patient in rigid and restrictive patterns, it would be particularly helpful to have a slightly more objective report on how the therapeutic task had been managed. The parents might impose some restrictions on the Identified Patient's behavior at home, and then report to the therapist that this did not work at all and only led to increased arguments. The therapeutic ally might report, however, that his parents laid down several rules but in a very tentative and confusing manner, and rescinded these on the first whine of protest from the Identified Patient. Further, he might describe how his father had wanted to persist with the plan while his mother was very anxious about what the Identified Patient might do as a result of being thwarted. Family evaluation is based on drawing out and then combining multiple perspectives on a given situation, and the use of the therapeutic ally helps the therapist achieve that goal.

The therapeutic ally is initially the therapist's main positive connection with the family which has one or more members who are unable to enter directly into a therapeutic alliance. These are typically families in crisis, with one or more members who are experiencing acute symptoms that require immediate attention. The therapeutic ally helps the therapist to accomplish the task of crisis management, and to obtain more time in which to ally with the others in the family, including the Identified Patient.

As this general alliance building develops, the therapeutic ally comes to assume a less special role in the family treatment. If the ally has been drawn into service in a discreet and subtle manner, then the transition back to a status equivalent to the other family members is a smooth and painless one. The therapeutic ally is always first a member of the family, helping the therapist to help the family as a whole, and is never to be considered a co-therapist.

But what of families with an Identified Patient that have no therapeutic ally, who offer no "beachhead" from which the therapist can comfortably conduct the evaluation and perhaps the treatment as well? First, consider the P. family just presented with the same parents and Identified Patient, but for the 22-year-old therapeutic ally substitute instead a 10-year-old brother. Age, then, eliminates this boy as a fulcrum for the evaluation, and the Identified Patient is uncooperative at the very least. Mother will be hard for the therapist to reach since she is likely to feel anxious and guilty about making any changes in the treatment of her daughter, and her husband cannot be relied on to support her (as a therapeutic ally might in the original scenario). The father will remain exasperated until he sees some results, but also will need some support to stay involved with his wife in initiating some changes with their daughter.

Without a therapeutic ally, the Identified Patient might easily refuse to attend follow-up sessions, and both parents might quickly end up confirmed in the attitudes and approaches they demonstrated on initial presentation. Some of this could occur even with the presence of an active therapeutic ally, but the therapist's chances of success go up considerably when (s)he is not working alone.

The Therapeutic Ally in Families with Uncooperative Members

Each member of a particular family enters the evaluation process with his or her own combination of attitudes and feelings about being there. There is always a range of emotion present concerning the evaluation within the family. Some members may feel very optimistic, others may be mildly skeptical, while others may feel desperate and frightened about what will happen if this approach is not useful. There are a large number of possible variations and combinations of attitudes toward evaluation within a family, but cases which reveal a wide polarization of feeling between at least two members offer special opportunities for alliance building.

These are cases in which one or more family members are moderately or strongly resistant to the evaluation and where at least one family member is motivated to have the family take part in the sessions. If everyone else were neutral or apathetic about the evaluation, then one very negative family member would likely be sufficient either to insure that the evaluation session never takes place or to sabotage the process if it gets underway. In such cases, a negative member would not be confronted or challenged by another family member who was in favor of the evaluation.

Without such an internal clash of perspectives, there would be little to slow the family's exit from evaluation other than the therapist's own success in allying with them. If the therapist could make a connection with the resistant member, or strengthen other members' confidence in the evaluation process, then the work could continue. But the therapist will often find in such cases that his or her attempts at building alliances will go unrecognized or unappreciated. (S)he cannot get through to the family.

But if at least one member is receptive to their efforts to work with the family, that person's influence on the family can often lead to a successful engagement in evaluation and treatment. These are instances where the "therapeutic ally" serves as a bridge to the rest of the family, buying the therapist time to build other alliances and to defuse pockets of resistance. When the therapist is confronted with such a family, one guiding principle should be: "Do nothing to jeopardize relationships with early allies." The therapeutic ally is a crucial figure in this type of family's initial session(s).

The therapist should, of course, ignore no one in the family and should attempt to build rapport with all. But there is no need for the therapist to feel compelled at all costs to win over an uncooperative family member in the early part of the evaluation. Such a major effort may be offensive to an already resistant or uncomfortable family member or may be interpreted as "high-pressure salesmanship." If the therapist is polite and respectful, an uncooperative family member is very unlikely to feel an increasing pressure to sabotage the evaluation. The evaluation can withstand the skepticism or resistance of several members if there is at least one significant potential ally in the group. The therapeutic ally must not be taken for granted, because if this family resource is squandered, then the evaluation may indeed be jeopardized.

The Y. family, consisting of parents, both age 40, a son age 13, and a daughter age 15, were seen for evaluation at the mother's request. She stated that she and her children could not tolerate Mr. Y.'s negativity and moodiness, and added that Mr. Y. only came to the evaluation session when Mrs. Y. threatened to divorce him if he refused to attend. Mr. Y.'s initial attitude was only mildly cooperative. He accepted full responsibility for all family problems, seemed beaten in spirit, and was generally quiet throughout the session. He would attend a follow-up session at his wife's request.

Efforts to build an alliance with Mr. Y. had to be handled delicately so as not to alienate Mrs. Y., the early therapeutic ally. If the therapist had gone to extremes in the first meeting to demonstrate an understanding of Mr. Y.'s feelings, or attempted to reframe them in a positive light, it is likely that Mrs. Y. would have felt misunderstood and mistreated. She might feel, "Here I had to coerce him to come to the session and he gets all the sympathy and understanding." Even if the therapist tried to balance the scales by attending equally to Mrs. Y., the challenge to the family interpretation of the problem would have been too rapid and extreme. Mrs. Y. could be expected to pull out of therapy, perhaps by precipitating a crisis that would restore the negative focus to Mr. Y.

Instead, the therapist used Mrs. Y.'s influential position to insure that her husband attended a subsequent individual meeting. Here more direct alliance building could take place without threatening Mrs. Y. or placing her in a negative light in her husband's eyes. The therapist told Mr. Y., based on information obtained in the first family evaluation session, that he saw him as a man cut off from his family who had become so accustomed to this role that he did not challenge it or even experience himself as being upset by it. The therapist said that Mr. Y.'s caring for his family was evident in his attending the sessions against his wishes when faced with the possibility of a breakup of the family.

This type of support allowed Mr. Y. to discuss his feelings regarding his wife's reliance on their children for her emotional intimacy and his chronic jealousy, guilt, and resentment as a result. He talked about his desire for closeness with his family, as well as his emotional deprivation in his family or origin. The therapist could then make plans to see the family and/or couple again, with a positive alliance made with Mr. Y. and a continuing alliance with Mrs. Y. In the next session, the therapist carefully balanced his support and solidified both alliances. Mrs. Y. was instrumental in arranging the evaluation and insuring her husband's early attendance, but soon she and her husband had both established working alliances with the therapist.

In other cases, the therapeutic ally is the key to getting the evaluation started, and remains the central figure throughout the evaluation and treatment. The A. family was seen for evaluation as a result of the parents' difficulty in setting limits on the behavior of their 14-year-old son. This young man was frequently skipping school and defying his parents at home. Also living at home were an older brother and sister, ages 17 and 20, who themselves expressed frustration and discouragement over their younger brother's behavior.

Mr. A. was very interested in the family being evaluated and was concerned about other aspects of family life as well (e.g., his daughter's problem in establishing relationships, his older son's withdrawn style). Mr. A. was the acknowledged authority in the family, although his job kept him away from home for long hours. Mrs. A. was primarily responsible for managing the family, and she was not optimistic or positive about their being seen for a family evaluation. She focused exclusively on the Identified Patient, with whom she appeared overinvolved and extremely discouraged.

The therapist did his best to communicate an understanding of Mrs. A.'s feelings, but the major goal of the early evaluation was to solidify an alliance with Mr. A. He could continue to arrange for the family's ongoing attendance which would allow the therapist to complete a thorough evaluation. If the therapist's recommendations were to include ongoing family therapy, as in this case they did, then Mr. A., the therapeutic ally, could help ease the family into therapy itself.

In this case, Mr. A. remained more comfortable with the family format throughout treatment, but eventually a "good-enough" alliance was established with Mrs. A. The couple was helped to clarify their perceptions of their children and coordinate their attempts at limit setting. Without the early therapeutic ally, it is likely that the A. family would not have followed through with a family evaluation and would have continued to look solely for individual help for the Identified Patient.

ALLIANCE FAILURE

With a number of families no therapeutic ally can be found and the family members are at least moderately resistant to family evaluation. These represent cases of "alliance failure." Certain families present themselves as "nonallying," and the therapist needs to be aware of this in order to assess prognosis properly and to decide what to do about treatment. As our example, let us consider the D. family, consisting of parents (father, age 39, mother, age 36), a 17-year-old daughter (the Identified Patient), and three younger children, ages 13 and 11 (boys), and 6 (a girl). The Identified Patient was hospitalized for several weeks following an acute psychotic episode, with the family being seen for evaluation during the latter stages of her hospitalization. In this case, the Identified Patient's symptoms left her in a rather fragile condition even after some improvement on medication. The therapist took a gentle, supportive approach with her, and she was able to participate in the evaluation sessions and to contribute to the description of life in the family. At the time of evaluation, however, her insight and judgment would have had to be rated as fair at best.

The Identified Patient's siblings impressed the therapist as being both young and naive, upset over recent family events, and allied with their mother in most matters. The family evaluation revealed a great deal of prior and current marital conflict, with mother and the children united in opposition to father. He was reported by everyone to be an alcoholic, although he minimized the extent of his drinking problem. Father stated that he wanted to become part of the family again, but both the chronicity of the marital conflict and its level of intensity mitigated against this change occurring. The father was cooperative with appointment setting and such, but the therapist never felt he made a strong connection with him.

The therapist had a sense that he could not really trust the father and mother in this family, that their statements and actions seemed to mask more than they disclosed. Such early impressions should be tested by further experience with the family member(s) in question, but the ability to generate a succession of ideas and beliefs about the people in the family is one of the essential components of the therapist's repertoire. The key here is to avoid finalizing beliefs prematurely, to be open to new information or to the discovery that one was simply "wrong."

In the case of the D. family, the marital conflict was chronic and severe, and the couple alternated between separation and living together. There was a pattern of the father wanting to "repent" and join the family emotionally, mother passively agreeing to this plan, and father soon thereafter being emotionally and/or physically expelled from the family because of a "transgression." Through all of this, the 17-year-old Identified Patient was in the middle. She had the only consistently supportive relationship with father, yet also felt strongly allied with her mother and siblings. With father in or out of the house, the Identified Patient was in a split-loyalty position.

The therapist could not establish or develop a therapeutic ally among the younger siblings because of their ages and consequent lack of maturity and judgment. Because of the extent of her symptomatology, the therapist would have to work carefully and slowly to build an alliance with the Identified Patient and would need to have some way of accurately monitoring the improvement in the Identified Patient's symptoms. Early in the evaluation, the therapist would not be able to rely on the Identified Patient's overall judgment of the family process. While both parents said the "right thing" in the evaluation sessions, they did not appear to be aware of the specific effect of the family conflict on their oldest child. They seemed primarily interested in placing blame on each other, and neither seemed to be making an active request to the therapist. The therapist could not easily become a part of this family, have some immediate access to information, and some early, modest control over their life situation. The therapist remained an outsider, being absorbed into the couple's and family's destructive patterns as a "bit player" or "extra."

It is important to establish that it was not primarily the severity of the marital/family disturbance that made the D. family so difficult to work with. It was the couple's lack of motivation and capacity to change, their degree of absorption in the destructive family patterns, that led to the failure to establish therapeutic alliances with them. Another couple, equally conflicted, but more open to the individual approach of the therapist, more willing to consider the state of their marriage directly, would enable the therapist to begin to work inside the family.

A similar family in which the Identified Patient had an older sibling who was sensitive to the family issues and could serve as the therapeutic ally would also improve the prognostic picture. The therapeutic ally could focus the family's attention on patterns and connections that would otherwise go unnoticed and could be the therapist's bridge to the family for a time. The therapeutic ally could likely be far more effective than the therapist in reminding the family of the real issues and keeping them in evaluation and treatment.

The D. family, however, falls into the "alliance failure" category. The therapist should determine whether any potential therapeutic allies exist in the family or its immediate social network, and should, as always, do his or her best to make a positive, individual connection with each family member. These actions will take place throughout the evaluation, and the therapist's determination that the family is a nonallying group, such as the D. family, will significantly affect the treatment recommendations and prognostic forecast.

It would be foolish to recommend a family treatment to a family group that has shown little ability to ally with the therapist and limited willingness to examine family life. In the case of the D. family, the therapist might recommend individual treatment for the Identified Patient, and individual and/or marital treatment for the parents. If the Identified Patient's symptoms improve and one or both parents are helped to deal more directly with their role in the family problems, then a treatment involving the whole family in some capacity might be recommended. Family evaluations can be effectively conducted with nonallying families, but conjoint family treatment is not usually recommended in such cases.

As we shall discuss in more detail in the next chapter, alliance failure in the evaluation sessions points to a generally poor prognosis for positive individual or family system change. It will take time to work one's way into even the most benign nonallying group, and during that time the problems continue and the therapist has no control over the situation. Certain cases, of course, will permit no entry at all by a therapist, and individual treatment with the Identified Patient may not even serve as an effective holding action.

SUMMARY

In examining three kinds of patterns that can confront therapists in attempting to build alliances with families, the underlying premise has been that the therapist will have to work to accomplish this goal. The therapist's personal style, qualities, and character are important, but are not sufficient to ensure alliance formation even with the most cooperative group. The therapist must use his or her skills as a clinician to generate constantly developing impressions of the individuals in the family that is being evaluated. The therapist's approach to the family must take into account their style, needs, and idiosyncracies. The therapist is not in effect saying, "Here is what I have to offer. Take it or leave it." (S)he is saying to him or herself, "What does each separate person in this family want or need, and how can I authentically present what I have to offer to match those needs?"

A delicate, frequently unspoken negotiation process characterizes the relationship between therapist and family during the evaluation period. This culminates at the end of the evaluation when the therapist will offer his or her recommendations to the family. In closing the evaluation, the therapist not only has to offer the family recommendations, but must do so in a way that (1) is understandable to the family, (2) fits their individual and joint needs and is therefore likely to be accepted by them, (3) is not personally compromising to any family members, and (4) leaves the family with an increased sense of hope and confidence about the therapist and their own future as well. The end of the evaluation process is obviously a time when the therapist must choose words, tone of voice, and content in a very careful and sensitive manner. These few minutes of the evaluation sequence will be considered carefully, then, in the next chapter.

8
Closing the Evaluation

Most families enter the first evaluation session with apprehension and uncertainty, gradually settle into the more comfortable middle portion of the evaluation, and then once again are brought to expectant attentiveness at the close of the evaluation. Family members are typically alert and listen carefully as the evaluation winds down. They are waiting to see what will happen next, and are wondering what the therapist is going to do or say.

At the conclusion of the evaluation session or sessions, the spotlight shifts from the family to the therapist. It is now the therapist's responsibility to present a verbal summary of what the evaluation has yielded and to offer specific treatment recommendations that will be of help to the family. The basis for such an evaluative summary and set of treatment recommendations is the therapist's formulation of the case, the fitting together of the pieces of information developed during the evaluation into a coherent whole.

DEVELOPING A FAMILY FORMULATION

There is an intellectual challenge implicit in developing a formulation of any given case. The presenting problem needs to be understood in all its complexity and in the richness of its context. What has contributed to the problem's development, what processes help to maintain it, and, most intriguing, what purpose the problem might serve in the life of the family? What is the individual meaning of the problem for the Identified Patient and for other family members? How are family relationships affected by the problem?

The therapist's detective work must draw on information from a variety of sources and from several levels of analysis. The family's structure, its roles, boundaries, and subsystems, must be understood and examined. Communication patterns in the family must be observed and included in the developing formulative hypotheses. As we have reviewed in detail in Chapter 2, the therapist needs to be aware of the family's stage of development, the predictable stresses of such a point in family life and the role they might play in the current presenting problem, and must assess how well the family has coped with this and previous developmental crises. If the family was unable to resolve the crises of one stage (e.g., creating a boundary around the early marital relationship), then it will face increased difficulty in subsequent stages (e.g., managing the arrival of children).

Thinking in terms of developmental stages provides a kind of diagnostic baseline for the therapist, and allows for differentiation between: (1) normal, acute, stage-specific difficulties, (2) maladaptive responses to the specific demands of the given developmental stage, and (3) "chronic" problems related primarily to unresolved prior developmental stresses. In developing a formulation, the therapist must also be aware of the family's particular manner of experiencing and expressing dynamics of loyalty and obligation, or reciprocity and fairness.

The therapist needs to understand the position and perceptions of each family member. Individual needs, conflicts, and perspectives are important, but in family formulation these are all placed in the context of the family system. Impressions are combined, blended, into a set of hypotheses that do justice to the individuals and to the family group alike.

A family formulation is a beginning answer to the questions: (1) how does the family work? and (2) how are the problem and the family system connected or intertwined with each other? We noted earlier the particular information the therapist should routinely obtain about the development and current impact of the presenting problem (see Chapter 5). The therapist begins tentatively to develop a formulation even during the early minutes of the evaluation. These early hunches or hypotheses are then refined as more information about the problem, the family members, and the family system is obtained. The therapist temporarily settles on an overall case formulation at the end of the formal evaluation period, but of course develops and reshapes these ideas as the case continues and his or her awareness and understanding of the family increases.

The art of family formulation is in the linking of symptom and system in the mind of the therapist. The system can maintain the presenting problem in a variety of ways. At a purely behavioral level, family members may inadvertently reinforce precisely those actions of a child that they wish to eliminate. At the level of identity and role complementarity, a husband may resist attempts to reduce his wife's phobias and anxieties. Despite his complaints about her symptomatology, he may depend on her identity as "the weak one" to maintain his own identity as "the strong one." And his wife may actually play her part in keeping her husband "strong" by being "weak." Symptom and system here maintain each other and are richly interconnected.

At the level of whole-family structural patterns, the parents of a rebellious, scapegoated Identified Patient may continue to encourage his or her behavior subtly in order to "detour" submerged marital conflicts. The Identified Patient may help preserve the family "harmony" and marital "unity" by placing him or herself in the spotlight as the problem. A child's truancy may be implicitly encouraged by a dependent, lonely parent. The Identified Patient's problem behavior in this case, then, would in part represent an act of loyalty toward this parent. An adult woman's psychiatric symptoms, which interfere with her ability to care for her children, may allow her own parents to absorb responsibilities for child care, thereby postponing the "empty-nest" crisis in their own lives. Threads of role complementarity and dynamics of loyalty would need to be pursued in formulating and treating such a case.

These reciprocal and interrelated actions are not usually consciously planned, and so there are few real "villains" or "victims" in family life. There are usually just individuals operating within complex patterns of relationships that are frequently mystifying to them.

In each of these examples, it is the connection between the presenting problem and the family context which clarifies major sources of the problem, factors maintaining it, and directions for change. Such multilevel formulations are not meant to replace or contradict individual formulations, but most often complement these. In the case of the phobic wife described above, there may be clear historical and psychodynamic origins to her fears, which dovetail with her husband's personal need for an emotionally crippled spouse. The truant child may have genuine fears and symptoms related to school which complement the mother's need for a companion in the home. A family evaluation which includes individual, subsystem, and whole-family assessment is most likely to capture this fit between individual and relational forces.

As we have seen, a formulation may involve a "reframing" of the presenting problem. The therapist's understanding of what is creating stress in the family may be very different from that presented by the family, and the therapist does the family a disservice if (s)he does not reserve the right to reconceptualize the presenting problem. One reason why the family seeks professional help is to get an outside perspective because they are all too close to the problem to see it clearly. They may have met with little success in solving the problem because they are trying to solve the wrong one. What looked like teenage rebelliousness may in fact be familial loyalty. What was presented as constant conflict and fighting may in fact reflect an overly close family. What appeared to be a problem with a reclusive, fearful child may primarily involve a depressed and needy parent.

TAILORING AN EVALUATIVE SUMMARY

While formulating a case is a largely intellectual task, choosing what to present to the family, how to present it, and with what treatment recommendations requires therapeutic skill, judgment, and an awareness of the therapist's own style and interactions with the family. The summary statement represents the therapist's conscious decision as to what the family is currently able to understand and accept as an explanation of the problem. Most therapists are familiar with the notion of individual defenses and resistance. Families, too, have their own forms of defense and resistance. They can close ranks and seal themselves off from the therapist who poses an immediate, serious threat to their current patterns of relationships.

The therapist's evaluative summary is not intended to be a complete case formulation. It is being offered to the family, not to professional colleagues, and therefore cannot include many potentially difficult or threatening impressions or hypotheses. A case or a family formulation represents the therapist's working understanding of the problem at the point of evaluation. The therapist's summary statement is shaped from the broader family formulation, and represents the selective use the therapist makes of the formulation in order to help the family understand and accept the forthcoming treatment recommendations and therefore to engage in treatment.

Overly confrontative or provocative formulations would jeopardize the family's comfort with the therapist and acceptance of his or her recommendations. As the treatment continued, the therapist would hope to work more and more directly and openly on family issues. But this is always dictated by the needs and abilities of family members to work productively in this manner, and many families make significant progress without all members being equally aware of the family dynamics at equal levels of sophistication.

The therapist will run into trouble if (s)he lets slip any vague comments or goes too far in offering relational hypotheses to the family. Mysterious, ambiguous, or confusing statements made by the therapist will be picked up and pursued by the family members, who will logically ask for an explanation. Already in too deeply, the therapist will then be in the embarrassing position of avoiding the question, trying to cover his or her tracks and not go into more detail. Most families, however, can freely accept the notion that specific tensions and pressures could have played a part in one member's developing symptoms, and that one person's problems could have likewise caused stress for the remainder of the family. Ideas of mutual concern and mutual influence are logical and point to a caring relationship among family members, and these concepts are therefore frequently incorporated into the therapist's evaluative summary.

By way of contrast, consider the formulative statement that one member's symptoms are serving the purpose of holding the family together and are successfully detouring the family away from some other serious problems. Even if accurate, this statement would likely be viewed as a foreign, upsetting, and offensive theory by most families during the evaluative sessions. It would be a case of too much, too soon, with too little preparation, finesse, or thought of what this stage of the evaluation is really meant to accomplish.

The therapist's summary should be geared as much as possible to be in keeping with the individual views and needs of family members. This, once again, would facilitate the family's acceptance of a therapist's ideas and increase their confidence and hopefulness about future treatment. In all of his or her adjustments of language and choices of concepts and themes, the therapist is of course holding to his or her genuine assessment of the family. The therapist's summary expresses what (s)he believes to be true about the family. Alliance building should not occur at the expense of truth or accuracy, but within the general confines of "the truth," the therapist should feel free to be very selective in what (s)he chooses to present to the family.

The therapist needs to take care that what (s)he does say is not personally compromising to one or more family members. No one should be blamed, of course, or provided with support for blaming another. Embarrassing past behaviors, either symptomatic behavior or the actions of any family member should not be emphasized or dwelt upon, and if dealt with, should be placed in the most positive light possible. Many families feel they are being labeled as defective because of the problems they have been experiencing, and this can lead them to have a defensive, clearly hostile, or depressed tone or style. The therapist can counteract the family's initial anxiety by emphasizing whatever resources (s)he observes in the family. Their caring or mutual concern, for example, is very often there in some form, if only in the fact that they have all come in together for the evaluation. This enables the therapist to indicate to the family that they are being seen together in part because they are, or can become, positive resources for each other.

Such positive formulations or reframings may actually provide a good deal of relief for family members. For example, in a family which presents accusatory complaints about hostile and destructive interactions, the therapist can sometimes emphasize the genuine presence of mutual concern. (S)he may comment on the well-intentioned statements which repeatedly get miscommunicated, as if somehow the "wires got crossed." Similarly, based on the earlier discussion of previous family crises and recent precipitants to the presenting problem, the therapist may be able to highlight the real stresses that the family has faced and compliment the family for having coped as well as they did. These positive reframings, of course, reflect the therapist's honest judgment about the family, and effectively serve to build the family's alliance with the therapist and enhance their compliance with the treatment recommendations.

PERFORMANCE CONSIDERATIONS

Like the beginning, the ending of the evaluation is a crucial time for the therapist to communicate clearly and effectively because the family is looking to the therapist to do something at these moments. At this sensitive point in the evaluation, a therapist's mistakes can readily jeopardize the family's cooperativeness or workability. The family—in need, at least mildly anxious, and decidedly alert—meets or confronts the therapist face to face to the greatest extent at the opening and the close of the evaluation. It is wise for the therapist to give careful thought to how he or she wishes to handle these brief, yet critical encounters.

As was the case at the opening of the session, the closing of the evaluation provides an ideal opportunity for building and strengthening alliances with the members of the family. But because the therapist is at this point going to provide a summary of the evaluation and make certain recommendations, the closing of the evaluation also offers an opportunity to enhance the family's hopefulness about their problem being resolved and their confidence in the therapist's ability to be of help to them.

The therapist needs to be skilled in utilizing him or herself to influence the attitudes and beliefs of the members of the family. In delivering a summary statement, the therapist should be aware of his or her vocabulary, tone of voice, and phrasing. Most basically, the family has literally to understand what the therapist is saying. The therapist develops an impression of the family's verbal skills and educational level, and makes moderate adjustments in his or her own vocabulary and phrasing as a result.

As a general rule the therapist should avoid highly technical, sophisticated language, and should refrain as well from "talking down" to patients. Words such as "modality," "dynamics," "interface," "parameters," "enmeshment," and "process" (as in "content versus process") rarely have a place in the evaluation sessions. The therapist should be able to use language that sounds intelligent and professional, but is generally understandable and in everyday use. "Closeness" is understood while "enmeshment" is not. "Process" is mystifying while the statement, "I'd like to get a better idea of what goes on between all of you when such an event occurs," conveys a clear message.

Some therapists make the mistake of speaking too casually or informally to patients. Slang expressions ("cop out," "vibes," "spaced out") are to be avoided at all times in family evaluation sessions. The therapist who says "pissed off" instead of "angry" or "annoyed" will not usually win the patient's or family's respect or admiration. Blurring the personal/professional boundary with such language reduces the clinician's therapeutic presence. While it may temporarily make one or two family members more comfortable, it runs the decided risk of alienating other family members. They may not share the particular language employed and expect the therapist to speak as a professional, not an acquaintance.

The therapist should speak in a clear and confident manner at the close of the evaluation. His or her tone should be sure and should have some life in it. Speaking in a monotone, speaking too softly, or with long pauses or frequent starts and stops, will reduce the family's comfort with and confidence in the therapist. There is a performance aspect to clinical work, especially seeing groups of people together, and the therapist is always being quietly reviewed by the family. Modulating and varying one's tone of voice, keeping up a good verbal pace, and speaking clearly and in an organized fashion help cement therapeutic alliances and increase the family's confidence in the therapist. These therapeutic skills can be practiced and learned, and are invaluable to the clinician.

In all stages of the family evaluation, the therapist needs to be continually monitoring the individual reactions of family members, and should be especially sensitive to nonverbal cues. This is certainly true during the closing phase, and as the therapist speaks, he or she should be gauging how each family member is responding to the summary statement. Is anyone frowning? Sighing? Is anyone looking confused? Disinterested? Frustrated? Like any speaker sensitive to the response of the audience, the therapist can and should make immediate slight adjustments in the summary statement as it is being delivered. If the last point was greeted by a chorus of quizzical looks, for example, the therapist should, without missing a beat, stay on that subject and attempt another brief explanation.

Adjustments can be made most easily during the delivery of the summary statement if the therapist is faced with a clear consensus of family reaction. If everyone in the family seems confused or bored or angry, the therapist will feel confident responding accordingly, even commenting openly on the group's reaction and exploring it. If only one person seems bored, or angry or upset, or if different family members show different troublesome reactions, the therapist's task is more complicated.

In such instances, the therapist would want to be sure that any modifications made in the summary for the benefit of one family member did not cause additional problems for another family member. For example, if one person seems confused and the therapist attempts a further explanation, this might end up confusing others; so, only quite brief ad lib reactions or explanations are in order when only one family member is having a particular problem with the therapist's summary.

At the end of the summary statement, the therapist should have noted the nonverbal reactions of various family members and should always ask if the family has any questions or reactions to what has been said. By responding in a clear, supportive way to any questions raised at this time, the therapist can correct misimpressions, relieve anxiety, and enlist the family members' cooperation. But there are instances when family members who appear bothered or troubled do not speak up in the group format, or a family member or members' reactions are still a concern to the therapist even after their questions have been answered.

When brief attempts to clarify impressions or reduce confusion are not sufficient, the therapist should once again think of the option that is of such value at various points in the evaluation—meeting with individuals or subgroups. In an individual meeting the therapist can come directly to an understanding of the family member's feelings and can take the time to respond in a supportive and relevant manner. Such individual meetings help strengthen therapeutic alliances and increase the chances that the therapist's recommendations will be accepted and followed.

As an example, consider the S. family of five members who were evaluated after the 17-year-old son experienced an acute psychotic episode. In this family, the father was the acknowledged dominant figure, and the mother was heavily involved with her children, almost as a peer. The formulation centered around the Identified Patient's sense of loyalty, both to his mother (he was her confidant) and to the rest of his family, and the conflictual situation in which this placed him. The therapist's summary statement did not include such formulative comments, but centered on providing the family with an understandable explanation of the Identified Patient's symptoms and preparing them for the recommendation of family therapy:

It's certainly clear that you are all concerned for each other and have all been very upset over Peter's [the Identified Patient] recent symptoms. Peter, you have been described by everyone as the "sensitive" one in the family, "the worrier," and you have all mentioned several recent family pressures that have caused worry; like Mrs. S.'s mother's recent surgery and problems in the family's grocery business. It makes sense then that Peter was worried about such things, along with dealing with the normal pressures of being in the last year of high school and facing graduation. And being worried about each other's welfare, while it's a good thing, a sign of caring, it can also take its toll on people, especially in combination with other pressures or factors.
Because you are all naturally involved in each other's lives and care about each other and react to each other's good and bad times, I feel it would be helpful to continue meeting for a time as a family to discuss these family-wide pressures and Peter's recent problems. Peter, I think individual meetings will also help you to maintain the progress you have been making. How does that sound to you all?

All through the therapist's statement the family group listened closely and appeared to understand. The only troublesome reaction was the steady frown on the father's face, and this was noted by the therapist while he spoke. He decided not to pursue that expression in the group format but instead added on individual meetings for each parent and for the sibling subgroup at the end of the session. One cannot just arrange an individual meeting with the family member in question, because this singling out would raise questions in all family member's minds as to what was happening and would run the risk of being greatly misinterpreted (e.g., "He's meeting with Dad because he won't level with the rest of us"). If an individual meeting is needed with one person, it helps to balance by having brief meetings with others so that such meetings seem to be a perfectly routine part of the evaluation and thereby eliminate suspicion and speculation.

In the individual meeting with the father in this family, the therapist led off by saying that the father appeared troubled during the last several minutes of the family session. The father then verbalized his concern: that family sessions were being recommended because the therapist felt the family had caused his son's problems. The therapist was aware of the father's strong leadership position in the family, and so in the father's mind, the therapist had implied that he, the father, had been responsible for his son's problems. The therapist could then comment directly on that concern and reassure the father that he was not being blamed or accused. A lengthier statement about the role which the patient's worries regarding family members played in his developing symptoms, and clear recognition of the parents' investment in helping any of their children served to reassure the father to a moderate extent.

It should be noted that the therapist does not have to win over all family members completely at all times. By avoiding major confrontations, suspicions, and resistances, the therapist facilitates the acceptance of the treatment plan and assures that the sessions continue. During the course of any subsequent sessions, the alliance issue remains central to the therapy, and the therapist continues to work actively to maintain at least a "good-enough" connection with each family member.

The formulation and resultant summary statement serve as preface for the therapist's specific treatment recommendations to the family. If therapeutic alliances have been successfully established and maintained, and if the summary statement has clearly prepared the family for the type of recommendation which will follow, then the therapist can expect a cooperative response from the family. The summary statement that said nothing about family pressures or tensions or about how family members can help each other, but instead emphasized only individual factors in the identified patient's problem, would leave the family ill prepared and probably resistant to a recommendation of family therapy. The summary should reduce the element of surprise in the therapist's treatment recommendation; it prepares the family for what is to come.

THE B. FAMILY: THE THERAPIST'S SUMMARY STATEMENT

In Chapter 5, "Opening Moves," the first minutes of a family evaluation session with the B. family was presented in transcript form. You may recall that this was the family of eight members in which the father had died suddenly the week before evaluation, where the Identified Patient was the 12-year-old son, Larry, who had gotten into a physical argument with his mother after the father's funeral. In the evaluative summary at the end of this session, the therapist wanted to point out the numerous changes the family had experienced in the past year or more, with the death of the father being the most recent and most traumatic. He then planned on reiterating the family's observation that Larry had become the lightning rod of the family's anger and upset, that because of his past behavior and history he became the logical safety valve for the family's level of stress. Briefly mentioning the Identified Patient's individual problems as well as their role in the family patterns was intended to pave the way for future recommendations of individual sessions for that person. Here now is the therapist's actual summary statement and recommendations made at the end of the family evaluation session with the B. family:

Well I'm particularly struck with the number of changes the family has been through in the past year or year and a half. A year and a half ago Maria leaves home. Last year you [Phil] entered college. Last April you're [Larry] diagnosed as having epilepsy. In June the family splits up, one group is left up here. You've changed schools this year; in addition to having difficulty adjusting to the epilepsy there have been school problems. There's also been a new group down there, the four of you, and then culminating in your father's death on Friday which came as a shock to you all.
That's an awful lot of changes for any individuals or any group to put up with without some very painful feelings, without some explosions or difficulty adjusting. It sounds like that's what's been happening. It's all connected. It's a cumulative effect as well as just a recent loss.
My sense of that also is that you're all concerned about each other. With all the fighting that you talked about, the family sounds like a very connected group. You are concerned about each other, you've been a real support to each other through all these things.
I think the whole group has been under an awful lot of stress. There has been a lot of tension, a lot of upset feelings, a lot of anger since last Friday, and then they just sort of erupted with Larry as the focus of it.
And Larry you've been having problems of your own over the past year, with the epilepsy and the move, so it's all sort of natural for you to be the focus.
But I think it would be quite useful for the whole group to continue at least through the next several weeks, through the crisis period, at least with as many of you as are available, with sessions such as these. I think you can be a real help to each other, and that such meetings would be important and useful to all of you, not just Larry.

With such a comment, the therapist was able to emphasize some of the family's strengths (mutual concern, trying to cope with change) and to sound a positive note in a period of doubt and pain for the family. The effect of numerous changes on the family as a whole was raised as an issue, and it could then be further developed in later sessions. Larry, the

Identified Patient, was given support by being seen as fulfilling a role in the family with his recent temper outbursts, but the therapist also did not minimize the extent of his individual conflicts and problems in the past year. The family had functioned well in the evaluation session, and so were likely to accept a recommendation to come in for several more family meetings.

It is important to recognize that selected key elements of the therapist's early formulative thinking were intentionally excluded from the summary statement. The therapist did not allude to the intensity and chronicity of the conflict between the mother and Larry, the Identified Patient, nor did he comment on the difficulty all the siblings appeared to have in separating from the family unit and establishing independent lives of their own. Such areas would likely be addressed in later therapy sessions, but the family would not be prepared to accept such interpretations at the end of the evaluation session. The therapist's summary statement included some mention of positive resources as well as some clear problem areas to focus on, and thereby increased the family's likelihood of cooperating with treatment and working towards the eventual discussion of more stressful or complex goals.

Individual sessions for Larry were not immediately recommended because at that point he would have refused them outright and once again been labeled "uncooperative". Individual meeting times could easily be arranged for Larry or any other family member during the early weeks of the family sessions, and a formal recommendation for regular individual sessions might be indicated and accepted by him at such a later date. The therapist spoke clearly with some modulation of tone in his voice, and his statement was organized and contained no long pauses or choppy sections. He made eye contact with each family member as he spoke, noting their reactions and keeping their attention. The family readily accepted the treatment recommendations, and left the session less anxious, clearer about the incident that had occurred, and with some confidence about the immediate future.

ASSESSING PROGNOSIS

One additional task for the therapist, which is directly related to deciding upon and making the summary and treatment recommendations, is the establishment of a prognosis for the family. Evaluating prognosis, which is essentially anticipating the outcome of treatment, is a surprisingly rare practice in family therapy. Its rarity may derive from the lack of specific, agreed-upon criteria for making prognostic judgments. Like so many of the areas assessed during the process of family evaluation, prognosis is determined to a good degree by the therapist's experience, judgment, and intuition. It is useful and important, however, to organize one's impressions around certain key characteristics of the family, characteristics that point to both good and poor prognoses.

During the family evaluation session, the therapist should monitor the family's level of mutual concern, level of hope, and level of trust. The presence of these attitudes point toward a good prognosis. In some families, relationships appear either malignantly conflicted, or "burned out" and devoid of life. In either instance, the family's willingness and ability to work on common problems or to be of help to each other is more likely to be limited as is the prognosis for improvement.

The therapist also looks at the level of trust within the family as well as the extent to which they seem able to trust the therapist. If the family keeps the therapist at arms' length, questions his or her motives and approach, and remains skeptical and hostile towards the therapist and the session, the prognosis is usually poor. While a good number of families may express these attitudes early in the evaluation, what is prognostically relevant is the persistence and calcification of their position regardless of a therapist's attempts to build therapeutic alliances. Such cases of "alliance failure" were described in Chapter 7.

The probe questions that assess family alliances and coalitions, patterns of closeness within the family, are useful to the therapist in gauging the family's level of mutual concern and trust. Do the family members express concern for each other, report that they go to others in the family for help or support with personal problems, or state that they experience a special closeness with another or others in the family? Probe questions such as "Who spends time with whom in the family?"; "Who are each of you most likely to talk to when something is on your mind?"; "Who sticks up for whom?"; "Who do you worry about most in the family?" help reveal such information.

The therapist's observations of the family's nonverbal behavior during the session is, as always, crucial to the evaluative process. Do family members listen to each other? Do certain members appear especially sensitive to and concerned about another member's statement? Do family members come to each other's defense at key points in the evaluation? The therapist is constantly looking for positive or potentially positive connections between family members. The lack of connection or interest, or the connection based primarily on angry or destructive feelings, usually suggests a more guarded prognosis.

Many families who are seen for evaluation have lost a good deal of hope for their future together. The existence of problems over a period of time and the failure of their own efforts or prior treatment attempts to improve the situation contribute to the diminishing of the family's hopefulness. In gathering impressions about this type of family attitude, the therapist looks less for positively expressed optimism than for signs or flickers of potential hopefulness. The probe questions which tap the family's ideas about possible desired changes in family life provide the therapist with an indication of the group's attitude towards the future.

Some families will think of things they would like to see changed, and are somewhat optimistic that they can find a way to accomplish such goals. Other families can think of desired changes, but express little hope that they can achieve these either on their own or with professional assistance. Still other families cannot even think of desired changes; they feel beyond such speculation. In their own eyes, the situation is past saving.

Clearly the last group of families offers the therapist little hope to work with, and the group preceding it, only a small amount more. Hope is a quality the therapist can do much to enhance, support, and keep alive. (S)he cannot create it by an act of will. If some mutual concern exists and if the family has some motivation to keep trying, then they are demonstrating at least minimal hopefulness for the therapist to respond to and develop.

The presence of positive prognostic indicators, such as concern, trust, and hope allows the therapist to ally successfully with the members of the family. The family's interest in each other and their willingness to hold out for the possibility of positive change, opens the door to the therapist and his or her task of building alliances during the evaluation and finally making treatment recommendations to the family. One general positive prognostic indicator, then, is the therapist's ability to create a working relationship with many, if not all, of the family members.

One frequently cited poor prognostic indicator is chronicity of disturbance. Most authorities would agree that chronicity reduces one's hopefulness about therapeutic change. If a marriage has been conflicted in the same way for thirty years, the basic style of marital interaction is considerably less likely to change. The therapist therefore looks carefully at the duration of the problem behaviors when obtaining information about the presenting problem.

Frequently, an acute, treatable disturbance occurs in the context of a chronically troubled family. The key, then, is to identify, understand, and treat the crisis situation and not immediately try to make adjustments in the basic and longstanding familial pattern. The therapist must be realistic in assessing where to begin working and what the initial treatment goal should be. It is a sound clinical principle to work initially towards the smallest possible goals that, if achieved, will effect a positive change in the family. The therapist can always go on to expand the work of therapy, but moving on from success to success, modest or not, is a more effective tactic than initially overestimating the family's capacity for change and then having to regroup and cut back the scope of the treatment goals. The latter route is filled with discouragement and disappointment, while the route of small successes creates an atmosphere of optimism and confidence.

This conservative and realistic approach to determining a prognosis and establishing treatment goals is built on the assumption that the therapist's impressions and assessments develop over time. The formal evaluation leads to specific initial recommendations and treatment, but as treatment continues, the therapist continues to adjust and deepen his or her understanding of the family and its capacity and desire for change. It is important to recognize that prognostic impressions can develop and change over time, and are not fixed or final statements about the family and its attitudes.

TREATMENT RECOMMENDATIONS

Turning from prognostic considerations to the area of specific treatment recommendations, we find that the most frequent recommendations made after family evaluation are for family therapy, marital therapy, individual therapy, or some combination thereof. What is particularly interesting from the perspective of maintaining the family's cooperation is the match between the family's request as they began the evaluation and the therapist's eventual treatment recommendation. One simple way of categorizing families is to divide them into two distinct groups: those who come into the evaluation seeking family therapy and those who do not.

In our experience, families who enter the evaluation requesting family therapy are in the minority. They are not rare, but it is far more common for a family simply to request help with a particular presenting problem. If a family has arranged the evaluation with family therapy in mind, and if that is the therapist's recommendation, then the summary/recommendation phase of the evaluation can proceed quickly and smoothly, and at times almost imperceptibly. There is often no need for a detailed summary establishing the principles of family influence, or a formal announcement of recommendations. The therapist can literally slide into the treatment and begin work on the key issues revealed by the evaluation.

But here, as always, it is advisable for the therapist to be attentive to alliance building with the family. A brief remark about the family's resources, strengths, and mutual concern sets the proper positive tone and enhances the family's confidence. Addressing the family as a group after the evaluation has been conducted is a perfect opportunity for the therapist to say something positive to them. The family is usually well aware of its deficiencies at such a point in its life and is often clear about tensions, resentments, and bad feelings that exist within the group. They have often lost touch, however, with their strengths, their caring, their mutual concern, and their hope for the future. The therapist can and should remind the family of such qualities and attitudes, basing his or her comments on specific impressions of the group and its life together. As always, the therapist's remark should be genuine and grounded in the evaluation of the family, but the family's positive qualities should not be overlooked by the therapist simply because they are not prominent or initially evident. Families need to be reminded of their strengths, and the therapist would be foolish, from both an alliance-building and hope-generating standpoint, to remain silent in this respect.

When the family has asked for family treatment and the therapist has recommended it, the therapist's only additional remark about the treatment often concerns its length. Families who have made clear their anxiety over getting caught up in an endless series of sessions are often relieved to be offered a recommendation for a specific number of sessions. Most other families do not require such a formal agreement, but are often helped by the therapist's general estimate of the duration of therapy.

One recommendation that can always be safely made at the end of the evaluation session is for the family to come in for a certain number of weeks, at which time they and the therapist will reevaluate where to go from there. Because of the reevaluation clause, the particular number of weeks specified is not crucial. Some manageable and nonintimidating number (four to eight) works best in our experience. Yet it should be noted once again that when there is a clear match between the family's and the therapist's expectations for treatment, the therapist can frequently just begin the treatment without commenting directly on the probable duration.

As an example, consider a family of four who were referred for family therapy after the psychiatric hospitalization of their 16-year-old daughter for anorexia nervosa. Both the Identified Patient, her parents, and her 14-year-old brother had been included in preliminary family therapy meetings during the hospitalization, and were well prepared for continuing with the family therapy approach. The new therapist met with the whole family for several initial sessions, conducting his own evaluation, and then just continued with the work of therapy. The therapist's summary statement in this case went as follows:

As you know, our primary purpose in seeing you is to help Margaret [the Identified Patient] continue to make progress with her symptoms. It has been found in cases like these that family tensions or pressures can contribute to the patient's symptoms and that family members can be very helpful to each other in dealing with the problems. I am impressed with your willingness to come in together and work on the problem, and you obviously care a good deal about each other. So I think it makes good sense to continue the work you all started in the hospital and for you all to come in as a family on a weekly basis.

In another case, parents, a 16-year-old boy (the Identified Patient), and his two sisters (ages 5 and 12) were referred for family evaluation and treatment after the Identified Patient had undergone a very unsuccessful six-month course of individual therapy for school behavior problems. The evaluation revealed some clear dysfunction in the relationship between the parents and the Identified Patient, some chronic marital tension, and a number of individual concerns and problems on the part of the Identified Patient. After several whole-family evaluation sessions, the therapist delivered his summary statement:

You all have clearly been under a lot of strain recently, and Mr. and Mrs. Q, things have clearly been very rocky between both of you and Tommy [the Identified Patient]. Tommy, you all said your individual treatment sessions really didn't accomplish much, and I think it's fair to say that both you and your folks need to be seen together in order to help with this problem. I hear how angry everybody has been, but in my experience what lies behind a good deal of anger is hurt, and I think you are all hurting at this point. I would like to try to be of help to you with the problem, because it seems to me that you all do care about each other, even if that doesn't come out too directly. It has been very helpful getting together with all of you for these first few sessions, and I would like to feel able to call on any of you again, but for the next several weeks I would like to see Mr. and Mrs. Q. and Tommy together to focus in on the recent problems.

If the family is expecting to receive family therapy and the therapist's recommendation is for an alternate mode of treatment, then the therapist must be sure to explain the change of plans properly and so reestablish the family's cooperation with the treatment plan. This occurs infrequently, because family therapy can take many forms and can coexist with other treatment approaches. But very occasionally the family is requesting family therapy and the therapist will feel that no family work of any type should occur at that time.

One such instance would be a father calling for family therapy because of his 22-year-old daughter's recent depression. He felt this had a great deal to do with her living at home, her relationships within the family, and while this may have been in part quite true, the Identified Patient was unable to speak freely in family group sessions (with her parents alone, or with the whole family including three younger siblings). While reaffirming the family's concern and caring, the therapist recommended a course of individual therapy for the Identified Patient and presented this as being indicated by the need for rapid, symptomatic improvement. It was hoped that the family, in particular the father, would be less upset about being excluded from the initial series of sessions by the therapist's mentioning that he would plan to get together with the whole group again in six to eight weeks.

Another example of redirecting a prospective family therapy case occurred when parents in their mid-30s arranged a family session because of their concern over chronic disagreements between their two daughters, ages 8 and 10. When evaluated as a group, the daughters did not appear particularly hostile towards each other, and instead both impressed the therapist as looking depressed. In the sessions, they silently sat and listened to their parent's bitter arguments about child rearing and many other matters. The therapist's recommendations here were delivered in a session with just the parents, because of the nature of the recommendation and the ages of the children. Once again, in this case, their concern for their children and family was cited and complimented, and they were reassured about their daughters' relationship with each other. The therapist then commented on the evident marital conflicts, and suggested a four-week trial of marital sessions to focus on that area in particular.

Other families are motivated by a more general desire to have the presenting problem treated successfully. Most frequently, these families call in order to get help for the Identified Patient, or the Identified Patient calls for him or herself, and the eventual request for the whole-family evaluation session comes from the therapist. These are the cases where the therapist needs to be especially sensitive to the family member's verbal and nonverbal reactions to his statements, since the notion of being seen as a family for sessions may be confusing and threatening to the group.

The therapist's summary statement in these cases follows the principles described earlier, and it is clear that some explanation of the treatment recommendation is indicated in every one of these cases, since the family had not requested family therapy. A family of parents and three daughters, ages 25, 22, and 18 were seen after mother called complaining of her youngest daughter's "rebellious" behavior at school and home. On evaluation, it appeared that the family had longstanding concerns about the 18-year-old's functioning, identifying her as mildly retarded, with a history of academic difficulties and immature behavior. Psychological testing records confirmed the diagnosis of mild mental retardation. There were clashes between the Identified Patient and parents over the degree of independence she was allowed, and the patient's sisters were able to comment on what they saw as both their sister's and their parents' difficulties adjusting to the Identified Patient's growing up. Additionally, the Identified Patient appeared mildly depressed and seemed in need of a supportive, individual therapeutic relationship to discuss her personal issues. The therapist's summary statement and recommendations were as follows:

You've all given me a lot of information to go on, and as you know I've also seen Donna's [the Identified Patient's] school records and such. Mr. and Mrs. W., you and Donna seem to have been in a struggle over the past year about rules and regulations at home, and this normal type of struggle seems to have occurred with your other daughters when they were about the same age. But with Donna, because she's the youngest, and because you see her as being a young 18, the struggle has been more difficult. Also, Donna, you've had a bunch of questions about where your life is headed, what to do after high school graduation, and you've been worried about all of this. Worries can make you depressed and irritable, and this can make the arguments at home seem a lot worse.

I'd like to make several recommendations to all of you. You obviously all care a great deal for each other. It comes through clearly in the sessions here. And no matter what hard feelings have cropped up at home, I think it's important to realize that they're based on your concern and worry about each other. Because you want to help each other, and I think you can help each other, I'd like to continue the whole family meetings for the next four weeks and then see where we are. I think you both [indicating the Identified Patient's sisters] can be very helpful in those discussions, because you and your parents have gone through similar issues before. Discussing the tensions at home with Donna as a family group will hopefully help you all make the kind of changes you'd like in those situations.

Also it seems to me that Donna, as the youngest, is in a special spot right now with its own pressures. Donna, I'd like to get together with you individually for several weeks to see if those kind of meetings are a help to you. Well, you've all listened quietly through my long speech, now it's your turn. Does anyone have any particular questions or reactions to what I've been saying?

Some cases begin with an individual's presenting problem, followed by the therapist's arranging a family evaluation, followed by a treatment recommendation which does not include family therapy. A 20-year-old man came in for an initial outpatient appointment complaining of symptoms of anxiety and depression, and described much conflict between him and his father at home. Others at home included the younger brother, 15, and the patient's mother. Two older brothers (25, 28) were married and lived outside the home. A whole-family evaluation session (including the two older brothers) was suggested and arranged by the therapist, with the therapist explaining his need to gather information from all those who were centrally involved with the patient and the home situation.

The family evaluation session revealed much chronic marital discord, and an implicit consensus among all the siblings and the patient's mother that the father in this family was an extremely anxious, intrusive, and stubborn individual. While they were cooperative with the evaluation process, neither the father nor other family members showed much capacity for therapeutic work, in that they had a very hard time listening to anyone else and did not readily establish working alliances with the therapist. In addition, the Identified Patient was extremely anxious and quiet during the family session, which only served to fuel the father's questioning and criticizing of him. For these reasons, the therapist's treatment recommendation was initially for individual therapy for the Identified Patient. The therapist stated:

It's been very helpful for me to meet with all of you to better understand the way Joe's [the Identified Patient's] been feeling recently. I think you've demonstrated a real willingness to be of help to Joe by your willingness to come in here, and it's clear that you care about each other's well-being. For now, I'd like to plan on continuing seeing Joe alone on a weekly basis. I'd like to feel free, though, to recontact any or all of you at some point in the future and invite you in to another session. Also, if any of you would like to return for another session at some point, please feel free to contact me.

Leaving All Your Options Open

The therapist's last comment in the above summary falls under the general heading of "leaving all your options open." It is certainly to the therapist's advantage to have access to everyone in the family at any time. The case that begins as an individual therapy may need to be expanded to include the family or certain subgroups in the family. When whole families are seen in an initial series of sessions, it is wise to inform them early on that the format of the sessions may change at various points and range from seeing the whole group, to subgroups, to individuals. The breaking down into smaller groups or individual sections that may have taken place as part of the basic family evaluation also helps prepare the family for future therapeutic recastings. Such open requests for future cooperation allow the therapist much freedom of movement during the weeks of treatment, and once again, constitute one of those early, small-scale therapeutic moves that help prevent future confrontations or resistances from developing.

SUMMARY

We have now examined the family evaluation process from the time of the first phone contact with the family to the time of the therapist's summary statement and treatment recommendations. These practical approaches have been grounded in our general understanding of families and family life, presented in the first section of this book. While the techniques and guidelines we have discussed will, we hope, allow for a smooth evaluation process, of course in the real world problems and pitfalls can occur. Anticipating the possibility of such trouble spots in the evaluation process can serve a preventive function and will certainly be of help if the therapist finds him or herself contending with such a problem during the evaluation. We turn now to several chapters devoted to potential obstacles which may be encountered in conducting family evaluations.

Part III
DEALING WITH OBSTACLES

9
Obstacles for the Therapist

We have attempted thus far to provide a structure for family evaluation sessions, with a format for organizing the session and a number of specific questions designed to assess various areas. But no matter how well prepared the therapist, (s)he is almost certain to be presented with challenging and difficult situations in the session itself. A variety of obstacles can complicate the therapist's efforts in the evaluation sessions or even prevent the evaluation from occurring in the first place.

Some obstacles are inherent in the very nature of the situation. An evaluation session with several family members automatically raises potential threats, in terms of managing multiple alliances, confidentiality and secrecy, support and confrontation. Other obstacles derive from the feelings and actions of the therapist. Still others may be generated by the particular family being evaluated. Regardless of their origins, all share the potential to work against the best interests of the family as well as the therapist.

Some obstacles are so idiosyncratic as to defy anticipation completely. Some families, in fact, can be relied upon effortlessly to produce many and more complicated dilemmas in one session than most therapists could process and react to in a week of leisurely planning. This, incidentally, is one rationale for a co-therapy team in some cases, since two therapists working together can usually accomplish more than twice what they might individually, in terms of recognizing and managing these pitfalls.

There are, however, some fairly common problems which occur in the context of family evaluation, as well as family therapy, which can be anticipated and, more often than not, either prevented or corrected. Chapters 9, 10 and 11 will describe and illustrate some of these most common obstacles, examine any special considerations or likely consequences for each, and whenever possible, suggest guidelines and techniques for their management. The discussion is based on the assumption that a person learning to sail, for example, cannot be expected to be prepared for a once-in-a-decade ocean storm, but that there is a good deal (s)he can learn about sudden wind changes, waves from the wake of fast-moving power boats, and what to do if a passenger falls overboard.

A critical point for the therapist to keep in mind when reading about each of these obstacles and when trying to manage them in the actual session is that "success" is always the approximation of success, never its final accomplishment. It is unlikely that an important family member will never be overlooked in arranging a session, that the family will never be confronted with too much force, or that a "dominating member" will never gain control of a session. The therapist can, however, expect to become more skillful at avoiding certain pitfalls and at being able to recoup quickly and gracefully after an initial misreading or miscalculation. To move from our nautical to an aeronautic metaphor, we might note that student pilots quickly learn that there is really no such thing as perfectly smooth flying, that flying is always a continuous series of small corrections. The analogy will, we hope, help therapists feel more at ease with the inevitable bumps and disruptions of their own family sessions.

In a sense, the most potent obstacles are those which can prevent therapists altogether from seeing families for evaluation. These factors often operate within the therapist and outside the family evaluation session itself. One of the most common of these factors is the therapist's "fear of children."

FEAR OF CHILDREN

To suggest that therapists are afraid of children may seem either laughable or immediately recognizable for many therapists who work individually with adult patients. It is not as easily recognized and discussed as are, for example, therapists' angry countertransference reactions with certain patients or their own difficulties with termination. But it is a theme which runs through consultations and conversations about family work with family therapists in training and with nonfamily therapists. The most common remarks of this type boil down to a sense of not knowing what to do with children. Therapists with some training and experience in child therapy may feel less at sea doing therapy with children alone but still feel unsure of how to handle them in whole-family meetings. Other therapists may feel at a loss with children in any situation.

Origins

Many individually oriented therapists are fairly comfortable seeing couples in marital therapy but draw the line when children are involved. On a theoretical level, this may reflect the inroads that have been made by interpersonally oriented theories in individual psychotherapy over the past twenty years and the much greater lag in acceptance of whole systems approaches. But on another level, recognizable in the casual comments made by many novice family as well as nonfamily therapists, is the sense of bewilderment and instantaneous incompetence engendered in many therapists at the thought of doing therapy with children.

At least one component of this reaction seems to stem from the importance of verbal skills in most forms of therapy. Many therapists become involved in and feel suited to clinical work partially in relation to their verbal strengths. And, until recently, most forms of psychotherapy have required a good deal of verbal ability on the part of the patient as well. This helps to explain the relative comfort of individually oriented therapists with couples, since both partners can presumably talk about their thoughts and feelings with each other as well as with the therapist. Children, however, are another story. They are not likely to be as facile as adults in articulating their inner experience and therapists are rightfully aware that often they cannot be approached in the same way one would approach an adult.

Reasons for Including Children

The reasons for including children in at least the evaluation sessions are both numerous and compelling. At the simplest level, the more members of the system present, the fuller the picture presented to the therapist. The participation of each family member provides at least four levels of information for the therapist: the person's stated experience as a participant in the system; his or her description as an observer of the system; the therapist's own impression of the person's character, role, and position in the family; and the interactions between the person and other family members. Any one of these areas would be difficult for someone interested in understanding the family (or a particular Identified Patient within it) to dispense with casually. Together, all four levels, which can be drawn from children when they are approached correctly, become invaluable.

Beyond the simple addition of information which comes from adding any member, children may provide especially useful material through a phenomenon which is suggested in the cliché, "out of the mouths of babes. . . ." They may demonstrate the "honesty of innocents" to the extent that they are less enculturated or less sophisticated in the arts of impression management (Goffman, 1959). The more embarrassing aspects of this phenomenon are recognizable in the popular culture's fondness for stories in which children innocently "blow the whistle" on their parents when company is present—"Mommy, when are you gonna get rid of Mr. Morgan like you said you would?" Similarly, in family sessions, children can be "truth tellers" in ways which reveal information that the family may have tried to conceal. When they do, the therapist should do everything possible to minimize the potential feelings of disloyalty this may engender in the child. For example, (s)he may make a comment about the child's efforts to help the family and then turn to the parents or older children (either in the whole-family session or later in separate meetings) for elaboration, instead of encouraging the child to compound his or her sense of having been "disloyal."

The honesty of children, however, need not always point out weaknesses in the family. It is just as likely to reveal hidden strengths of particular members or of the family as a whole. In one family, for example, father, who is admittedly alcoholic, might be portrayed by other family members as a good for nothing who contributes little and is looked to for nothing by other family members. One of the children might at some point remark that as soon as father comes home from work, he is bombarded with all the problems which arose that day. In so doing, the child provides the specific information which can at some point be used to contradict the attributions made about father and to support his positive contribution to the family.

The major reason for including children at least in family evaluation sessions follows from one of the ethical bases of family therapy, as opposed to the more pragmatic considerations discussed so far. This concerns the therapist's responsibility for all members of the family and relates to the preventive aspects of family work. Treatment which focuses on changes in a whole family, as opposed to an individual alone, automatically has a greater potential for preventive therapeutic impact on family members who have not yet developed problems or have not yet been identified as problem bearers. When an individual or marital therapist works towards improved functioning of a parent or improved cooperation within a marriage, (s)he is at least implicitly working for the health of the children. The family therapist does this more deliberately and with more active monitoring of the actual impact of his or her interventions on the children. This is part of the preventive dividend which, one hopes, accompanies the curative efforts of family treatment. In other words, the child needs an advocate. Children should be present—to tell their side, to describe or perhaps only display the impact of other problems on them, and to be evaluated in terms of their strengths, needs, level of functioning, and potential problems.

Finally, even when children contribute nothing verbally to a session (especially in the case of infants or toddlers who are in no position to make verbal contributions), their presence even for only a part of the session can shed a good deal of light on the family through observations of parental (and sibling) interaction, caretaking, and discipline of the child.

The therapist can simply observe what the family does in these areas or (s)he can create situations which highlight them. For example, if only one parent is attending to the child during the session, the therapist might ask that the child be shifted to the other parent for a while. If a parent is setting no limits on a very active child in the session, the therapist might ask that greater limits be set and observe the parents' efforts to do so. If an infant can be included at the outset of the session and later watched by a friend or relative in another room, the therapist may be able to glean additional information in a number of these areas without needing to have the child remain for the entire session.

Guidelines for Including Children

When children are included in the session, the following guidelines for their participation can be expected to decrease anxiety on the part of the parents, the therapist, and the child. Because children, depending on their age and intelligence, may not be as skillful as adults in responding to abstract and open-ended questions, it may help to be specific and to use more closed-ended (yes or no) questions with them. Asking how the child felt when daddy left may be much more stressful and difficult than asking what they did or were they sad, angry, etc.

Because of their simplicity and specificity, many of the probe questions discussed earlier are well suited to eliciting useful information from children. Generally, they respond eagerly and easily to questions about who gets up first in the morning and what they do in the evening; about their chores, their best and worst times at home; about who they would go to with a problem and who "sticks up" for whom. Children may be especially responsive to tasks they can fulfill during the session, such as using a table or a piece of paper to show the therapist the seating arrangement around the dinner table at home. These tasks let children get up and move around and feel good about a job they can do well.

If a child is being evaluated individually as part of the family assessment, again depending on age, there are similarly simple but rich probe questions which can clarify the child's needs, level of functioning, problems, and self-concept. The therapist can ask about hobbies and leisure activities, favorite television or comic book heroes, what the child will do when grown up (and what sorts of things those people do). Will (s)he marry? What will be the best and worst parts of marriage? Will (s)he have children? Boys, girls? How many of each? What would the child do if given three wishes? The therapist can inquire about school—best and worst parts; about friendships—how many, is there a best friend?; and about good and bad dreams. (Chapman, 1974; Simmons, 1974). This discussion is clearly not intended as a format for a thorough individual child assessment. Its purpose is to give the therapist some avenues for evaluating children, both with the family or separately, within the context of the whole-family evaluation.

Finally, the therapist can help all involved by knowing when and how to take the child "off the hook." When a child seems unable to answer a question, the therapist should not be afraid to change tracks instead of leaving the child to agonize as everyone else waits for a response. The child's silence may indicate that the question was too hard or unclear. The therapist might try to rephrase the question more simply or switch to another topic or family member. Alternatively, taking the blame on one's self for a fuzzy question may help the therapist reassure the child. (S)he can also encourage the child to bring up the topic again if he or she gets any new ideas.

A preventive, as opposed to reparative, approach by the therapist to the problem of getting the child off the hook involves a willingness to ignore the child when certain questions are asked. No iron rule of family therapy insists that every family member must be polled on every topic. Families usually react quite naturally when small children are omitted from a discussion of more adult topics among parents and adolescents or older children. With experience, therapists can become more knowledgeable about the kinds of questions which can be presented to children in general, and to specific children of different ages. Having children of one's own helps but is certainly not essential in accomplishing this.

All of this is simply to stress that children are as much or more in need of the therapist's attention as are other family members. They are potentially valuable contributors to and, for the most part, manageable participants in the family evaluation session.

FEAR OF GRANDPARENTS*

If many therapists are reluctant to include small children in evaluation sessions, they are often even more reluctant to include the parent(s) of the adult patient, that is, the grandparents of the nuclear family. Recently, a colleague described a case to us in which a woman in her late 20s whom the therapist had seen for a few months in individual treatment, repeatedly complained about her relationship with her mother. She had in fact made a medically serious suicide attempt recently in response to problems with her mother but was quite negative to the suggestion of having her mother come in for any sessions. What was most noteworthy was that the therapist was quite unsure of how hard to push on this, although she would have had no doubts if the complaint had been about a spouse instead of a parent. It is precisely this difference in how many therapists would react to these two situations—adult patient and parent versus adult patient and spouse—which highlights the generally unrecognized values and biases to be discussed here.

Origins

The therapist's recognition of the importance of including a spouse who is heavily involved in the problems of an Identified Patient reflects, as stated earlier, the inroads which have been made by interpersonally oriented theories in individual psychotherapy. The greater rarity of such an approach with an adult's parents again reflects in part the lag in integration of whole systems approaches. But more would appear to be involved here. This marked reluctance to include the parents of the adult patient seems to reflect a myth of generational discontinuity, of separation or independence, which may be held by the patient and shared by the therapist, and which is certainly prevalent in the culture at large.

The patient may have many reasons for wanting to exclude a parent

---

* For the sake of brevity, the parent of the adult patient may be referred to in the following discussion as the "grandparent."

from treatment, even if only from a whole-family evaluation. (S)he may have concealed and may be ashamed to reveal actually being in treatment to the parent. (S)he may want to preempt the attention and sympathy the parent might receive from the therapist or to prevent the therapist from seeing the parent's side of the problem. The patient may want to cling to an impasse with the parent, to prevent any changes in the status quo, to avoid having to confront or forgive the parent. (S)he may deny that any significant relationship exists with the parent at all and resent the suggestion, which inclusion of the parent carries, that this is not so. In sum, a patient's resistance in this area should be neither mysterious nor surprising.

The reasons for the therapist's reluctance or ambivalence are somewhat harder to spell out, but are nonetheless real. These reasons may involve a relationship with his or her own parents which may be similarly denied or painfully stalemated. They may simply reflect a lack of conviction that such relationships are of significance in an individual patient's problems, or that the participation of a parent in evaluation can provide considerable leverage towards increased clarity, and hopefully, progress in treatment.

It is certainly not hard to understand such a lack of conviction, given the power of the myth of generational discontinuity in our culture. In the emphasis on nuclear as opposed to extended families and the increasing trend of care for the elderly in institutions away from the home, the society demonstrates its insistence that adult children are unconnected to their own parents. The very recency of family (as opposed to individual) therapy and its development largely in terms of marital and nuclear family treatment testifies to the power of these biases in the mental health field itself. It is often a convergence of such forces within the patient, the therapist, the ideologies of the mental health field, and the culture at large which prevents the inclusion of an adult patient's parents, even when this is indicated clinically, in the process of family evaluation.

Reasons for Including Grandparents

The reasons for including grandparents in the evaluation session largely parallel those for including children. The addition of any family member provides more information to the therapist on a variety of levels and so contributes to a more complete picture of the family (and the Identified Patient, if there is one). And the therapist's responsibility to side with all members of the family suggests the utility of meetings with and advocating for grandparents as well as children.

One important added consideration involves the potential ability of the parent to influence the patient—either to oppose and sabotage or to support and encourage treatment. This possible influence highlights the importance of, at worst, "knowing the opposition" and, at best, securing a potentially powerful therapeutic ally. It is probably a good idea at least to consider including parents of the adult Identified Patient in the evaluation process, if available, unless otherwise indicated. This will partially balance the counterforces described above. Beyond this basic consideration, there is a range of situations in which the inclusion of grandparents is variably indicated. In general, the priority of including grandparents increases with: (1) increased frequency of regular contact between grandparents and nuclear family, (2) increased references by the patient to the grandparents' participation in his or her personal and family life, (3) increased complaints by the patient about the grandparent or praise for his or her availability and helpfulness, (4) increased accessibility in terms of proximity, and (5) increased need for a therapeutic ally (patient unreliable; children uncared for or in danger; suicide risk; couples' inability to control violent explosions).

Guidelines for Including Grandparents

The therapist can request the grandparents' participation on general grounds of wanting a full and more complete picture of the family and/or presenting problem. Because the grandparent is likely to be concerned about the problem and to want to help, (s)he can be valuable as an historian and an observer. It is neither necessary nor helpful to insist before a grandparent has even been seen that (s)he come in because (s)he is part of the problem (unless this has been dramatically demonstrated and is clearly already assumed by all family members, especially the grandparent). Once a therapist has met with the grandparent, an approach can be developed to help encourage the grandparent to share more responsibility for a problem in which (s)he is involved. But the unsophisticated message that the grandparent come in because (s)he is somehow at fault for the problem, whether communicated explicitly or implied indirectly, is likely to help neither the Identified Patient, the grandparent, nor the therapist.

A major consideration in the inclusion of grandparents for sessions should be, as in all clinical work, to avoid or at least to minimize blame. One variation of a "blaming" message is that the grandparent him or herself "has problems" and "needs treatment." Often, because of general attitudes about the mental health field, even when the therapist makes no such implication, the grandparent may nevertheless assume this is the message. If this seems to be the case, the therapist should strive to correct it. The grandparent is being asked in as a helper, not as a patient. This is an important point especially when there is a conflictual relationship between the adult Identified Patient and his or her parent. In such an instance, if the Identified Patient is delegated to include the parent, (s)he may sabotage the process with just such a message. "The doctor says he wants to see you. He must think you've got a problem." If this seems a likely danger, the therapist should contact the grandparent him or herself and take care to avoid this implication. Once in the session itself, the therapist will be much freer to ally with the grandparent without alienating the Identified Patient.

Once the decision has been made to include the grandparents in the evaluation, the question arises as to how to include them. Should they be seen together with the family as a whole? Alone? Alone with the Identified Patient? Decisions in this area should reflect: the family's own self-definition (as best the therapist can surmise), the nature of the presenting problem, and the therapist's own sense of healthy family boundaries. The following situations describe some fairly clear-cut cases in order to provide at least the extremes of the continuum.

When a grandparent lives in the home (or nearby) and appears, from initial contacts, to be very closely involved with the single Identified Patient, (s)he can be included in a conjoint evaluation meeting as would any other family member. When the Identified Patient is married, if the grandparent lives in the home and gets along well with both spouses, the same holds true. For example:

A 24-year-old single woman, living with her 60-year-old widowed mother and working as an office clerk, was seen in a hospital emergency room following a first acute psychotic episode. She had one married brother and a single sister, both in their 30s, living out of the home. Initial evaluation in the emergency room suggested that the patient, the youngest child, was quite infantilized, living a somewhat marginal existence and relying heavily on her mother, brother, and sister-in-law. When the case was referred for outpatient treatment, arrangements were made to start off with a full-family evaluation including the patient, mother, sister, brother, and his wife. Following this, the patient and her mother were both seen individually and her brother and his wife, identified as strongly therapeutic allies in the full group evaluation, were seen together.

In another case:

A 34-year-old divorced mother of four children was admitted to a psychiatric inpatient unit with complaints of severe depression and suicidal ideation. The patient's children ranged in age from 7 to 16 years old. Their father and the patient had divorced seven years previously and the patient's mother lived in the home and clearly functioned as a substitute parent for the children. In view of the patient's long-term symptomatology, grandmother in fact impressed staff as the more competent and reliable parent-figure. When a family evaluation was requested by unit staff, the group was seen as a whole, with the visibly enmeshed grandmother and mother being seen together and individually without the children afterwards.

When the grandparent is regularly involved with his or her child's family but a more distinct boundary seems to be drawn by the family members, when his or her role is more that of a helpful, concerned member of the extended family and less that of a quasiparental replacement, the therapist may choose to follow the family's lead and see the nuclear family as a whole and the grandparent separately. For example:

A 15-year-old boy was admitted to the pediatrics unit of a hospital following an acute psychotic episode with a history of increasing withdrawal, minor offenses, and poor school performance over the preceding year. The parents had been divorced for some years. The boy lived with his mother, younger brother, and sister and had regular contact with his father. The mother's parents lived in an apartment upstairs. The sequence of initial evaluation meetings was: Identified Patient alone; present nuclear family (mother and all three children); grandparents together; father and his second wife.

When the grandparent has only episodic contact with the family, has a poor relationship with the daughter- or son-in-law and the presenting problem involves a good deal of marital conflict, it is probably best to see the grandparent separately from the family as a whole. For example:

A 42-year-old, twice-married mother of three children, ages 5, 12, and 17, was seen in a hospital emergency room following an acute psychotic episode. The patient and her husband had a long history of marital problems and, in particular, fought over the patient's 17-year-old daughter by her previous marriage. This daughter spent a good deal of time out of the home with her maternal grandmother who was on very bad terms with the son-in-law. The sequence of meetings for the family evaluation was: nuclear family (Identified Patient, husband, and all three children); Identified Patient individually; husband individually; and, on a later occasion, maternal grandmother individually.

Finally, when the primary problem is described as between the adult patient and his or her parent, the therapist will want to meet with them together as well as separately and with a larger family grouping to provide some context. For example:

A 30-year-old divorced mother of two children, ages 3 and 7, was seen for evaluation in an outpatient clinic. Her primary complaint concerned problems in her relationship with her mother. She had lived next to her mother for two years after returning from another part of the country and complained of a chronically conflicted relationship. Most recently, the patient had become friends with a woman who was also a friend of her mother's. A good deal of mutual jealousy, hostility and verbal conflict ensued. The patient, who called requesting treatment, was seen individually first. Following this, the patient's mother was seen individually;

they were seen together; and one meeting was held including the Identified Patient, her mother, mother's second husband, and the patient's 16-year-old sister living with mother.

While clearly far from exhaustive, the cases discussed above suggest some of the options and rationales the therapist can consider and perhaps employ in specific cases. Having discussed the therapist's fear of children and grandparents, we can now move to a discussion of one other factor which seems to prevent many therapists from evaluating families. We refer to this last factor as "the cult of compulsory flamboyance."

COMPULSORY FLAMBOYANCE

It is quite common for therapists to approach family work with a sense that they will have to be highly active, dramatic, provocative, even a bit outrageous in the sessions. They may imagine themselves suddenly ordering the family to change seats or sidling up to a parent for an intimate chat at one moment while taking a child on their laps at another. In general, they respond to an unspoken assumption that they will have to act in an unpredictable, surprising, dramatic, almost shocking way. Usually the therapist's immediate reaction is a sense of inadequacy: "I could never do that. I'm not loose enough. I'm not that . . . charismatic." This sense that family work requires charisma, this "cult of compulsory flamboyance"—stronger in certain orientations and training centers than others, but on the whole quite widespread—is one of the more intriguing and unfortunate developments in the family field. The following factors seem to be at least partially involved in the evolution of this view.

Origins

Working with whole families does necessarily involve more sources of input and more sheer stimulation, requiring more structure and organization on the part of the therapist. This may select for individuals who are likely to be more active, controlling, perhaps even overpowering during sessions. This may in turn contribute to the fact that the field of family therapy as a whole has been dominated by a number of highly charismatic and provocative figures. These individuals are often seen as flip, confrontative, crusty, and rarely timid about their opinions. The high visibility as well as the relatively large proportion of such figures in the field contributes to a psychological (and often institutional) set which makes trainees feel illegitimate if they do not possess these traits and operate clinically in this style.

Additional factors may include the accidental but extremely influential convergence of family therapy with videotape as a clinical and training aid, and the emphasis in family work on case observation and live supervision. Family therapy and the development of videotape capability emerged at roughly the same time, and certainly many other schools of therapy have made extensive use of video. But it seems fair to say that no other form of therapy has so totally used the medium and been so deeply influenced by it as has family work. Certainly, credit should be given for the efforts made by those using videotape to demystify their treatment, to open their work for observation, to share skills and teach techniques on a wide scale. However, the emphasis on live observation and videotape sessions may inadvertently lend itself to a certain "spectacular" (in the sense of the spectacle), or theatrical, mentality.

Finally, perhaps in part because of the relative ease of reproduction and dissemination of videotapes, the charismatic figures described above have emerged as a pantheon of "Masters" in an almost religious sense. This in itself is not unusual in many schools of therapy, but it seems likely that many more therapists, even nonfamily therapists, have seen Minuchin, Whitaker, or Satir at work than have seen Howard Searles, John Rosen, or Albert Ellis.

Nor is emulation in the form of imitation of a "Master" unique to this field of therapy. Certainly, psychoanalysts have attempted to reproduce aspects of Freud's method of work as well as his personality for decades. And this is the crux of the issue—where to separate personality from technique. Our feeling is that in psychoanalytic treatment as well as family work a certain baseline in terms of technique is dictated by the nature of the clinical work involved. Beyond this, however, much that is attributed to the inherent demands of the work in fact reflects the institutionalization of fairly arbitrary personality factors. Every analyst must, to some extent, retain enough ambiguity to facilitate a "transference cure." But some of the most skillful and effective analysts allow their own feelings and personalities (and, it should be noted, very different feelings and personalities) to enter into and facilitate the treatment.

Therapeutic Use of Self

We can look at this particular obstacle in two ways. From one angle, it is the feeling of illegitimacy as a family therapist if one is not a mini-version of a particular Master—the sense that you can't be a family therapist and still be yourself. But from another angle, it represents a therapist's own retreat from the problem of therapeutic use of self, which is a major task of clinical work. This task involves discovering and developing who the therapist is and how (s)he can use him or herself as part of the clinical process. From this angle the more self-conscious forms of imitating a Master represent a retreat from a basic struggle for clinical and personal growth.

The complexity of family work, stemming from the presence of many persons and consequent increase of information, observations, and inter-actions, requires a baseline of active structuring and organization on the therapist's part. But to assert beyond this that therapists need to be pro-vocative, brusque, or theatrical in order to be effective is simply mistaken. Some may claim that the therapist must be overpowering in order to break through the family's often rigid and formidable defenses. What is true is that for purposes of family evaluation, the therapist needs: (1) to prove him or herself trustworthy to the family, (2) to exert enough control over the session to be able to assess the necessary areas, and (3) to have some influence or impact on the family when discussing recommendations for treatment. There are in fact as many ways to accomplish these goals as there are therapists in practice. For example, imagine four therapists confronted with the exact same situation in the course of a family eval-uation session.

A 9-year-old boy has been describing a painful incident in the home when he begins to cry. One therapist might focus on the boy in a sym-pathetic way and reflect the feelings of hurt and frustration. Another might joke with the boy (and with the family indirectly) in a gruff but affectionate and sensitive way, in an effort to lighten the mood, but with-out losing the content of the boy's statement. A third might react to an older sister's look of concern and might nod, giving her permission to help the boy, and thereby giving him permission to cry and the family per-mission to mobilize its own resources. A fourth therapist might respond to a sense that what the boy wants most is to be "out of the spotlight" and so may make an appropriate but discreet transitional comment in order to ask another family member about the boy's comment. Each of these very different responses is likely to achieve very similar results. They take different routes to accomplish the basic goals of the evaluation session. Together, they suggest that the therapist will be most successful when most him or herself.

10
Problems
with Family
Members

If we assume that the therapist has mastered his or her own fears of bringing in certain family members and worked through unhelpful stereotypes of what a family therapist should be, we can also assume that (s)he is now prepared to start dealing with obstacles generated by the family and the evaluation itself. In describing these problems, we will move from the general to the specific. The first to be discussed—regulating stress on the family—is inherent to all evaluation sessions. Those which follow represent more specific problems which may be generated by some families but not others.

REGULATING STESS ON THE FAMILY

The family comes in with a problem or with several problems. Associated with the problem(s) may be: feelings of guilt, shame, resentment, blame; secrets, old wounds or losses; members' unconscious fears of their own or another's implication in the problem. There may be significant past events which involve unfairness unforgiven, sacrifices unrecognized, and misdeeds regretted but unrepaired. There are activities, alliances, rights, and responsibilities which are jealously guarded, and familiar ways of doing things which, even if not always the best, are the family's own creation, providing them with some sense of shared identity. When the therapist touches on any of these sensitive areas (s)he will elicit a response which in some way warns, "Hands off."

The Family's Fears

These are moments in which the family (or particular family members) are feeling threatened. For most families, the very act of participating in the evaluation is inherently threatening, to varying degrees. This operates on a variety of levels. At the conscious, individual level, family members may be reluctant or unwilling to discuss certain subjects, to entertain certain notions, or to hear certain statements. At the interactional level, the family may resist attempts to alter certain fixed interactional patterns (e.g., one parent talking for everyone in the family). At an unconscious, group-fantasy level, the therapist may appear as an "intruder" and may trigger a primitive sense of threat to self and system, that is, to the family members' sense of the integrity of their relational world. R. D. Laing (1969) makes a useful distinction between the family—that is, the group of actual persons who make up the family—and the "family"—that is, the picture of the family as a whole which exists internally in its members as something which is "inside" them yet which they are "inside." It is the "family" which members are discussing when they say, "It seemed like the family was falling apart," or, "Our family was like a team, but then it exploded." The threat posed by the family evaluation sessions may be experienced and expressed at any or all of these levels.

Balancing Confrontation and Reassurance

In managing the opening of the session as described in Chapter 5, the therapist is working to defuse this initial sense of threat by fostering a relaxed and accepting atmosphere. But if (s)he is to do his or her job, the therapist cannot afford to maintain this tone without variation throughout the evaluation. It is highly unlikely that the therapist can gather the impressions and information needed without stressing the family to some extent. The question is, to what extent? What is the point of stress or discomfort at which the therapist has access to the material which matters in a particular family but which they can still tolerate without significant resistance?

It is this point of tolerable discomfort for which the therapist is aiming. At some point during the evaluation session(s), some if not all family members should feel, in the words which are often used, "a little on the spot." If no one in the family experiences this at some point during the evaluation, the chances are good that the therapist will have learned little of value at its close. If, on the other hand, the level of discomfort or stress is too high, the family's resistance will intensify and the evaluation may be either interrupted or aborted.

Warning Signs

There are a variety of ways in which the family may signal its discomfort or displeasure with developments in the session. Members may simply become evasive and vague. They may launch into long chatty monologues meant to convey that things are "all right." The therapist may observe nonverbal messages from one member which seem to silence another. Or, less subtly, family members may become openly hostile towards the therapist. What all of these reactions share is their common effect of making the therapist feel more hesitant, more cautious, perhaps more timid in his or her explorations.

An important point to remember is that typically the less overt—that is, the more subtle and subliminal—the signals given by the family, the more powerful the reaction in the therapist. These responses make their impact on the therapist more indirectly. They "creep up" on the therapist and are often more difficult to recognize since the family is at least ostensibly being cooperative. They are more easily misinterpreted and are therefore more difficult to respond to.

On the other hand, if the therapist feels that the discussion is vague and, for the most part, superficial throughout the session; if, as the session goes on, (s)he feels that almost nothing of significance has been learned about the presenting problem and the family as a whole; if, above all, the therapist has at no point during the session had the sense of "treading on shaky ground," of taking a risk, then most likely (s)he has stayed too much in "safe waters." The obvious consequences are that little sensitive information will have been obtained in the evaluation and that the family's ability to tolerate stress or confrontation in treatment will not have been assessed. An additional consequence may be the family's lack of engagement in treatment. This may occur if they feel that the session has been a waste of time, or sense that the therapist has nothing to offer or is clearly no match for them. In such an instance, the real tragedy is that in an effort to ally with the family by not causing anyone to become upset, the therapist actually loses the case.

Overloading the Family

There are lots of ways of being too confrontative, depending on the particular family being evaluated. For some families or individuals, this may involve bringing up certain topics which are completely taboo in the family or bringing up slightly less stressful issues with certain family members present. It may involve an interpretation on the therapist's part that requires the family to look at something about themselves, such as highlighting a scapegoating process by parents towards the Identified Patient. It may involve making or breaking boundaries in the family structure by prescribing or proscribing certain interactional sequences. For example, the therapist might forbid a highly dependent, fused child to sit on his mother's lap. Or, (s)he might ask the child to sit on his father's lap instead when upset.

Finally, although it occurs less frequently, the therapist may get the sense that unless prevented, the family may break its own rules. In these cases, an interaction, commonly called a "runaway," can escalate to the point where previously unspoken but shared rules are violated. A good example of the difference between repetitious and homeostatically secure conflicts and those which move the family too precipitously towards dangerous new ground can be seen in the difference between the chronic, routinely cruel games played by Martha and George in Edward Albee's *Who's Afraid of Virginia Woolf?* (1963), and the final scene in which Martha breaks all previous rules by "killing" their "child." Family therapists sometimes choose deliberately to provoke a runaway if they feel this may help to introduce change into a stagnant, repetitious pattern. But in an evaluation (as opposed to a therapy) session, the therapist needs to be aware that unless (s)he controls such an escalation, (s)he and the evaluation may be blamed for its consequences.

Guidelines for Regulating Stress

Regardless of its sources, the obvious consequence of overloading the family is that the therapist may win the battle but lose the war. Important information may be obtained but the family may be alienated from treatment. The following guidelines and techniques are aimed at helping the therapist to avoid both overloading and overprotecting the family. The overriding principle is to move slowly and in gradual steps over the course of the evaluation session(s). The recommendation given earlier to open the session with relatively harmless identifying data before discussion of the presenting problem is in part designed with this principle in mind. The organization of general probe questions, starting with the most innocuous and proceeding to the potentially more provocative, is another example of a gradual, careful approach.

The therapist should exercise care not to short-circuit his or her own sense of pace in approaching stressful material; (s)he should resist the "bait" that is sometimes offered by family members to do likewise. If, for example, in the middle of general introductions, one family member hints at a potential bombshell, the therapist may want to suggest holding off discussion of this for a while and then returning to it later when (s)he knows better what to expect of the family and when they too are presumably better prepared for it. Ideally, the therapist sets a pace in response to his or her overall sense of the family and discourages both "stalling," when the session can be moved to another level of risk, as well as "runaways," which can plunge the family into an overwhelming sense of threat.

The therapist's careful use of language which is nonloaded, discreet, even euphemistic, making particular use of any such language introduced by the family itself, may make otherwise highly threatening discussions much more tolerable. Again, some of the probe questions discussed earlier are designed with this consideration in mind, such as asking about "gripes" instead of conflicts, asking who "spends time with" whom and who "sticks up for" whom instead of who is close to whom, or who likes/dislikes whom.

Beyond these standard probes, the therapist should always look for the expression or phrase which is likely to be most acceptable to the family. For example, if the topic of the parents' sexual relationship comes up in the family meeting and the therapist feels it is worth pursuing this only insofar as it affects boundaries within the family, the therapist might ask what the parents do when they want "privacy."

In one family consisting of a 48-year-old mother, and a son and daughter both in their 20s, all members described, with a mixture of openness, embarrassment, and laughter, their regular, simultaneous use of the bathroom. The therapist noted to himself the relative unusualness of the practice as well as its implications for boundaries within the family, but took care to reflect the family's own attitude by referring, with a bit of humor, as though joining the fun, to their "efficient use of the bathroom."

In another case:

A 13-year-old boy was being interviewed individually with observation through a one-way mirror of which he was aware. On the topic of dreams, he made clear allusions to several erotic dreams with some pride in his new interest in sex but discomfort with what seemed to be the aspect of nocturnal emissions. The therapist let him make his statement but tried to take him off the hook, with language he would be most likely to use himself, by completing a sentence he'd left hanging with a reference to the "sexy stuff." The boy's reaction indicated satisfaction at having been understood and relief at not having to talk about it anymore at that point.

In this way, the therapist strengthened his alliance with the boy and encouraged him to take similar risks in the future by demonstrating the relative safety of doing so.

The examples above suggest two more factors in helping family members to discuss difficult areas or to accept stressful interventions with tolerable discomfort. The first is the therapist's general tone and style which, when possible and appropriate, should convey relaxation, reassurance, and naturalness. Serious crises and highly emotional interactions may require a different stance, but the therapist should try as much as possible not to convey nonverbally a sense of "uh oh"—of dark secrets, hidden pathology, or terrible truths.

The second factor involves the use of humor. Probably a whole chapter could and should be devoted to the uses of humor in family work or in all kinds of clinical work. Our intention here is merely to highlight humor as a tool which, when it is a natural part of the therapist's repertoire, should be carefully cultivated. Warm humor, friendly humor, as opposed to hostile, critical humor, often works as a sort of grease which can make otherwise bumpy, or threatening interactions go much more smoothly. Humor conveys warmth and informality, strengthens alliances, and can help set the relaxed tone described above. As in other settings, when humor is successfully employed, it "disarms" people. It makes them less defensive and more able to tolerate potential threats.

Lastly, the therapist can make some uncomfortable discussions more comfortable simply by pursuing them in individual or subsystem as opposed to whole-family meetings. This can relieve at least those discomforts which stem from uneasiness about discussing certain things in the presence of many family members or of particular family members. A teenager may feel more comfortable discussing needs for autonomy and independence with the therapist alone, rather than with the parents present. Parents may find it much easier to describe their hostile responses to an adolescent Identified Patient's provocations without the adolescent present.

Proceeding from more general to more specific problems in family evaluations, we move now to a consideration of destructive interactions in the evaluation sessions.

DESTRUCTIVE INTERACTIONS

Before discussing the problem of destructive interactions between family members in the evaluation session, a brief word is in order on the topic of too much interaction of any kind.

How Much Interaction?

Perhaps because interaction is such an important component of relational systems (it is certainly the most visible component when one considers the shift from individual to family therapy), it has at times been considered virtually the essence of family therapy. It is probably safe to say that most novice family therapists, when they look forward to their future careers, imagine themselves directing one family member to discuss a certain topic with another member. In other words, they see themselves fostering interaction. Our experiences, both in our own training and in the supervision of other trainees, suggests that this is, in fact, what beginning therapists most often do, especially in the absence of any other clear direction.

But while interaction between family members is an essential component of all family treatment, it is one component among many. Especially in the context of an evaluation, its role and function can change considerably. There is a natural tendency for family members to interact, despite the uniqueness of the situation, in fairly stereotypical ways during the evaluation. The patterns, alliances, and dynamics these interactions suggest are, as we've indicated previously, one of several valuable sources of information available to the clinician.

The danger in this, however, involves the therapist's allowing too much time for such interaction and subsequently finding him or herself with only a limited amount of time left for the rest of the evaluation. (S)he may then have very little idea who these people really are and why they've come for the evaluation. (S)he may not have had enough time to inquire about the history and particulars of the presenting problem, about previous family crises and current stage of development, about recent stresses and attempted solutions within the family. In other words, (s)he may have failed to assess the relational and historical context which would make the presenting problem and the interactional sequences displayed comprehensible.

Often, the kinds of interactional patterns one sees in an evaluation session are fairly stereotyped and repetitive in each particular family—that is, the process of the family tends to run along already well-worn channels. For example, they might involve: a pattern of chronic bickering between two members; an aggressive but futile "interrogation" by one "pursuing" member of another "distancing" member; a "ganging up" by two members against another; an expression of cheerful consensus by all members on any topic. The point is that such patterns can usually be discerned fairly quickly and that, beyond the point at which the therapist feels (s)he can see the pattern, allowing it to continue can be both time-consuming and counterproductive.

Aside from his or her own needs to assess multiple areas for a clear and complete picture of the family, the therapist wants to offer the family something more than a chance to replay in the interview room the same old patterns which have continued with little resolution or success outside the session. (S)he also wants to be sure the family knows that (s)he has more than this to offer.

To summarize, observing or fostering interactions between family members is one component of family therapy and evaluation. Useful both as a source of information and as a technique for change, it is nonetheless only one among many. By itself, it is not family therapy and is certainly not a substitute for a thorough evaluation. It can be used by the therapist in a deliberate fashion in order to learn about the family in general and to assess specific areas and resources, but it should be used in balance with other components of the evaluation process. Therapists who conduct family evaluation sessions need to be assertive enough to interrupt prolonged, repetitive interactions and to budget time in order to insure as thorough an assessment as possible on a variety of levels. This point being made, we can move to a discussion of the more specific problem of destructive interactions in the evaluation.

Consequences of Destructive Interactions

Destructive interactions are those which elicit feelings of shame, guilt, blame, and pain in one or more participants with no discernible benefit. They typically diminish individual and relational resources, such as trust, hope, self-respect, willingness to be vulnerable and to engage in dialogue and willingness to look at one's own role in problems. They may take the form of angry accusations or sarcastically sweet provocations. Or they may simply involve the withholding of something by one member—approval, acknowledgment, affection—that another member is begging for. Destructive interactions may shame one member before other members and the therapist; they may involve using the therapist's words against the other. They may be subtly guilt inducing or simply belligerent. They are most often blaming or accusatory.

If it were possible to isolate such an interaction from its context, it would not necessarily be said that it was inherently destructive. Taken in the context of a family therapy session in the middle of treatment, for example, what began as this type of interaction might lead to a significant and very therapeutic breakthrough. Such an interaction might be a necessary turning point in the whole course of treatment. But, like any form of interaction, it takes on a very different meaning in the context of the evaluation session.

When such an interaction "succeeds"—that is, when it contributes to therapeutic goals—in the course of family therapy, it does so because certain preconditions are present. These include a measure of trust and rapport between therapist and family, some degree of commitment on the part of family members to solving the problem, and some degree of hope that this can be accomplished. *None of these can be taken for granted at the point of evaluation.* This means that their probable absence makes such interactions extremely risky and that such interactions may in fact preclude the development of trust, commitment, and hope.

When these interactions take place and go unrepaired in an evaluation meeting, family members are more likely to feel attacked, unprotected, and unsupported. They are more likely to see the therapist as either unable or unwilling to prevent such episodes—that is, as either weak and ineffectual or, for some reason, unmotivated to protect family members. This is likely to decrease hopefulness and to reinforce whatever resistance to treatment already exists. It may substantiate common fears among family members that treatment will involve a good deal of unproductive pain. So, unless prevented or repaired, destructive interactions may diminish a variety of potential resources for treatment and preclude others from developing, with no significant gains of any kind.

Approaches

We can divide approaches to this trap into preventive and reparative interventions. Preventive moves involve the therapist's exerting careful control over the quality, pace, and intensity of interactions in the session. This can be done implicitly by gently but firmly intervening to head off building confrontations and to slow down what seem likely to become "runaway" interactions. When family members are relatively cooperative, this can be done simply by politely interrupting certain sequences, changing subjects or moving to a related aspect of the particular content.

If this approach meets with only minimal success, the therapist can move to a more explicit intervention by stating some ground rules for the session. (S)he may, for example, ask the family members, for the next five to ten minutes or for the rest of the session, to speak only to him or her and not to each other. (S)he may explain this in terms of his or her own difficulty following so much information or by appealing to the need to do something different in the interview than what has already repeatedly occurred at home. (S)he may also point out that many old problems exist and that few, if any, will be settled once and for all in this meeting but that perhaps some directions will be established for improving things in the future.

These ground rules and explanations may result in the family's monitoring their own process and preventing or at least curtailing destructive interactions. However, the force of the unresolved issues and the probable rigidity of these patterns make it much more likely, instead, that these ground rules will simply make the family more receptive to subsequent interventions by the therapist. Such ground rules in fact rarely succeed on a one-shot basis. They must be followed with repeated, active interventions to head off what promise to be unhelpful interactions. If the therapist does not respect and enforce his or her own rules, it is unlike that the family will either. If all else fails and it becomes clear that destructive interactions cannot be contained as long as the "combatants" are together in one room (this is often true of *Virginia Woolf*-type couples), the therapist can separate them for individual or subgroup meetings.

Destructive interactions cannot always be prevented or "nipped in the bud." But even when the therapist is presented with a *fait accompli*—that is, when the harm has already been done—there are still therapeutic interventions which are both possible and necessary in an attempt to repair the damage and recoup to some extent.

For the most part, these interventions involve allying with the victim (as soon as possible) without attacking or criticizing the initiator. The therapist tries to take the victim "off the hook," to support or defend him or her, to see things from his or her side, without taking sides against the initiator. In other words, (s)he tries as much as possible to *dilute blame* against both initiator and victim. This becomes easier if the therapist can find something positive to support from the content of the interaction in both the victim and the initiator.

For example, in an evaluation session including mother, father, and 15-year-old daughter, daughter is describing how she has always been "caught between" her parents:

Daughter: My mother used to give me money and she used to tell me not to tell my father and I used to feel guilty because it was his money. . . . My mother used to tell me not to say anything to my father, about what she did for me, giving me his money.
Therapist: Even though that was her way of trying to see that you got things. . . .

Daughter: Yeah.
Therapist: But it still was hard on you because you wound up feeling guilty.
Daughter: Yeah.

In other words, whenever possible, the therapist reframes the accusation so that both the object of attack and the attack itself are seen in as sympathetic a way as possible (without overly straining credulity).

Even when this is not possible, the therapist can express receptivity in a more general way for the victim who presumably is hurting the most at that moment. (S)he can ask how (s)he sees the issue, giving the message that (s)he is receptive to his or her side of things and will clear a space for him or her to defend him or herself. What matters is for the therapist, in whatever way possible, to demonstrate a willingness to take all members' sides and to minimize painful and destructive interactions in the session.

Obviously, there are exceptions to this rule. Even in an evaluation session, a therapist may decide at some point to allow what appears to be a destructive interaction, for example, in order to jolt a particularly complacent family member, to assess the family's ability to tolerate conflict, or because intervening would appear to be so confrontative in this case that its negative consequence would likely exceed that of the interaction itself. In these cases, however, reparative moves are strongly indicated at a later point when the therapist feels they will be more easily accepted.

One special but highly common type of destructive interaction involves verbal combat between warring spouses. Any therapist who even occasionally sees couples or families in treatment has almost certainly been faced with this type of interaction. In a purely marital evaluation, besides the couple themselves, there is no one but the therapist to react to these scenes. In the family evaluation, when this type of marital combat goes uncontained, it is likely to generate feelings of anxiety, embarrassment, frustration, or hopelessness in the couple's children. A therapist rarely needs more than one or two minutes in order to be able to identify such an interaction and, unless (s)he has a specific rationale for allowing it to continue, the interests of the family are best served by his or her curtailing the conflict and allowing other areas to be assessed.

The approaches to interrupting this type of interaction are essentially the same as those discussed thus far. The therapist can try to modulate the affective tone of the meeting by using a calm and soothing tone. This may reassure and deescalate the partners in conflict. In many if not most cases, however, more forceful interventions will be necessary. This is one type of situation where, if not flamboyant, the therapist certainly has to be able to take an active, assertive approach. (S)he needs to feel entitled and unafraid to interrupt these patterns and to refocus discussion in ways (s)he feels will be more productive. The family expects the therapist to be in charge of the meeting; (s)he needs to be willing to take action sympathetically but forcefully to prevent time from being wasted or the tone of the session deteriorating into a grudge match.

The therapist can try simply interrupting the sequence when necessary. If this is unsuccessful, (s)he can suggest ground rules such as directing further comments to the therapist instead of each other, as discussed earlier. (S)he can appeal to the need to have something different happen in this meeting than what routinely occurs at home. (S)he can use physical activity and proximity to control the participants, either by moving one or both partners closer to him or herself or by seating him or herself briefly next to one or another of them. Finally, if all else fails, (s)he can split up the warring partners into separate individual or subgroup meetings in order to assure that the major purposes of the evaluation are not sacrificed to the ongoing struggle between the parents.

DISTRACTING SUBGROUPS

Another form of potentially harmful interaction—less dramatic but not necessarily less powerful than those discussed in the previous section—involves distracting subgroups. As the number of people involved in the evaluation increases, so does the potential for subgroups splitting off within the session. These groups, often pairs, may huddle, whisper, giggle, and chat together or exchange meaningful looks in a silent commentary on the proceedings in the session. Children and adolescents are understandably often the worst offenders.* And often, such pairing is a naturally protective move, faced with the anxieties and uncertainties presented by this first meeting. Nevertheless, it is hard to overestimate the extent of the disruption this activity can have on the session.

Consequences

The session with an obvious distracting subgroup is not so much shattered (as often occurs with a provocative challenger or an acutely psychotic patient) as it is slowly worn down, like a person under water

* It should be remembered that this is a description of the behavior of some children and adolescents in some cases. Obviously, it is not intended to describe the attitudes of children in general. Therapists often find that even small children may approach family therapy and family problems, at times, with more concern, conviction, and courage than their parents. This discussion applies only to those cases in which their subgroup interactions constitute an interference with the goals of the session.

torture. At the very least, the low buzz of sound created can make other conversations more difficult to hear for all involved, distract the therapist's attention from other family members, and create a mildly chaotic, confusing atmosphere. But the *psychological* impact of such activity far exceeds its actual stimulus value. The visible and audible presence of this little sphere of activity drains attention and involvement away from whatever else is happening in the session. The therapist's attention is divided. It becomes more difficult to focus oneself on the other family members speaking or on the information being imparted. Family members, as well, become divided between their discussions with the therapist on the one hand, and the distracting subgroup on the other. Often, both therapist and family members find themselves preoccupied with whether to do anything about the problem and, if so, what.

Parents may feel responsible for the children's behavior but unclear about the norms of the meeting. They may wonder if they should step in. If they do not, will they look too lax? If they do, too strict? Should they let the therapist handle this, since (s)he's running the meeting?

While the parents may be preoccupied with these questions, the therapist faces a related but significantly different dilemma. In a sense, (s)he is in a position like that of a teacher on the first day of school with some marginal disruptions in the class. The disruptions in both cases often represent a sort of test or provocation on the part of the participants. How much will the person in authority tolerate? Will (s)he allow the subgroup to do whatever it wants? Will (s)he try to ignore the distraction, as if afraid to engage in a confrontation? Or will (s)he come down hard in an angry or authoritarian way?

This is precisely the dilemma presented to the therapist—how to assert control over such behavior without being seen as an angry or authoritarian figure. Allowing it to continue beyond a certain point interferes with gathering information as well as forming alliances and is likely to reduce the therapist's perceived effectiveness in the eyes of family members. Coming down on the subgroup members in a forceful punitive manner or with poorly concealed irritation is likely to impair alliances with them and perhaps with other family members as well. The therapist can no more afford to stand by helplessly while the energy for the session is diffused than (s)he can risk rapport by overreacting to an ostensibly minor disturbance.

Approaches

As with other dilemmas discussed so far, it is best for the therapist to react in a way which is consonant with his or her own personal style.

And there are certainly a variety of approaches and styles of approach to this problem. Since controlling distracting subgroups requires, on some level, a confrontation, the general guideline concerning confrontations pertains here. Start with as gentle an intervention as possible and move to more forceful ones, as necessary, using responses to earlier interventions as guides.

The therapist can, of course, simply ask the distractors to be quiet since (s)he needs to be able to hear other family members who may be speaking. This approach is certainly straightforward and not overly harsh, and it has the advantage of giving an explanation for the request. However, particularly if the therapist is annoyed, it may be difficult to carry off without a somewhat punitive, chastising tone.

Another set of approaches involves a combination of humor, and, paradoxically, calling even more attention to the distraction. For example, the therapist might stop whatever is happening in the session and call the whole group's attention to the whispering or chatting. (S)he might apologize for having missed what was said by the distractors, or let them know that (s)he is very interested in what they have to say and doesn't want to miss anything. This will rarely result in the conversation actually being shared with the group since it was, most likely, not intended for "publication" anyway. But precisely for this reason, such a move makes the distractors less likely to continue, once they know that the spotlight will be turned on them at each repetition. These interventions which call attention to the distraction can be accomplished with just a hint of irony or with very broad humor. As long as it's done in a friendly, good-natured way which the children or adolescents can understand, it amounts to a sort of harmless teasing and the therapist's point is made clearly.

Silent conversations, such as those carried by an exchange of knowing winks, nods, and long-suffering raised eyebrows, can also be put in the spotlight if they have an inhibiting or intrusive impact on other family members. Often, a mere comment by the therapist about how well the two or three members can communicate without words will be sufficient to diminish this activity. In more serious or intractable situations, the therapist may want to note out loud the effect this seems to have on the other member(s).

An alternative approach to distracting subgroups involves changing the seating arrangement of the session in order to break up such subgroups. The therapist can ask one or both of the members to move so that they are no longer sitting together. (S)he may move one member to a seat beside him or herself where (s)he will probably be more responsive to verbal and nonverbal control by the therapist. No verbal explanations for such a move are necessary on the therapist's part. (S)he is presumed to be in charge of the session by family members and, in our experience, such moves rarely meet with any resistance.

Finally, if all else fails, the therapist can resort to the already discussed option of splitting up the session. In almost all instances, such subgroups will prove more helpful and less divisive when seen either individually or even together but without other family members present.

THE DOMINATING MEMBER

One very common problem involving a specific type of family member will usually become apparent within the first five minutes of the session. This is the "Dominating Member." The Dominating Member is one who, in a variety of ways, dominates or tries to dominate the session, monopolizes the therapist's attention and, if dealt with unsuccessfully, blocks the therapist's attempts to join with and assess the whole family. At the extreme, sessions in which the Dominating Member is unrestrained degenerate into a closed conversation between the therapist and the Dominating Member, with other family members often bored or frustrated in the background.

The category of Dominating Member is not monolithic. Dominating Members come in many different forms and cover a range from the less to the more difficult to manage. Perhaps the most common forms are: (1) the *switchboard*, (2) the long-winded *circumstantial member*, (3) the pressured *agitated member*, and (4) the *challenger*. Obviously these are not pure forms. A particular family member may be characterized by more than one such term. However, we will discuss each separately in order to make identification easier and to clarify particular patterns and approaches associated with each of them.

The Switchboard

What is often referred to as the *switchboard* role may be the most common form taken by the Dominating Member. The switchboard speaks for other members and acts as a translator between the therapist and other family members. (S)he often identifies him or herself at the opening of the session by responding to the therapist's initiating introductions. The switchboard will usually tell the therapist who each member of the family is instead of letting them introduce themselves. (S)he may "help" the therapist talk to certain family members by repeating or rephrasing the therapist's questions, sometimes in ways which unfortunately change their intent or implications.

For example, a therapist's neutral question about what kinds of problems the family has been having can become a punitive and shaming "Go on, Johnny, tell her what you did." Or, without any change in words at all, the therapist's question to the Identified Patient about particular symptomatology, carefully phrased to be casual, neutral, and accepting, can be repeated in a tone which conveys embarrassment, shamefulness, or condescending "understanding." The switchboard may follow the therapist's question to a particularly quiet member with such a barrage of "helpful" questions that the member withdraws even further. In each of these cases, the therapist is prevented from having a simple give and take with the other member. Nothing (s)he says reaches the member in pure form. Instead it is altered, perhaps distorted, by the switchboard coming in on the therapist's coattails.

Obviously, not all such behaviors constitute obstacles. Often, a family member may genuinely help other members communicate with the therapist, clarifying or rephrasing statements in a successful way. Such characteristics in fact often indicate family members who can function as "therapeutic allies." When a poor or difficult relationship between the therapist and a family member is aided and strengthened by another member, the aims of the session are facilitated. However, when the therapist is unable even to begin to form a relationship with other members or when perfectly workable relationships are blocked, what might have been help becomes obstruction. It is these situations which are under discussion here.

The switchboard's domination seems to be dynamically and relationally motivated. (S)he has a strong need for control which often dovetails with some if not all other family members' readiness to be controlled, coaxed, and directed. His or her domination then is individually and systemically fueled. Attempts by the therapist to contain the switchboard's activity are felt as and therefore constitute confrontations and potential power struggles.

The Circumstantial Member

The *circumstantial*, long-winded member on the other hand, often appears to dominate unintentionally, more by dint of style than anything else, and frequently tends to be oblivious of the dominating impact of his or her monologues. Attempts by the therapist to limit this member's impact feel much less threatening and are often accepted more easily, perhaps even with some self-deprecating humor. They may be experienced as a small criticism but are less likely to be felt as a basic threat to the person's identity and position in the family.

The Agitated Member

Similar to the circumstantial family member (in terms of the largely stylistic as opposed to dynamic factors in their domination) but usually more difficult to manage is the pressured, *agitated* member who interrupts frequently with a strong sense of urgency and upset. Such members often remain fixated on one topic, leading to their common description as sounding like a "broken record." The agitated member has a pressing agenda which makes discussion of any other area, either with or between the therapist and other family members, difficult at best. Often the therapist tries to meet the ostensible demands of the agenda but finds that the agitated member persists in spite of this or switches immediately to a new urgent demand. In these cases, it often becomes clear that the pressure does not, in fact, lie in the particular agenda presented but may instead reflect either other concerns, situational anxiety, or personality style. Each of these suggests a somewhat different approach as will be discussed below.

Aside from the negative impact which the agitated member has on information gathering, (s)he also interferes with the therapist's attempts to form alliances with all family members. The urgency of the agenda may polarize the session in such a way that the therapist's attending to this family member is very much at the expense of other members, and vice versa.

The Challenger

When the agenda of the Dominating Member has less of a complaining and more of a demanding flavor, when the therapist feels it is more like an attack or a challenge than a cry for help, the Dominating Member can most likely be characterized as a *challenger.* Of the various types of Dominating Members discussed here, the challenger is most explicitly involved in a power struggle with the therapist. Often (s)he identifies him or herself at the very start of the session or when first contacted by the therapist by, so to speak, "throwing down the glove" with a head-on confrontation.

Such a confrontation may take the form of a question: a rather stiff inquiry into the therapist's professional credentials, experience, or age; a withering "request" to "please tell us what possible good you expect to come of discussing my son's escapades in this way"; an angry demand to "know why the youngsters have to be subjected to this." Or the challenge may take the form of a simple refusal to participate in some aspect of the evaluation. For example, the therapist's innocent question about the length of the marriage may elicit a response such as, "I fail to see what my marriage has to do with this and I have no intention of discussing it."

Challenges may also take the form of direct interventions between the therapist and other family members, such as refusing to let a member answer one of the therapist's questions or preventing a member from making or finishing a particular statement.

The challenger acts as if (s)he has a "chip on the shoulder" and is daring the therapist to knock it off. For those therapists who have not yet been confronted with a challenger, it is difficult to convey the sheer power and emotional impact of such assaults, which often feel like a "slap," a "blast," or a "barrage." The therapist, whose task is to ally with family members, is at a unique disadvantage since his or her psychological set is to try to join, not to oppose. So, in contrast to a trial lawyer for example, (s)he is less prepared for the onslaught and may, therefore, be much more taken aback. Many a novice therapist has left a therapy or evaluation session with the sense of having been "mowed down" or "beaten senseless" by a challenger and the violence of such metaphors attests to the verbal and emotional force of these challenges in some instances. The difficult part of managing the challenger involves neither capitulating to their moves for control nor retaliating in a similarly aggressive way. Their attempts to threaten and provoke the therapist often make such a response far from easy.

Consequences

The consequences of the therapist's failure to manage the Dominating Member are potentially quite serious. They include the obvious decrease in information, impressions, and interactions which can be elicited by the therapist and the disruption of the therapist's attempts to form alliances with all family members. In the worst instances, this can lead to a state in which the therapist loses the Dominating Member as well as all other family members. The therapist's inability to set limits in some way on the Dominating Member is not likely to improve rapport between them and is almost certain to impair it. A typical pattern is for the therapist to sit through the Dominating Member's activity with decreasing sympathy and increasing irritation until his or her anger is communicated to the Dominating Member, which only increases the emotional distance between them. In this sense, the therapist's attempt to assess the reasons for the Dominating Member's activity and the most effective means of controlling it represent, at least in part, an attempt to build rapport with him or her. Finally, when the therapist is unable to prevent the Dominating Member from monopolizing the session, the family is more likely to see the therapist as helpless and ineffectual and to have correspondingly decreased hopefulness about the possible benefits of treatment.

Special Considerations

The most important consideration concerning the Dominating Member involves the causes or reasons for his or her monopolizing behavior, since the therapist's understanding of this will dictate the approaches that are designed to control it. A general principle of all clinical work, which is especially applicable here, involves the therapist's attempt, when confronted with what seems negative or destructive in a patient, to look for the positive force behind it. So, for example, a patient's highly critical, rejecting behavior becomes easier to sympathize with, to tolerate, and to manage if the therapist can see a strong wish to be accepted and an even stronger fear of rejection in the patient. Another patient's belittling of the therapist's efforts and effectiveness might become similarly easier to tolerate and to work with if it is understood as reflecting an invisible loyalty to a parent who may have tried unsuccessfully to help the patient.

In terms of the therapist's management of the Dominating Member, there are two overall guidelines which should inform any particular strategies and techniques. To the extent that setting limits on the Dominating Member represents one form of confrontation with the family, the principle of moving carefully and in gradual steps is particularly useful in this context. The therapist can be more comfortable with and more sure of particular moves as (s)he gets to know the person better. (S)he can better gauge what sorts of moves are likely to be most successful, and, in general, how much (s)he can "get away with" in dealing with the Dominating Member. For this reason, especially if the therapist is forced to set limits very early in the session (for example, if the switchboard tries to short-circuit introductions by simply identifying each family member), (s)he should use more gentle and less provocative techniques first. Not only are these less likely to alienate the person but the responses they elicit will guide subsequent moves by the therapist.

Secondly, when all else fails (or, with a more preventive slant in mind, looks likely to fail), the therapist can move to a smaller group or individual meeting. If the therapist feels that protracted efforts to meet the Dominating Member's needs are alienating other family members, or that his or her freedom to use alternative approaches with the Dominating Member is limited by their presence, (s)he can ask to meet with the Dominating Member (or, if the Dominating Member is a parent, perhaps with both parents) alone. For example, if a challenging parent demands to know if the therapist feels that an acting-out adolescent Identified Patient should be allowed to do such-and-such, the therapist may find it much easier to advocate for the Identified Patient in the parents' own terms without the Identified Patient present since (s)he might react negatively to these terms. Stated differently, when the Dominating Member's agenda pressures the therapist to take sides in a family conflict, multiple alliances are facilitated by separate meetings since the therapist can more easily speak to each member's or subgroup's needs without alienating the others.

Some readers may feel that such relatively spontaneous decisions to split up the session might unduly disturb family members, or perhaps seem like an admission of defeat. In fact, this is rarely the case. The family expects the therapist to be in charge and to guide the session. When requests such as these are made in a casual tone which conveys that this is a normal, everyday aspect of the evaluation session, families usually react with mild surprise but quick acceptance.

Approaches

Obviously, there are a multitude of possible reasons for monopolizing behavior on the part of a family member. Since all such behavior on some level puts the Dominating Member in opposition to the therapist, an important distinction among different forms of this behavior involves the degree of flexibility it leaves the therapist to react without opposing the Dominating Member in return. More simply put, can the therapist meet the Dominating Member's particular needs in such a way as to diminish or contain monopolizing behavior, or do the Dominating Member's needs leave the therapist no way to ally with the person and still fulfill the demands of the evaluation session? Some of what are assumed to be the more common reasons for monopolizing behavior are presented below with this distinction in mind, and with one or more techniques designed to manage such behavior most effectively.

When the Dominating Member has an agenda that (s)he keeps bringing up in ways which interfere with everything else in the session, as is often the case with the agitated member or the challenger, the therapist should listen carefully for (s)he may discover a very real and specific concern. For example, a mother keeps interrupting early information gathering to ask if the therapist plans to use medication for her adolescent daughter. A brief exploration of the question reveals that mother's sister was at one time treated with psychotropic medication, unfortunately with numerous complications and side effects, contributing to a fear on mother's part that this may do her daughter even more harm. As this example suggests, such agendas often involve misconceptions about psychiatric treatment: will a family member be committed to a hospital? Is the Identified Patient a schizophrenic? Is the therapist part of some state agency which can take children from the home?

When approached correctly, these sorts of concerns can not only be quickly nullified, but can, in the process, largely eliminate monopolizing behavior and strengthen rapport between the initially Dominating Member and the therapist. A hoped-for comment from this individual afterwards might be, "Nobody really ever took it seriously before." The therapist should not try to answer questions prematurely—for example, concerning an Identified Patient's diagnosis, prognosis, or course of treatment. (S)he can, however, often do much to reassure family members without compromising him or herself.

When this type of concern involves some aspect of treatment, it may be that the family has received poor treatment in the past. In this case, one member may be expressing the family's reaction to this in behavior typical of a challenger or an agitated member. This situation can also be fairly easily remedied by the therapist's taking these concerns seriously and reacting appropriately. In addition to the benefits described above, this may also give the therapist extra information about how to approach this family in treatment most successfully.

In other cases, it may become apparent that the Dominating Member's behavior reflects not so much any one important concern as a characteristic response to situational anxiety, created here most likely by the session itself. In these cases as in the others just described, there is still likely to be a good deal of flexibility in the pattern so that the therapist can expect the monopolizing behavior to diminish as (s)he succeeds in lowering the person's anxiety. This might be true of any of the four types of Dominating Members discussed above. The therapist might try to reduce anxiety by stepping back from the particular content of the session for more informal interaction, by using humor or bringing up a loosely related anecdote from his or her own life, or by focusing on a different family member for a few moments. All of these moves are intended to set a more casual, relaxed tone for the session, to demonstrate that the therapist "does not bite," that (s)he is not out to blame but to understand and side with family members. If his or her guess about the source of the monopolizing behavior is correct, (s)he should see it diminish. If not, the formulation needs to be revised and a new strategy devised.

In other cases, the Dominating Member's behavior simply reflects long-term stylistic factors which do not indicate any particular agenda and which would be observable at roughly the same level outside the session in the person's daily life. The Dominating Member may well want to help and cooperate with the therapist but, as in the cases of the circumstantial and the agitated members, may only be able to do so in either a tangential or a pressured and insistent fashion. Often in these cases, as noted earlier, there is a convergence between an individual family member's personality style and the structure of relationships within the family. This is perhaps most clear in the case of the switchboard who often meets his or her own needs and the needs of family members by being the "organizer" of the family. In comparison with the patterns discussed thus far, managing the Dominating Member in these cases requires more care and effort since it is less a question of any one agenda or situational reaction than of a personal and interpersonal style. However, these cases are usually less difficult to manage than those in which the Dominating Member's monopolizing is not only stylistic but is *aimed*, consciously or unconsciously, *at* the therapist.

When the Dominating Member's monopolizing behavior reflects general stylistic factors, the therapist can use a variety of techniques to try to ensure more balanced participation among the family members. The simplest and most straightforward approach is for the therapist to make clear that (s)he wants to hear from *all* members of the family. Obviously, this is most likely to succeed when stated clearly but in a friendly and casual way, with as little as possible of a chastising tone toward the Dominating Member.

Or, once again, (if the therapist feels comfortable enough and senses that the family will respond to this), the use of humor may help to smooth over what might otherwise be a somewhat touchy interaction. (S)he might tease the Dominating Member (and the family as a whole) by protesting that the Dominating Member is "overworked" and should get a five minute break or that (s)he is being too generous in letting other family members "off the hook" while (s)he does all the work. When the Dominating Member acts as a switchboard, the therapist can highlight this by referring to the Dominating Member as such or as a "translator."

Similarly, these or any other shorthand codes which encapsulate the monopolizing behavior are usually quite helpful, *when agreed upon* by the therapist and the Dominating Member. They allow the therapist to identify the behavior simply, quickly, and in terms the Dominating Member can accept. For example, the therapist might point out that the circumstantial member seems to be the kind of person who never takes the main road because (s)he likes the side streets so much. If this description is accepted by the circumstantial member, the therapist may need only to mention "side streets" when this person becomes particularly tangential in order to get things back on track. The therapist should *not*, however, use humor if (s)he senses or knows (from an earlier probe) that the family will respond poorly to this or if (s)he is angry or irritated with the Dominating Member. If the therapist is angry, his or her humor is more likely to have a blaming, critical, or aggressive edge to it, with predictably poor results.

An alternative approach to the Dominating Member involves an effort to *channel* instead of simply containing the monopolizing behavior. The therapist can, for example, give the Dominating Member a circumscribed task such as describing a typical day in the family. Such "assignments" can be given in the context of several assignments for several family members. For example, the therapist may say, "I'd like Mrs. J. to describe what people in the family do in the evenings and Bobby to tell us about weekends at home." This, one hopes, will give the Dominating Member freedom to talk at length on one topic while being made more aware of the limits which are necessary in order for all members to participate.

Once the Dominating Member's monopolizing behavior has been commented on in any of the above ways in the session, the therapist may be able to interrupt later instances with nonverbal signals to the person. If this approach seems insufficient, the therapist may want to move the Dominating Member physically so that (s)he is seated next to or nearby the therapist. Increasing proximity usually makes the Dominating Member somewhat easier to control. It makes possible physical contact, such as a hand on the person's arm, which can be especially useful with children. But even without such contact, mere proximity will usually have a constraining effect on the Dominating Member.

Finally, as we suggested earlier, if all these approaches are unsuccessful in assuring more balanced participation, the therapist can vary the membership of the meeting, that is, break the family into smaller groups and individual meetings. This allows more wholehearted attention on the therapist's part towards the Dominating Member when they are together, as well as more balanced participation among other family members when the therapist meets with them separately.

The Dominating Member is even more difficult to manage when the personality factors driving his or her monopolizing behavior involve a need to retain control and a fear of losing power, either to the therapist or in the family. These cases most often involve the switchboard or the challenger, although they may develop in agitated or circumstantial members as well. Here, the Dominating Member has a more rigid need to exert control in ways which interfere with the requirements of the evaluation session. For example, the person who must be the "hub" of all possible relationships will prevent direct, one-to-one relationships between the therapist and other family members. The person who becomes threatened when family members respond autonomously or in disagreement with him or her will need to "help," disqualify, or "correct" them until their statements are more acceptable. The person who is threatened by the discussion of certain topics will need to minimize, disrupt, or divert attention until the focus is shifted. In these cases, the Dominating Member (often not without ambivalence) has an investment in thwarting the therapist's agendas which make his or her management much more difficult than in the other situations described thus far.

In these cases, the therapist may try some of the gentler approaches discussed above. In fact, (s)he will probably need to do so if for no other reason than to determine the relatively greater resistance of these patterns. It is more likely, though, that these situations will require stronger measures, such as separate meetings. Since in many of these cases the Dominating Member's opposition to the therapist is likely to be partial and unconscious (that is, automatic as opposed to deliberate), with some real intention to cooperate with the therapist, it will most likely *not* be useful to call attention to such opposition. Instead, separate meetings can be used as described above—that is, for greater freedom on the therapist's part, both to attend to the Dominating Member and to deal more easily with other family members.

Finally, the Dominating Member may quite simply be consciously and deliberately dead set against the purposes of the evaluation. Whether this is stated explicitly (as is sometimes the case with the challenger) or acted out behaviorally, the therapist obviously has fewer options and very little room to move in managing such a person. In the spectrum of possible motives for monopolizing behavior we have presented here, this clearly represents the extreme of the inflexible, hard-to-manage case. Again, separate meetings are almost certainly called for. But in these cases, where the Dominating Member has made no attempt to conceal his or her opposition to the therapist, the most productive approach in a separate meeting will probably involve discussing his or her feelings about the evaluation openly. In general, the therapist's goal will be to see if there is some framework (s)he and the Dominating Member can agree upon for at least completing the evaluation. If this is successfully negotiated, the Dominating Member can be expected to be more cooperative when a decision is reached to return to a full-family evaluation format.

A more complex and potentially deceptive picture involves those cases in which the Dominating Member (often a challenger), ostensibly acting individually, has in fact been collusively "delegated" by the family to oppose the therapist. These cases unfortunately are usually not detected until the therapist tries to bypass the Dominating Member in an effort to ally with other family members only to discover that it is the family as a whole, not just the Dominating Member, that is arrayed against him or her. In these cases, the therapist has very little chance of success in forming a working alliance with family members, let alone managing the behavior of the Dominating Member.

Ending this discussion of the spectrum of monopolizing behavior with the most difficult cases may have a discouraging impact on the reader. (S)he should remember that the Dominating Member in a particular family may resemble any of the subtypes described here or, as is often the case, more than one of them. Someone who initially presents as a Dominating Member may resist all efforts on the therapist's part or (s)he may develop into a major therapeutic ally. The Dominating Member is, after all, there in the flesh for the evaluation, which in most cases bespeaks at least some degree of motivation, hope, and willingness to cooperate. It is the therapist's job, then, not to squander and, as much as possible, to nurture these potential resources.

THE "FUNCTIONALLY MUTE" ADOLESCENT

Therapists who work either with families or individually with adolescents are familiar with a particular type of adolescent in treatment. These young men and women appear angry, sullen, or pouty. They approach encounters with adults and authority figures, which certainly includes the therapist, with an attitude of angry defiance. They present initially (and in some cases, perpetually) as though "on strike." They remind one of those Hollywood war heroes who refuse to give their enemy interrogators anything but "name, rank, and serial number." Obviously, adolescents have no monopoly on this stance. A child, parent, or grandparent can behave in this way in the session. However, this pattern is much more common with adolescents and, in view of the problems it can create in the evaluation, merits discussion in its own right.

Consequences

When such an adolescent is not central to the presenting problem (for example, a sibling of the Identified Patient), (s)he poses no particular management problem. The therapist can simply resign him or herself to getting little help from this adolescent and concentrate instead on more compliant family members. However, when the resistant adolescent is the Identified Patient, (s)he is likely to have a more disturbing and disruptive effect on the evaluation session. His or her noncompliance can create uneasiness and resentment in other family members, who often feel that they are there because of the adolescent's problem. His or her silence can undermine the participation of others and often has the effect of slowing down or deadening the session. Others may be less likely to describe their side of issues if the adolescent will not defend his or her own. They may feel that there is no purpose to the session if the Identified Patient won't even take part. In other words, the typical behavior of the "functionally mute" adolescent may well generate tension, frustration, resentment, guilt, uncertainty, or pessimism in other family members.

Special Considerations

The first consideration in dealing with these adolescents is to be reasonably sure that one's assessment is accurate. The therapist needs to be sure that (s)he is not in fact dealing with a teenager who is psychotic, catatonic, dissociated, or organically impaired. The severity of any of these conditions would necessitate more thorough individual assessment and immediate therapeutic intervention. In addition, the approaches which might help manage the "on-strike" adolescent in the session would likely be ineffectual, and perhaps even harmful, in any of these cases.

In general, disorientation, impaired attention and memory, or any sudden and drastic changes in mood and behavior should heighten one's suspicion for organic involvement, as should a recent history of an accident or injury to the head, high fever, or drug ingestion. Suspicion for psychosis should be heightened if friends or relatives describe having observed recent episodes of bizarre behavior or conversation, of the person talking to him or herself, or of appearing to be listening or responding to voices. Previous history for any of these symptoms should also raise the therapist's suspicions in this area. Evidence that the adolescent is appropriately oriented, clear, and talkative in at least certain relationships (e.g., friends or siblings) suggests the picture we have described above, the adolescent who is temporarily on a "sit-down strike." The scope of this book precludes more extensive discussion of methods for arriving at these differential diagnoses. The reader is referred to basic texts in clinical diagnosis for further description of these conditions and their assessment.

The therapist should also be careful not to confuse this type of adolescent with one who is not so much on strike as genuinely afraid of incriminating either him or herself or some other member of the family in some way if (s)he speaks. Perhaps the clearest examples of this latter situation involve families in which there has been unreported physical or sexual abuse of children by a family member or trusted adult. Often, the feeling-tone expressed by these adolescents is significantly different from more resistant adolescents. In the former case, the adolescent is more likely to communicate, either verbally or nonverbally, "I can't talk," rather than "I won't." The therapist is then presented with a dilemma which involves managing family secrets (see Chapter 11) rather than a resistant adolescent.

This type of situation also serves to remind us that the difficult-to-manage adolescent may, like any other difficult-to-manage family member, be reacting to legitimate issues, agendas, or anxieties. If the adolescent is willing to cooperate even minimally, the therapist should take into consideration the points raised in earlier sections of this chapter for managing such issues in the evaluation session. It may well be that the adolescent's resistance reflects a legitimate concern, such as anticipated mistreatment based on a previous negative experience with treatment or misconceptions concerning the purpose of the evaluation. In these cases, the therapist's sympathetic attention and reassurance may do more than anything else to defuse resistance.

If, however, the therapist has ruled out these other presenting pictures and feels confident that (s)he is in fact dealing with a resistant adolescent, all efforts at therapeutic management are guided by one basic premise. This is the recognition that *the adolescent is involved in a power struggle which (s)he can easily win, simply by doing nothing.* We have tried thus far in this book to deemphasize the preoccupation among some family therapists with issues of power and conflict, but it does little good to ignore power dynamics where they are prominent. The power struggle in which these teenagers engage the therapist may well originate in an invisible loyalty to a parent. It may be accompanied by nuances of ambivalence and even longing for help. But unless this power struggle is recognized and managed effectively, the therapist runs a high risk of being caught in an unproductive and debilitating combat with the adolescent.

Typically, such combat takes the following form: The therapist invites the adolescent to speak; the adolescent declines, either with a flat refusal, or by giving vague, monosyllabic, or inaudible replies. The therapist tries harder to "reach" the adolescent who either hunkers down, digging heels further in place, or skips gracefully out of the therapist's reach. The therapist may become more frustrated; if this is the case, the adolescent often becomes more satisfied with his or her success. The therapist may try to convince, cajole, beg, or threaten the adolescent, again with no success. The therapist's own building anger and resentment may become visible and may lead to critical, punitive responses. In some cases, the therapist may finally give up only to have his or her hopes and efforts rekindled by an encouraging sign from the teenager. Predictably, if the therapist takes the bait, (s)he most often runs up against a brick wall again.

Aside from the sheer frustration this engenders in the therapist, it is of little help and has the potential of doing real harm to the family. Deprived of an opportunity to see the adolescent's side of things, the therapist is less able to advocate for him or her and to understand the family and the presenting problem as a whole. If the therapist adopts one or more of a variety of essentially negative stances (authoritarian, transparently manipulative, lecturing, beseeching-bargaining, punitive) and continues to fail in his or her efforts, (s)he begins to lose face with the family and may be seen as less effectual and perhaps less trustworthy. This will most likely diminish hopefulness on the part of family members that something positive might emerge from the evaluation.

If the adolescent chooses to, (s)he can always win this struggle hands down. (S)he has merely to do nothing. The first sign of wisdom, then, in these situations is recognizing and accepting that the therapist is essentially powerless to make the adolescent participate actively in the session. But this does not mean that the therapist has to give up and accept defeat. There are a variety of more strategic approaches to this type of situation. These approaches involve efforts to minimize, rechannel, or eliminate the adolescent's resistance instead of merely trying to overpower it.

Readers will undoubtedly note an element of playfulness in the following discussion. At their best, strategic maneuvers by a therapist always contain some element of playfulness, since they are designed to deal with "game-playing" interactions. Like humor, this playfulness is most likely to succeed when the therapist is laughing (or playing) *with* the adolescent, as opposed to laughing *at* him or her. Undoubtedly, the more skillful of these adolescents will sorely test the therapist's ability to keep to the former approach. The job of the therapist is to do his or her best to pass such tests.

Approaches

We can roughly divide approaches to this group of adolescents into three categories: (1) attempts to minimize problems before the start of the session, (2) efforts to encourage greater participation from the adolescent in the session, and (3) techniques for managing the session if these efforts are unsuccessful.

Essentially, attempts to minimize problems before the start of the session involve "early detection" of the likelihood that such a pattern will develop and efforts to prevent or dilute it. This usually takes place in initial contacts aimed at setting up the session, in person or by telephone, between the therapist and the parents or other professionals already involved in the case.

The therapist may hear something which raises the possibility that the adolescent Identified Patient will fit this pattern. For example, a comment that (s)he is very negative about the session or a report that (s)he has behaved in exactly this way in one or more previous meetings elsewhere. If this occurs, the therapist tries to find out which factors, if any, are likely to make this response more or less probable. For example, (s)he may find out that the adolescent is resistant in whole-family meetings but more cooperative in individual meetings, or perhaps just the opposite. (S)he may discover that the adolescent is most cooperative when seen with a trusted sibling or with one parent. (S)he may find that the child only acts this way when a particular family member is present.

This information may help the therapist to structure the session so as to optimize chances for success. Since the therapist will often want to form his or her own impressions before changing the format of the evaluation, (s)he may begin the session with the format (s)he thinks most sensible, such as a full-family meeting, but switch to another format if this seems to promise greater success. If the adolescent is most likely to participate in a particular format which does not violate the ethics and constraints of evaluation, it is usually in the interest of the therapist and the family to incorporate and work around it. This is dictated by the priorities of gathering relevant information, seeing each person's side, and forming some alliance with the adolescent.

The therapist may not be able, however, to anticipate this pattern before the session. (S)he may simply be presented with it and have to make the best of it. The most important principle involves the therapist's not letting him or herself be goaded or seduced into a power struggle aimed at trying to *make* the adolescent talk. (S)he can, however, intervene in a variety of ways which aim at increasing the likelihood of the adolescent's participation while simultaneously assessing the flexibility of this stance and minimizing losses if unsuccessful.

One relatively safe therapeutic intervention involves decreasing expectations. These adolescents often have finely tuned radar for the needs and expectations of others (especially parents, parent-substitutes, and authority figures). Often they react immediately (and not necessarily voluntarily) by digging in their heels and in essence saying, "No."

This finely honed sensitivity and reflexive opposition often does as much harm to the adolescent him or herself as it does to anyone else. If the adolescent senses strong pressure from the therapist to participate, the very opposite is quite likely to occur. These are situations in which the therapist as "rescuer" is least likely to succeed.

The therapist may be able to avoid this trap by somehow communicating that (s)he is receptive and interested in what the adolescent has to say, but does not necessarily expect or demand that (s)he talk and that the therapist will not lose sleep over the adolescent's possible unresponsiveness. Because these adolescents are often reacting against overly involved parents who may express extreme reactions to whatever the adolescent does, this slightly disinterested tone is, paradoxically, likely to be more successful. This is not an encouragement for therapists to act smug, flippant, uninterested, or coldly indifferent. It is simply to say that the more the adolescent feels that the therapist is interested, in a warm, friendly but appropriately limited way in his or her participation, the more likely (s)he will be to participate in a more appropriate way.

How the therapist communicates this decrease in the pressure of expectations is largely a matter of metacommunication—a posture and tone of voice which convey a friendly but moderated interest. More explicitly, the therapist can also make comments which defend or validate the adolescent's reluctance to participate, essentially granting permission for his or her noncooperation. For example, (s)he might comment that the adolescent may not have much to say at a certain point and that (s)he should feel free to interrupt later if (s)he has something to add, at which point the therapist can move directly to another, more cooperative, member. Besides side-stepping the standard transactional pattern, this type of intervention may actively serve to encourage participation by channeling opposition into a form of therapeutic leverage. If the adolescent is set on opposing the therapist, (s)he can be guided into actually participating as an act of opposition. All this requires is that the therapist somehow convey that (s)he does not expect the adolescent to participate at all. Often, this type of adolescent finds it hard to resist such a challenge.

The therapist can also reframe the adolescent's silence so as to make it less acceptable to him or her. Any statement on the therapist's part which associates the silence with qualities which are usually seen as undesirable by teenagers may elicit the desired response. Examples might include relating the silence to fear ("That's okay. Johnnie may just be too afraid to really say what's on his mind"), uncertainty ("I think Debbie may just feel too unsure of herself to say how she really sees things"), emotionality ("Maybe it's better you don't talk for a while, because it looks like you're afraid you'd get real upset if you did"), or immaturity ("If Anne doesn't want to talk, I think she shouldn't be forced to. Sometimes some people feel like they're too young to make a real contribution").

This means that if the adolescent remains silent, (s)he is forced to accept the therapist's negative definition of the silence. This is considerably more uncomfortable than is simply thwarting the therapist by being "on strike." The teenager can only contest these definitions of his or her silence by breaking it, and often this in itself provides a first step towards greater discussion. In some cases, it may provide no more than that, and other approaches or repetitions of this one may be necessary. However, adolescents usually need to be either very cagey, very determined, or both, to resist the "bait" altogether in this type of intervention.

If the approaches discussed so far are even momentarily successful, the therapist must be consistent in his or her response to the adolescent's reaction. This means that (s)he cannot display too much enthusiasm or gratitude for the adolescent's contribution. If any of these approaches have worked to any extent, it is primarily because the therapist has played a little "hard to get," depriving the teenager of an opportunity to frustrate him or her. When the teenager does finally participate, the therapist should *casually* reinforce this participation by responding to it with moderate interest. (S)he should neither ignore it nor gratefully latch on to it, as this would undermine the strategy which elicited it in the first place.

If none of the above approaches is successful in drawing the adolescent into the evaluation session and if his or her resistance inteferes with the flow of the evaluation, the therapist retains the option of removing him or her from the session and testing to see if things go more smoothly in an individual session following the whole-family meeting. The therapist actually has several degrees of freedom here. If (s)he wishes to soften the impact of this move, (s)he may split the family in a different way. For example, all the children might be sent out while the therapist meets with the parents and later with the children, either together, individually, or in various smaller groups.

If the therapist does send the adolescent out of the interview room, it should be done casually, not punitively. In fact, the act of sending a child from the room so closely resembles a traditional parental punishment that the therapist needs to be particularly aware of presenting it differently. (S)he can casually refer to this as a routine part of the evaluation, just one instance of splitting the family up into various smaller groups. This leaves open the possibility for a more productive subgroup or individual meeting later. Lastly, if the therapist removes the adolescent from the room and plans not to try to see him or her until the next scheduled evaluation session, (s)he is probably better off making some kind of individual contact with the adolescent, no matter how brief, before the family leaves. This signals behaviorally that the therapist has not forgotten the adolescent altogether and has not counted him or her out of the evaluation. The therapist is still receptive to the adolescent and willing to make some efforts to meet him or her part way. Again, the therapist's tone should be interested and well meaning without being urgent or overinvolved. These adolescents will generally respond better to someone who presents a friendly "take it or leave it" attitude than one of excessive caring. The latter may often be what they most want; it is more rarely what they respond to cooperatively.

If the adolescent is absolutely determined to resist all therapeutic efforts and if his or her behavior is the major (or part of the major) presenting problem, the prognosis for treatment becomes more guarded. For the therapist to have essentially no therapeutic alliance with a major participant in the presenting problem almost always constitutes a major obstacle towards therapeutic change. This places even more importance on therapeutic alliances with other family members, especially parents. While it is usually more difficult to promote therapeutic change when the resistant Identified Patient is an adolescent rather than a child, it is not impossible. But where the therapist has no trustable alliance with either the adolescent Identified Patient or the parents, (s)he most likely has a case which will not respond to family treatment.

This does not rule out other forms of treatment, even when the therapist evaluating the family feels that they are less likely to be of significant therapeutic impact than successful family work might be. Even when the adolescent resists treatment and the parents appear largely unmotivated or unreliable, the family evaluation increases the likelihood that appropriate recommendations for treatment (or other interventions) can be made. Or, if nothing else, that possibly scant resources (in terms of time, money, and the therapists' emotional reserves) be put where they can do the most good.

Finally, therapists (especially those who are unfamiliar with the treatment of adolescents) need to remember that the style of cooperation in this age group is often quite different from that in other life stages. It is entirely normative for adolescents who are invested in and committed to some form of therapy to come as though under protest, with muttered complaints and expressions of contempt or boredom. Therapists who are experienced with adolescents in treatment tend to make little of these ritualistic protests. They recognize that, in most cases, if an adolescent comes with reasonable regularity to meetings, (s)he is sufficiently engaged and the work of evaluation or treatment can be done in spite of apparent complaints or indifference.

11
Family Secrets

Some of the most common, complex, and often anxiety-provoking dilemmas in family evaluation and treatment involve family secrets. Secrets can create dilemmas for the therapist at almost any point before, during, or after the evaluation session. A parent or previously involved professional can inform the therapist of a secret during the initial telephone contact and forbid him or her from using this information in the session. Particular family members may reveal a secret to the therapist at a subgroup meeting when certain members are absent or ask for a separate meeting in order to discuss "something private." Someone may take the therapist aside for a confidential comment at the end of the meeting, even as other family members are filing out of the room.

The consequences of mishandling secrets in the evaluation are potentially serious. The opportunities for doing so are perhaps greater than with many other traps because the dilemmas created by secrets are often more complex than those associated with other traps. This is because, in addition to management problems, they may raise more basic uncertainties in the therapist concerning therapeutic goals and fundamental ethical questions regarding family relationships and the limits of the therapist's responsibility.

When the therapist is trying to deal with a dominating member, for example, (s)he is usually quite clear on the goal, which is in some way to limit that member's control over the session in order to assure more balanced participation among all family members. With secrets, however, many therapists find themselves less certain even of their goals. Should the therapist go after a secret if it looks important? Is it really important for the therapist not to keep secrets? If a secret is impulsively shared with the therapist, is it fair to insist that it be shared with other family members? Is it fair not to share it? Issues of fairness aside, is it practical not to share it? And what if threatening to share it drives the family away from the evaluation? If it is to be shared, whose job is it—the one who told the therapist or the therapist him or herself? These and a host of related questions may immobilize the therapist who is likely to have much greater difficulty in deciding on tactics to manage the problem if (s)he can't decide on guidelines for management in the first place.

To a greater extent than for any of the other traps discussed thus far, the problems associated with secrets in the evaluation reflect significant relational issues in the family's life outside the evaluation. Difficulty with regulating stress on the family, with distracting subgroups and destructive interactions are problems that are inherent to the evaluation itself. They have no particular significance outside the evaluation. Even where this is less clear-cut, as in the cases of the dominating member and the "functionally mute" adolescent, there is reason to see these as epiphenomena of the evaluation, with possible but by no means inevitable importance in the dynamics of the family.

In this sense, the problems associated with secrets differ significantly from those associated with other traps. Therapists cannot manage secrets in the session without considering their place in the family. For this reason, we will explore common patterns associated with secrets in families before moving to a discussion of considerations and guidelines for therapeutic management in the evaluation. We begin with a brief word on terminology.

TERMINOLOGY

Secrets involve information that is either withheld or differentially shared between or among people. This definition suggests some of the more interesting aspects of secrets, especially for family theorists and therapists. The phrase "between or among people" signals that we are squarely in the realm of interpersonal relationships, and "withheld or

differentially shared" immediately suggests the notion of boundaries and
alliances—that is, the structuring of relational systems. The word "information" bears further discussion. Empirically, one is struck by the fact
that secrets tend, for the most part, not to be about feelings or thoughts,
but about *facts,* real happenings or incidents. Examples might involve an
extramarital affair, a prison record, incest, an abortion, the adoption of
a child. This is consistent with the importance of the factual dimension
of relationships, described earlier.

We can refer to the network of persons involved in the secret as the
awareness context. This refers to the network *as a whole* and includes
those who are unaware of the secret as well as those who know it. The
term is derived from the work of Glaser and Strauss on the awareness of
dying (1965).

A fairly simple typology of secrets can be drawn from the kinds of
boundaries created in the relational system. From this perspective, three
major types of family secrets emerge: (1) individual secrets; (2) internal
family secrets; and (3) shared family secrets.

Individual secrets involve those cases in which one person keeps a
secret from the other person or persons in the family. Examples might
include a spouse's secret extramarital affair or a mother's knowledge that
her husband is not their child's father. In both cases, one person's secret
is shared with no one else in the family. The boundary formed by the
secret is located between the person holding the secret and the other(s).

Internal family secrets involve those cases in which at least two people
keep a secret from at least one other. For example, both parents know
that their child is adopted, but the child does not. Or, a mother informs
her teenager daughter that she plans to file for divorce, but neither tells
the father. Internal family secrets create subgroupings within the family.

Last, *shared family secrets* involve those cases in which all members
of the family know the secret but are pledged to keep it from persons
outside the family. Examples might include a parent's alcoholism, a son's
homosexuality, or the birth of an illegitimate child to a daughter. Shared
family secrets strengthen the boundaries separating the family as a whole
from the outside world.

Finally, the following terms are suggested for different roles within
the awareness context. The person or persons who know and keep the
secret can be referred to as the *secret holder(s)* and the person who does
not know the secret as *the unaware.* The addition of one final role is
needed in order to round out an analysis of secrets. This is *the subject,*
meaning the person that the secret is about. Subject and secret holder
may be one and the same person, as in the case of a spouse's secret
infidelity. Or they may be different, as in the case of a mother (secret

holder) who keeps secret from her children (the unaware) that their now deceased father (subject) actually committed suicide.

The confusion that surrounds secrets may make it difficult in some cases to make absolute distinctions between knowing and not knowing a secret. For example, members may say, when the secret is finally discussed openly, that they didn't know but they "wondered" or "suspected." Some may have known parts but not all (and different members may have known different parts). Similarly, for some secret holders there may be absolute clarity about the fact that there is a secret, but others may be quite surprised to recognize the secret as such. A typical remark would be, "Well, it's funny. I always knew this was something I shouldn't talk about and I didn't really know whether my brother knew or not, but I never really thought of it as a secret before."

This last point suggests the need for a way to identify secrets, even when the secret holder is unaware of them as such. In this spirit, the following rule of thumb is offered only somewhat facetiously. The therapist should immediately consider the possible existence of secrets *any time the word "know" needs to be used more than once in a sentence* either by the patient or the therapist. For example, "I know but she doesn't know"; "I know you know"; "I don't know whether she knows."

SECRETS AND LOYALTY

It is nearly impossible to overemphasize the significance of loyalty dynamics in the creation, maintenance, and eventual facing of secrets in families. Often, the secret holder feels, or may actually be, "sworn to silence." (S)he owes it to the other person(s) to keep the secret. Disclosing the secret would be experienced as an act of betrayal and would arouse guilt over disloyalty. These are instances of loyalty to the secret holder(s). But the awareness context is further complicated by the fact that a secretholder may also feel loyalty to the unaware. For example, mother tells one son a secret about his brother and insists that he not tell his brother about this. By keeping the secret—that is, expressing loyalty to his mother—the son expresses disloyalty to his brother, but if he tells his brother, he betrays his mother. This represents what Boszormenyi-Nagy describes as a split-loyalty pattern. In summary, loyalty dynamics can contribute to the creation and maintenance of family secrets that, in turn, are likely to generate or exacerbate split-loyalty patterns.

SECRETS AND POWER

In some cases of secrets, there is an element of "one-upmanship"; the secret holder feels "one-up" on the unaware. This is expressed in its least subtle form when a young child crows to a friend or sibling, "I know something you don't know!" The power dynamics implied here exist in more subtle and often much more destructive forms in nominally more mature relationships; the secret holder gloats in his or her secret knowledge and the other's ignorance.

In addition to being one-up on the other, the secret holder has the threat of "unused ammunition." In the pattern of skirmishes and battles typical of the *Virginia Woolf* type of marital relationships, for example, the secret holder has a sort of relational nuclear bomb that can be kept for later use. There is a dangerous and unstable tension inherent in these power dynamics of secrets because, in order to be able to savor the full effect of the secret, to squeeze every ounce of cruelty from it, the secret holder must reveal it. Then (s)he can see the reaction of the other person when (s)he realizes (s)he has been deceived. There is, therefore, an inherent instability in such patterns, always pressing towards destructive disclosures.

SECRETS, BOUNDARIES, AND ALLIANCES

Internal family secrets create or strengthen boundaries and alliances within the family between secret holders. Estrangements develop between secret holders and the unaware in response to the secret holder's inability or unwillingness to discuss the secret and to the deception or mystification that often follows in the wake of secrets.

A curious fact about secrets is that the boundaries created by them depend not only upon who knows the secret but on *knowing who knows.* For example, a mother tells each of her two sons a secret about their sister. She does not tell either son that she has told the other and swears both to silence. Each son knows the secret, but neither knows that the other knows. In this case, *the boundary created between the two sons is just as real as that created between the secret holder and the unaware, even though both know the secret.*

When all members know the secret and, unlike the case above, know they all know, the secret serves to strengthen the boundary between the family and the outside world. In extreme cases, it may make alliances between family members and persons outside the family virtually impossible if they feel they can neither reveal the secret nor become involved emotionally without revealing the secret.

SECRECY VERSUS PRIVACY

When is something secret, and when it is simply private? Obviously, different families will define these terms differently. At the risk of oversimplification, one might guess that the more enmeshed the relational system, the more likely members are to think of private material as secret—that is, as something one should feel guilty for not sharing. At the extreme in such relationships, there is no such thing as privacy. All personal thoughts, feelings, and acts are expected to be shared.

Differences between families may reflect differences in the culture-at-large. For example, many of the values of the 1960s, particularly as expressed in the human potential movement, contributed to what might be regarded as a cult of *compulsive honesty*. In the extreme form, such a stance asserted that everything should be shared, everything divulged. In this form, such compulsive disclosures, even when well intentioned, often had disastrous results and when less well intentioned, served as a sanction for cruel and destructive behavior.

But the culture had little to offer as an alternative to this stance. Probably the clearest alternative involved what we would have to call an attitude of *cavalier deception*. This is most neatly summarized by the popular expression, "What he doesn't know won't hurt him." Under this banner, a serious consideration of what is and is not owed in relationships is dismissed by opting for the easiest way out, which is then rationalized as being in the best interests of the unaware!

Returning to the question of secrecy and privacy, we feel that this distinction hinges on the *relevance* of the information for the unaware. A current secret extramarital affair by one spouse is, in most cases, highly relevant to the other spouse, because it involves major issues of trust and trustworthiness, deception, and a violation of reciprocity. The question of one's biological parents or children is also relevant, as indicated by the tenacity with which adoptive children (often at great personal effort and cost) seek out their natural parents and vice versa. On the other hand, a traumatic episode in a parent's childhood, reasonably well resolved, with no significant effects on his or her own children, can more realistically be considered private. The parent may, of course, decide to share this material with the growing or grown child some day, but it is not *owed* to the child by its implications for him or her. Similarly, intimate details of one spouse's previous relationships that have no important implications for the current relationship are private, not secret. The fact that it is the secret holder who must make these decisions can be problematic, however, as will be discussed below.

This distinction leads to an alternative to the two stances—compulsive honesty and cavalier deception—described above. We can refer to this stance as *accountability with discretion* (Karpel, 1980). In practice, it involves:

- a serious consideration by the secret holder of the relevance of the material for the unaware.
- with an attempt to see this as much as possible from the viewpoint of the unaware,
- and with sensitivity to the timing and consequences of disclosure for the unaware.

This means, to use an everyday expression, trying to "put yourself in the other person's shoes," trying to understand what they need and what they are owed. It also means that when a decision to share is made, it takes the other's situation and likely reactions into account. For example, one does not reveal a secret that is likely to upset the other greatly in the midst of his or her surprise birthday party or when (s)he is already in crisis caused by an unrelated situation. This stance clearly reflects certain ethical values. They include, in this case, a respect for individuation, an effort to maximize trust and trustworthiness in relationships, and an attempt to balance the two fairly. More will be said later about the implications of this stance for the therapist's handling of family secrets.

SECRETS AND PROTECTION

It is virtually impossible to discuss secrets without the issue of protection being raised almost immediately. The question is, who is really being protected and from what? The answers are often difficult to obtain because the secret holder might be protecting him or herself, the subject, the unaware, or the awareness context as a whole. Consider the following situation:

The family consists of mother, father, and two children—an 8-year-old son and a 3-year-old daughter. Mother has a long history of somatic complaints, depression, and substance abuse. She is unavailable to the children and gives little to them. Father, a somewhat obsessive, constrained man, manages to give somewhat more than his wife to the children. In a family evaluation session, daughter is constantly near father or sitting on his lap. When the therapists ask mother to take the child, she does so but soon becomes irritated and daughter is passed back to the father. Mother later reveals to one therapist that, although he is completely unaware of this, her husband is not the father of the child and that she would never reveal this to him.

In this example, whom is the mother protecting? By keeping the secret, she may feel she is protecting her daughter from a possible withdrawal of love on her husband's part or both children from the ways he might react to such a disclosure—divorce or perhaps abandoning the family. She may be trying to protect herself from her husband's anticipated anger, withdrawal of love, or desire for revenge, or from her children's reactions to her if they were ever to find out. She may feel she is protecting her husband from feelings of pain, hurt, and betrayal. Bear in mind that she is not thereby protecting him from the betrayal itself, which has already occurred. This distinction has significance for the consequences of secrets, which are discussed below.

What bears comment is that when the secret holder claims to be trying to protect the unaware, (s)he does so without consulting the person him or herself. What may be extremely important decisions about a person's life are being made *for* the person, not *with* the person. And especially when the secret holder and subject are one and the same, as in the above case, there is reason to ask who really is being protected. When we look at secrets from the standpoint of relational debts and obligations, it appears that in many cases, the secret holder is at bottom protecting him or herself from a number of things, most important of which is taking responsibility for his or her own actions. Facing secrets involves facing personal responsibility for one's own actions and/or holding other(s) responsible for theirs. It requires an examination of the degree of fairness or unfairness in dealings with the other, the degree of respect for mutual obligations and entitlements, and the consequences of actions for the other. And family members are often as afraid of holding the other accountable for their actions as they are of facing their own.

In view of the fears and doubts that exist as to the outcome of such confrontations, facing secrets requires courage, conviction, and, for lack of a better word, strategy. The first two are self-reinforcing and self-explanatory. Strategy is involved in the attempt to minimize risk and possibly destructive outcomes—in the attempt to develop an approach to a particular secret in a particular family that least endangers and most likely contributes to mutual trust and trustworthiness.

CONSEQUENCES IN THE FAMILY

We can examine the consequences of secrets on a variety of levels. At a purely *informational* level, they result in deception, distortion, and mystification, as in the following example:

An 18-year-old woman was adopted at birth. The parents agreed never to reveal this to her. When she was 14, however, in the midst of a violent argument, her father blurted out angrily that she wasn't really their child. Mother's statement to the girl following this episode was [verbatim]: "Well, if he says he's not your father, then that's what he says. But I'm still your mother." The subject was never discussed again.

At an *emotional* level, secrets generate anxiety, regardless of position in the awareness context. Secret holders experience anxiety in their fear of disclosure, their discomfort when relevant topics are discussed, and their attempts to deceive or distort information. The unaware are likely to experience anxiety in relation to seemingly inexplicable tension that develops when areas relevant to the secret are discussed with the secret holders. They may also experience confusion and a variety of negative feelings in relation to the "explanations" they formulate in an attempt to understand this anxiety. Secrets perpetuate shame and guilt by sealing these feelings up within the secret holder, out of the reach of others who might help. And they may contribute to a vague but tenacious sense of shame or guilt in the unaware.

Individual family members and the family as a whole suffer from the loss of *relational resources* that results from secrets. Secrets interfere with the person-to-person relationships that are essential in differentiated and reciprocally balanced systems. They may contribute to pseudobonds instead of genuine alliances, and they create unnecessary estrangements. Secrets mean that trust is not in fact merited by trustworthiness, and for this reason, whether the secrets are revealed or not, they harm the balance of fairness, the overall structure of trust and trustworthiness, within the system. This violation of trust may constitute the most devastating consequence of secrets. The unaware is deprived, by those (s)he expects and is expected to trust, of information that may have profound bearing on his or her life.

One man who was informed of his illegitimacy and early adoption when he was 15 years old described, twenty years later, the anger and resentment of not having been told earlier. He said, "It was *my* background. I had a right to know." In a different case, a young man was informed in a family session of a secret that had had a clear and significant impact on the development of the family and particularly of the presenting problem. His sense of hurt at having been excluded and having had to struggle to understand, often incorrectly and with misplaced blame, what had happened in his family was obvious. In both cases, it was as though the person were saying, "How could you let me live a lie?" This might just as easily be said by the man whose wife has spared him the *feelings* of having been betrayed, but not the betrayal itself.

This expression—"living a lie"—perhaps better than any other captures the consequences of secrets for the ethical dimension of people's lives. Both the secret holder who deceives the unaware and the unaware him or herself are "living a lie." One knows it and the other does not, but this *fact* exists in both their lives. In the case of secrets, as opposed to mere privacy, contrary to the popular cliché, what we don't know *does* hurt us.

There is one final consequence of secrets at a *practical* level. That is the danger of unanticipated and destructive disclosure of the secret, by the subject, a secret holder, or an accidental discovery. So, for example, the classic case of the child who is tauntingly informed by other children (who have heard the gossip from their own parents) that his father did not "die in the war" but ran away from the family. Or the daughter in the example above whose adoptive father impulsively and angrily revealed her adoption. Or the husband who finds love letters to his wife in a drawer. This danger of unanticipated disclosure has special significance for the management of secrets in family and marital therapy, which is discussed below.

CONSEQUENCES IN FAMILY EVALUATION AND TREATMENT

The problems created by family secrets in the evaluation arise when the therapist is drawn into the awareness context by the secret holder(s) and is prevented from discussing the secret with the unaware. For example, a wife reveals a secret affair to the therapist and insists that (s)he not reveal this to her husband. A grown son reveals his father's stated plan to leave his mother to the therapist who is seeing the parental couple and swears the therapist to silence.

The specific strategies with which these types of cases can best be approached will be dictated by an appreciation of: (1) the consequences of these types of secrets in treatment; (2) relevant therapeutic considerations; and (3) the ethical stance of the therapist towards secrets. It will be helpful in the following discussion to think of the therapist as the *trustee* of the family secrets—that is, as *entrusted* by the family with the secrets as well as the hopes and fears that accompany them.

The consequences of such secrets in evaluation and treatment mirror those discussed earlier in families generally; they simply reflect the inclusion of the therapist into the awareness context.* In terms of *information,* the therapist is given important information, which, however, (s)he is unable to use openly. This involves the therapist in the web of deception and distortion and may tie his or her hands in such a way as to make any interventions virtually impossible. For example:

Husband and wife come in, both complaining of her unjustified suspiciousness and jealousy. She is genuinely apologetic about this and asks for help ridding herself of it. Husband reveals to the therapist in an individual meeting that he has had continuing affairs over the years but that he wants to maintain the marriage and so his wife must not be told.

Unless (s)he can find a way out of this trap, the therapist can neither reveal this, continue treatment as requested, or even terminate and honestly explain the reasons for termination. At a *strategic* level, therefore, secrets can make it difficult, perhaps impossible, for the therapist to operate effectively in the interests of the couple or family.

Emotionally, the therapist becomes susceptible to many of the feelings that permeate the awareness context. (S)he may feel guilty for deceiving the unaware, resentful of the secret holder for having revealed the secret, anxious about the complications developing in the case, and powerless to do anything about them. The catastrophic fears often associated with the thought of disclosing the secret are especially contagious in these cases. Therapists suddenly find themselves thinking that they cannot reveal the secret for fear of precipitating the disintegration of the family, suicide, or murder. Such fears may in some cases be justified; often they are not. This is a determination that the therapist must make and must translate into strategies that prevent or minimize possibly destructive outcomes.

Relationally, the therapist inevitably enters into a secret alliance with the secret holder(s) by virtue of the secret they now share. For this reason, (s)he is inevitably estranged from the unaware as any family member would be. The potential resources in the therapist's person-to-person relationship with the unaware are thus diminished. In terms of *power dynamics,* the therapist is trapped into colluding in the "one-up" status of the secret holder over the unaware.

Ethically, by colluding with the secret holder to deceive the unaware, the therapist endangers the family's *trust* in him or her. Considering that the basis of any successful therapy involves the patient's being asked and

---

* This discussion refers to those situations in which the therapist has been informed of a secret and simply obeys the injunction not to discuss it with the unaware.

being able to trust the therapist, this clearly runs the risk of undermining the enabling conditions of treatment. Therapists in these situations are often intuitively aware of this fact. Something *has* gone wrong with the treatment, and it transcends feelings and strategies. There is an ethical imbalance because the unaware is being asked to trust a therapist whose actions may not, for him or her, merit trust. The therapist's emotional reactions of guilt and anxiety are internal representations of his or her awareness, on some level, of this imbalance—an awareness that, unless remedied in some way, both therapist and patient are "living a lie" in the therapy.

Finally, at a *pragmatic* level, like any other secret holder, the therapist runs the risk of an unanticipated and destructive disclosure of the secret. Especially in cases that are characterized by the kinds of power dynamics discussed earlier, there is a serious risk that the very person who has sworn the therapist to silence will him or herself disclose the secret to the unaware. The unavoidable implication, whether verbalized by the secret holder or not, is: "and the therapist never even told you." In this sense, the therapist and the therapy can be blackmailed by the secret holder who has the power to expose the therapist's participation in the secret and to sabotage the treatment entirely.

Some distinction should be made between the consequences of secrets in the family evaluation and their consequences in family treatment. The degree of the distinction depends on the recommendations and course of action which follow the evaluation. When the evaluation leads to a recommendation to continue in family treatment with the therapist who is conducting the evaluation—that is, when the evaluation is simply the first stage of family therapy—the distinction is insignificant. In these cases, in which the therapist retains clinical responsibility and plans to meet with all family members, the consequences we have just described apply with equal weight. The therapist is no less likely to have his or her hands tied by the secret or to endanger the family's trust in him or her.

In those cases where the therapist opts to continue treatment but decides not to see the family as a whole, (s)he may have greater freedom to take a more gradual approach to the issue of managing the secret. For example, a brief series of individual meetings with the secret holder(s) might lead either to a decision to reveal the secret in time to the unaware or to the therapist's acceptance that keeping the secret does not violate trust and fairness, in the family or in treatment.

Finally, if the evaluation leads to a recommendation for treatment, of whatever form, with a different therapist, for other interventions instead of therapy, or for no interventions of any kind, the therapist has considerably more freedom to keep the secret without serious ethical or practical consequences. If the therapist will not be continuing with the family, there is no treatment to be impeded. And while the secret may impose some limits on what (s)he can do in the evaluation, these limits are likely to be much less significant in the evaluation than they would be in treatment. Just as the goals of the evaluation are more limited and the degree of trust and investment between family and therapist necessarily more limited in the evaluation (as opposed to in ongoing treatment), so the degree of obstacle posed by the secret is also more limited.

If anything, in those cases where the therapist will not be continuing with the family, the brevity of contact virtually dictates that the therapist not try to encourage disclosure of the secret at that point. This follows from the fact that the therapist will not be there to help the family deal with the risks and possible costs of disclosure. Therefore, when therapists know they will not be continuing with a case, they are more free to hear and keep secrets without fears of endangering treatment. They can allow the information they obtain to inform the specific recommendations they make to the family or to other professionals involved in the case without feeling obligated to manage the issue of whether the secret should be disclosed themselves.

In actual practice, therapists are unlikely to know which of these scenarios fits a certain case until fairly late in the course of the evaluation. For this reason, we turn now to therapeutic considerations and active strategies for managing secrets in the evaluation.

THERAPEUTIC CONSIDERATIONS

Faced with the consequences described above and their inevitably destructive effects, the therapist's responses are guided by several (sometimes competing) therapeutic considerations.

First is the therapist's need for any information that is highly relevant to the presenting problem or to the system as a whole—information that may significantly affect the formulation of the case and the recommendations that follow from it. Second, the therapist needs to demonstrate and maintain trustworthiness to all members of the system. (S)he must somehow communicate to all family members that (s)he is "on their side," has their interests at heart, and will act accordingly.

Much of the difficulty of managing secrets in treatment stems from the fact that these two considerations—the therapist's need to know and his or her obligation to maintain trustworthiness—are often in direct conflict. Even when both can be fulfilled, it is no easy matter and in some cases there is no alternative but to choose (at least temporarily) one or the other, as will be illustrated in the examples that follow. One final therapeutic consideration involves the therapist's need to manage crises with the least possible destruction and to avoid precipitating a second crisis within the crisis.

These considerations translate, in our view, into a specific therapeutic stance that is felt to be optimal in the management of family secrets. We can refer to this stance as we did earlier to a personal stance toward secrets as *accountability with discretion* because it reflects the application of this stance to the particular case of therapeutic relationships. In practice, it requires the therapist's efforts to balance his or her need to know with his or her obligation to maintain trustworthiness in a way that works for the best interests of all family members. When secrets are shared, it requires his or her consideration of the relevance of the secret for the unaware, arrived at as much as possible by trying to see this from the viewpoint of the unaware. And finally, it calls for sensitivity and planning as to the timing, circumstances, and consequences of disclosure for all family members in an effort to minimize possibly destructive outcomes.

APPLICATIONS

In the application of this therapeutic stance to particular cases, we can distinguish between *reparative* and *preventive* strategies.

Reparative strategies are necessary when the therapist is dragged into the awareness context without warning—that is, when the secret holder simply and suddenly reveals a secret.

Mr. and Mrs. L. seek psychiatric help for problems involving their 9-year-old son who is described as withdrawn and depressed, with a poor relationship with his father. Mr. L. is a successful architect who is heavily involved in community affairs. There are two teenage children. As part of a routine family evaluation, the parents are seen together and separately.

In her individual meeting with the therapist, Mrs. L. impulsively discloses that in the past her husband had been involved in homosexual extramarital affairs. He has not done so for several years, although she says she remains somewhat jealous and anxious about this recurring. She immediately regrets having disclosed this and asks the therapist not to reveal this knowledge to her husband. She makes a persuasive argument that her husband might be able to tolerate the therapist's knowing this once he knew and trusted the therapist more but that finding out at this early stage would almost certainly drive him and therefore the family from treatment.

The therapist makes clear to the wife that she will have to inform her husband of her disclosure to the therapist at some point; she agrees to try to do so at a later date. As Mr. L. gets more comfortable in treatment, he begins to hint at important material in his past. The therapist's hands are tied here because Mrs. L. has not yet spoken to her husband. In a brief individual meeting, the therapist makes clear to Mrs. L. that treatment cannot proceed beyond this point unless she talks to her husband. She does so that week with good results. In the next individual meeting with the therapist, Mr. L. reports that he was upset when she told him this but that he understands both his wife's and the therapist's positions. He goes on to discuss some personal material from his past that helps the therapist better understand the context of the current problem.

In this case, the secret holder's flexibility and willingness to cooperate allow the therapist to take a flexible approach. He is firm in asserting, for ethical and practical reasons, that the secret must be revealed, but is flexible in negotiating the circumstances and timing of such a disclosure. The specific decisions reached on these factors will depend upon what will make it easiest for the secret holder to open up and what will minimize possibly destructive outcomes.

For example, the therapist can offer his or her presence and moral support in a session to help the secret holder with this task, or (s)he can respect the secret holder's desire to do so with the unaware in private. (S)he may want to offer extra sessions in order to help the secret holder prepare for disclosing the secret, supporting the latter's courage and conviction that this is necessary, and helping to anticipate and thereby minimize destructive outcomes.

Cases in which the secret holder is essentially inflexible are more problematic. When the secret holder refuses to inform the unaware, the therapist must weigh the danger of contributing to the consequences described earlier, the likelihood that (s)he can be of real help to the family without the secret being revealed, and the risks and costs of refusing to treat the family unless there is some willingness to consider revealing the secret at some point. These are difficult decisions for the therapist, but they cannot be avoided. Once the therapist is inadvertently included in the awareness context, there is simply no way to avoid making a choice. The point is to make the best possible therapeutic decision based on the factors described above.

Preventive approaches to secrets can only be used when the therapist is informed that some kind of a secret exists but is able to respond before it is actually disclosed to him or her. This commonly happens when particular family members request a separate meeting with the therapist to discuss some as yet unspecified material. For example, in a marital evaluation, the husband may state that there are some things he would like to discuss with the therapist alone. Or a family member may call the therapist aside, either right before or after the session, hinting darkly at important but potentially explosive material.

A general preventive approach involves discussing the dangers and problems posed by special confidences in relational therapies and asking the individual, the couple, or the family how *they* would like the therapist to handle this.* For example, the therapist might describe the likely decrease in effectiveness that occurs when something important is known in therapy that can't be discussed. Having explained this, (s)he can ask how they would like this to be handled. It can also be made clear, if they sanction such confidences, that this arrangement may become unworkable at some point. If so, the therapist will tell them so and they will have to choose between disclosure and termination.

This presupposes that the therapist has ruled out the theoretical option of forcing a disclosure of the secret him or herself. We feel that, except in rare cases involving illegal, clearly harmful, or potentially harmful circumstances, the therapist cannot embody a stance of accountability with discretion by forcing a disclosure of the secret or by disclosing it him or herself. If the secret holders are unwilling or unable to face the consequences of disclosing the secret, the therapist cannot take responsibility for forcing the situation because all indications are that the necessary resources for minimizing destructive consequences would be insufficient. The therapist can encourage (literally, *give courage to*) family members to face secrets; (s)he cannot do it for them.

This is done most easily when the original request for a separate meeting and the therapist's response to it are made in the conjoint sessions, inasmuch as the therapist's communication automatically includes all members of the system who can then discuss and decide on this. Strategically, this increases the likelihood of eliminating the problem altogether and, ethically, it demonstrates the therapist's effort to maintain trustworthiness towards all members of the system.

Once the therapist takes this stance, any of the possible outcomes are virtually guaranteed to be more benign. It may prompt the person simply to reveal the secret. Or, if (s)he is given permission for a private discussion, the therapist may find that the "secret" is really more in the realm of the private and may drop the whole matter. If, at a later point, treatment cannot proceed without the secret being revealed, the therapist can say so. The members will have been forewarned of this and may be more able to tolerate disclosure. Even if they are not and the therapy terminates, they have had the experience of a trustworthy relationship and they know that they can seek this out in the future if the problems around the secret are resolved in one way or another. They are not further deprived of hope by feeling cheated or betrayed by what is supposed to be a helping agent.

---

* This approach was first suggested to the authors by Ms. Judy Fine, R.N., M.A., in a personal communication.

The situation is slightly more complicated when the original request is made in private. The therapist's response can be essentially the same except that if the secret holder opts for sanctioning secrecy, the therapist must insist that this at least be discussed with the unaware and agreed to by him or her (or them) before the therapist can proceed.

Obviously, the therapist can only take this stance *if (s)he feels it is possible not to be informed of the secret,* inasmuch as the member(s) may opt to keep the secret from the therapist if they feel that disclosure to the therapist may mean disclosure to the unaware. In those cases in which the therapist simply feels (s)he cannot afford not to know, it may be necessary to go along with the secret holder, or even press for the information to be revealed to the therapist.

An example of this situation, illustrating several principles of the therapeutic management of secrets, is described below:

Mrs. R. is a 25-year-old married mother of two. She is seen with her husband and her family of origin in consultation in the emergency room of a general hospital. The couple's 8-year-old daughter has died in an accident. Mrs. R. appears calm but seems to have dissociated the girl's death. Even following the funeral, she insists that the girl is waiting at home and needs to be fed. Family members report that this dissociative state has alternated with recognition of her child's death, accompanied by depression and vague suicidal threats. Mrs. R. has a history of two suicide attempts preceding this incident as well as alcohol and drug abuse and a generally impulsive style. One sister hints in the family evaluation session that she knows something that has bearing on Mrs. R.'s condition but that she feels she cannot reveal to other family members.

The therapists meet with the sister individually. She reports that, although no one else in the family knows it, the child had been left unattended by the mother at the time of her death. The therapists do not disclose this information to any other family members at this point. They arrange for a brief psychiatric hospitalization for the mother when family members make clear that they cannot manage her at home. The therapists do reveal the secret to the staff on the unit where the patient is to be admitted and recommend that efforts be made to further clarify and verify it. If verified, they suggest that this be discussed with Mrs. R. after her condition has stabilized but before her discharge from the hospital.

These therapeutic decisions illustrate several salient points. First, in the middle of a serious crisis with potentially harmful consequences (such as another suicide attempt by the mother), the therapists allow themselves to be drawn into the secret by the sister. They feel they simply cannot afford not to know. For this reason, without any qualification, they solicit the sister's secret.

Second, in an effort not to precipitate a second crisis within the already existing crisis, the therapists do not reveal their knowledge of this to Mr. and Mrs. R. or to any other family members. They allow the information to inform their own formulation and recommendations. They take care, however, to postpone further discussion of this with the family or the mother until the situation has stabilized, the mother is in a more secure environment, and continuity of treatment is assured so that the staff members who raise the issue can follow through on it with the patient.

Third, their recommendations are for further exploration of the sister's story before it is raised with the patient. The story might reflect the sister's misunderstanding, her misinformation, or simply her fabrication. Given the complexity and ambiguity surrounding taboo subjects, there is no reason for the therapist simply to assume that every situation identified as a secret is "the whole truth and nothing but the truth."

Finally, from a conviction that this woman will be unable to work through her reactions to the child's death unless possible feelings of guilt and responsibility are addressed, the therapists make a strong recommendation that, if reasonably well verified, the sister's information be shared with the mother. It is hoped that she would raise this herself in the context of a supportive relationship. If she does not, the therapists would most likely not feel justified in helping her to conceal or deny it—especially when an impulsive history of more than one suicide attempt and possibly overwhelming feelings of guilt and unworthiness might join in a potentially lethal combination of which most other family members would be ignorant.

What unites these different approaches to family secrets is the therapist's stance. Both examples represent a particular therapist's attempt to devise an approach to a particular situation that embodies a stance of accountability with discretion and that fulfills his or her own obligations as a trustee of the family's secrets.

References

Albee, E. *Who's afraid of Virginia Woolf?* New York: Pocket Books, 1963.

Bateson, G., Jackson, D. D., Haley, J., & Weakland, J. H. "Towards a theory of schizophrenia." *Behavioral Science, 1*, 1956, 251–264.

Bertalanffy, L. V. *General system theory: Foundations, development, applications.* New York: George Braziller, 1968.

Boszormenyi-Nagy, I. "A theory of relationships: Experience and transaction". In Boszormenyi-Nagy, I. and J. Framo, (Eds.), *Intensive family therapy: Theoretical and practical aspects.* New York: Harper and Row, 1965.

Boszormenyi-Nagy, I. and Krasner, B. R. "Trust-based therapy: A contextual approach." *American Journal of Psychiatry, 137*, 1980, 767–775.

Boszormenyi-Nagy, I. "Behavior change through family change." In Burton, A. (Ed.), *What makes behavior change possible?* New York: Brunner/Mazel, 1976.

Boszormenyi-Nagy, I. "Contextual therapy: Therapeutic leverages in mobilizing trust." In *The American Family.* Philadelphia: Smith, Kline and French Company, 1979.

Boszormenyi-Nagy I. "Loyalty implications of the transference model in psychotherapy." *Archives of General Psychiatry, 27*, 1972. 374-380.

Boszormenyi-Nagy, I. & Spark, G. *Invisible loyalties: Reciprocity in intergenerational family therapy.* New York: Harper & Row, 1973.

Boszormenyi-Nagy, I. & Ulrich, D. "Contextual family therapy," In Gurman, A. S. & Kniskren, D. P. (Eds.). *Handbook of family therapy.* New York: Brunner/Mazel, 1981.

Bowen, M. "Family therapy and family group therapy." In Kaplan, H. I. and B. J. Sadock, (Eds.), *Comprehensive group psychotherapy.* Baltimore: Williams and Wilkins, 1971.

Bowen, M. *Family therapy in clinical practice.* New York: Jason Aronson, 1978.

Buber, M. "Guilt and guilt feelings." *Psychiatry, 20,* 1957, 114–129.

Carter, E. A. & McGoldrick, M. "The family life cycle and family therapy: An overview." In Carter, E. A. & McGoldrick, M. (Eds.), *The family life cycle: A framework for family therapy,* New York: Gardner Press, 1980.

Carter, E. A. & McGoldrick, M. *The Family life cycle: A framework for family therapy.* New York: Gardner Press, 1980.

Chapman, A.H. *Management of emotional problems of children and adolescents.* Philadelphia: Lippincott, 1974.

Duvall, E. *Marriage and family development.* Philadelphia: Lippincott, 1977.

Erikson, E. *Identity and the life cycle.* New York: International Universities Press, 1959.

Freud, S. *A general introduction to psychoanalysis.* New York: Washington Square Press, 1952.

Glaser, B. G. & Strauss, A. L. *Awareness of dying.* New York: Aldine, 1965.

Goffman, E. *The presentation of self in everyday life.* Garden City, N.Y.: Doubleday Anchor, 1959.

Hadley, T., et al. "The relationship between family developmental crisis and the appearance of symptoms in a family member." *Family Process, 13,* 1974, 207–214.

Haley, J. "Toward a theory of pathological systems." In Watzlawick, P. and J. Weakland (Eds.), *The Interactional view:* Studies at the Mental Research Institute, Palo Alto, 1965-1974 New York: W. W. Norton, 1977.

Haley, J. *Uncommon therapy: The psychiatric techniques of Milton H. Erickson, M.D.* New York: W.W. Norton, 1973.

Hill, R. *Family development in three generations.* Cambridge, Mass.: Schenkman, 1970.

Hoffman, L. " 'Enmeshment' and the too richly cross-joined system." *Family Process, 14,* 1975, 457–468.

Hoffman, L. "The family life cycle and discontinuous change." In Carter, E.A. & McGoldrick, M. (Eds.), *The family life cycle: A framework for family therapy.* New York: Gardner Press, 1980.

Hoffman, L. *Foundations of family therapy: A conceptual framework for systems change.* New York: Basic Books, 1981.

Karpel, M. "Family secrets: I. Conceptual and ethical issues in the relational context. II. Ethical and practical considerations in therapeutic management." *Family Process, 19,* 1980, 295-306.

Karpel, M. "Individuation: From fusion to dialogue." *Family Process, 15,* 1976, 65–82.

Laing, R. D. *The politics of the family and other essays.* New York: Pantheon Books, 1969.

Laing, R. D. & Esterson, A. *Sanity, madness and the family.* London: Tavistock Publications, 1964.

Levinson, D. *The seasons of a man's life.* New York: Knopf, 1978.

McGoldrick, M. & Carter, E. A. "Forming a remarried family." In Carter, E.A. & McGoldrick, M. (Eds.), *The family life cycle: A framework for family therapy.* New York: Gardner Press, 1980.

Minuchin, S. *Families and family therapy.* Cambridge, Mass.: Harvard University Press, 1974.

Neugarten, B. "Adaptation and the life cycle." *The Counseling Psychologist, 6,* 1976, 16-20.

Paul, N. "The role of mourning and empathy in conjoint marital therapy." In Zuk, G. and I. Boszormenyi-Nagy (Eds.), *Family therapy and disturbed families*. Palo Alto, CA: Science and Behavior Books, 1967.

Rogers, R. "Proposed modifications of Duvall's family life cycle stages." Paper presented at the American Sociological Association Meeting, New York, August 1960.

Searles, H. F. *Collected papers on schizophrenia and related subjects*. New York: International Universities Press, 1965.

Simmons, J.E. *Psychiatric examination of children*. Philadelphia: Lea and Febiger, 1974.

Solomon, M. "A developmental, conceptual premise for family therapy." *Family Process*, 12, 1973, 179–188.

Stierlin, H. *Separating parents and adolescents: A perspective on running away, schizophrenia and waywardness*. New York: Quadrangle Books, 1974.

Stierlin, H. *Psychoanalysis and family therapy*. New York: Jason Aronson, 1977.

Weakland, J. "The 'double bind' hypothesis of schizophrenia and three-party interaction." In Sluzki, C. and D. Ransom (Eds.), *Double bind: The foundation of the communicational approach to the family*. New York: Grune and Stratton, 1976.

Watzlawick, P., Beavin, J. H., & Jackson, D. D. *Pragmatics of human communication*. New York: W. W. Norton, 1967.

Winnicott, D. W. *The maturational processes and the facilitating environment*. New York: International Universities Press, 1965.

Index

Bertalanffy, Ludwig von, 19, 20
Binding mode, the, 68
Biological family, the, 4-6
Birth, 13, 14, 17, 41, 51, 53
  circumstances of, 9
  of the first child, 54
  order, 8
Blame, 214
  diluting, 222
  minimizing, 207
Boszormenyi-Nagy, I., 7, 18, 23, 29, 31,
    32, 34, 36, 37, 39, 41, 44, 57, 248,
Boundaries, 7, 21-23, 52, 53, 54, 58,
    61, 68, 176, 209
  and secrets, 249
Bowen, Murray, 23, 29, 75
Buber, M., 41

Carter, Elizabeth A., 50, 51, 76, 77
Case management, 161
Cavalier deception, 250
"Challenger," the, 227, 229-230, 233
Chapman, A.H., 204
Charisma, 210
Child custody, 108
Child-focused problem, 59
Child's capacity for meaningful
    contribution, 57, 58
Children,
  as "truth tellers", 202
  birth of, 54-55
  departure of, 66-69, 92
  fear of, 200-205
  individuation of, 56-59
Chronicity of disturbance, 188
Circumstantial family member, the, 227,
    228
Claim, 33-35, 39, 42
Closeness, 142, 143
Confusing statements, 179
Collaborative families, 157, 158
Colloquialisms, 142
Colliding entitlements, 88
Commitment, 6, 30, 69
Communication, 23-26, 44, 87, 176
Compulsive honesty, 250
Compulsory flamboyance, cult of, 210
Confidentiality, 199
Confrontation, 199
Conjoint family treatment, 172
Conjoint sessions, 109
Conjunctive forces, 43, 91
Co-therapy, 113, 166, 200
Countertransference, 201
Crisis intervention, 112-112
Cut-off relationships, 34, 53

Death, 7, 11-14, 38, 146
  and aging of parents, 71-74
  of spouse, 72
Debt, 33, 36
Defenses, 18-19, 212
Delegating mode, the, 68
Dependability, 44
Depression, 17, 55, 59, 71
Detouring, 29
Devotion, 30, 74
Disagreements, 143-144
Disconfirmation, 25
Displacement, 37
Disqualification, 25
Divorce, 6, 12, 146
Double bind, 24
Duvall, E. 50

Editing, 159
Ellis, Albert, 211
Enmeshment, 86, 91
Entitlement, 7, 29, 31-33, 34, 36, 40
  colliding, 88
  of adolescents, 62
Empty-nest syndrome, 66-67, 70, 71,
    177
Erikson, Erik, 17, 49, 63
Esterson, A., 19, 64
Ethical balance, 33, 36, 43
Evaluation,
  as threat to the family, 214
  individual, 110
  marital, 109, 112, 223
  of children, 204
  opening minutes of, 117
  pace of, 217
  verbal summary of, 175
Existential indebtedness, 41
Expelling mode, the, 68
Exploitation, 30
Extended families, 22, 23, 38, 55, 56

Fairness, 30, 33, 36, 52, 252
  and unfairness, 29, 46
  capacity for, 44
  efforts to reassess the balances of,
    42
Family,
  as seen by members, 4-6
  definitions of, 4
  functional, 4-6
  "invisible" structure of, 7
  legal, 4-6
  of long-term coommittment, 4-6
  subsystems, 3, 7, 20, 54-55, 58, 73
  system theory, 14